THE WINGED PROPHET

From Hermes to Quetzalcoatl

The Journey of Venus through the Underworld: The planet is invisible after
its appearance as the Morning Star—77 days. In the center of this
circle-in-a-square (a Mesoamerican mandala) is the vase of the ashes of
Quetzalcoatl as Ce-Acatl (reed or cane), overflowing.

THE WINGED PROPHET

PROPHET

From Hermes to Quetzalcoatl

An Introduction to Mesoamerican Deities through the Tarot

Carol Miller & Guadalupe Rivera

SAMUEL WEISER, INC.

York Beach, Maine

First published in 1994 by
Samuel Weiser, Inc.
P. O. Box 612
York Beach, ME 03910-0612

Library of Congress Cataloging-in-Publication Data

Miller, Carol
    The winged prophet from Hermes to Quetzalcoatl : an introduc-
tion to the Mesoamerican deities through the Tarot / by Carol
Miller and Guadalupe Rivera.
        p.   cm.
    Includes bibliographical references and index.
    1. Tarot. 2. Indian mythology—Central America—Miscellanea.
3. Indian mythology—Mexico—Miscellanea. I. Rivera Marín,
Guadalupe II. Title.
BF1879.T2M64 1994
133.3'2424—dc20   94-18281
                                                          CIP

ISBN 0-87728-799-6
EB

Printed in the United States of America

99 98 97 96 95 94
10 9 8 7 6 5 4 3 2 1

Typeset in 11 point Palatino

The paper used in this publication meets the minimum requirements
of the American National Standard for Permanence of Paper for
Printed Library Materials Z39.48-1984.

To my husband, Tomás González, for his patience and understanding, and to my children, Alexandra and Fausto, because I love them so much.

—Carol Miller

To the memory of Dr. Ignacio Iturbe-Zabaleta, to whom we owe this project, and to my sons, Juan Pablo and Diego Julián.

—Guadalupe Rivera

TABLE OF CONTENTS

LIST OF ILLUSTRATIONS

PREFACE

BY GUADALUPE RIVERA

My late husband Ignacio Iturbe-Zabaleta and I began our research, under the name *The Tarot in the Mexican Codices*, toward the end of the 70s. It was our initial attempt at a correlation between the cultures of pre-Colombian America and those civilizations that had passed into the annals of world history under the generic heading, "Distant Civilizations, Primitive or Vanished."

We actually considered this a contemptuous assignment of terms, which resulted in patronizing cultures that since the beginning of evolution had developed within a framework of profound spirituality and the greatest harmony with the world around them, in the full awareness of their place in the Cosmos, peoples for whom "What lies above, lies below."

In the beginning, we wanted to explore those countries that we felt had produced cultures with affinitive characteristics, in whatever context, with the Olmec, Maya, Teotihuacan, and Aztec or Nahoa (also Nahua) peoples, specifically Egypt, China, Greece—in particular, Crete—and Peru.

We also attempted to solve a few of the riddles surrounding ancient cultures with a penchant for pyramids, similar to those that had existed in the territory known as Mesoamerica—a term encompassing archeological sites extending from Zacatecas in the north to the Petén, in Guatemala and down through Isthmus Central America—and Burma, Indochina, Babylon, Chaldea and Egypt in the Old World. Why so many similarities?

Why in China, India, and Tibet were there serpents and dragons with wings? Or tigers, like the jaguars of the Americas, that were venerated for their unique powers as much in pre-Hispanic Mexico, Peru, or Colombia as in Asia? Why did the creators of cultures that flourished five thousand years ago—between the Tropic of Cancer and the Tropic of Capricorn—develop similar sacred symbols, with as much emphasis on spirals, zigzags and crosses as cultures at the opposite end of the world? Why for every people on Earth, without exception, were the Big Dipper and the North Star equally sacrosanct?

For all these cultures the gods had come down from Heaven four times, to create and re-create humanity, once in each of the four Cosmic periods that preceeded our own. And the present and Fifth Era, all agreed, would bring the destruction of humanity.

During our travels we searched out answers to these questions, looking for anything that would bring us closer to a reasonable hypothesis. We discovered friends and teachers who indeed offered us wisdom through their instruction, arguments compatible to our own, and their own wealth of experience. Some of them shared our travels, others our quest. Still others were the authors of books that opened our eyes to a truth different from any we had previously imagined.

Among this reading and infinity of encounters someone introduced us to the tarot, as a medium for knowledge of esoteric teachings, said to be older than the oldest rites of Babylon. Its origins are attributed to the grand master, Hermes Trismegistus, known as Thot, thought by some to have been Babylonian, by others Egyptian. And then someone else showed us the way to the symbolism in the *Tonalamatl*, "The Book of Days," a resumé of ancient Maya divinatory wisdom adapted and applied by other Mesoamerican cultures – mainly the Aztec described in the pages that follow.

There was no doubt as to the common features in both, concealed within the diviner's art, as visible and apparent on the one continent as on the other. We penetrated to the depths of the obvious parallel and found an astonishing similarity, in the twenty-two major cards of the tarot and the twenty-two cards or lamatl that constitute a good part of the Borgia Codex, as well as the first section of the Bourbon Codex, books of history and wisdom devoted specifically to the ancient Mexica culture – those peoples of the Central Mexican plateau, now encompassed by present-day Mexico City.

The discovery, reduced here to a few words but in actual fact, a monumental experience, evolved after endless hours devoted to evaluating texts and documents, comparative mythology and Asiatic cosmology, as well as cosmological studies related by the Maya and Nahoa (Nahua). Yet even having deciphered the symbolism mysteriously shared by ancient Asia and indigenous America, we reached an impasse.

Then a phrase came to us, from the tarot as interpreted by the great Mouni Sadhu, and through its application we stumbled on our breakthrough – an ancient technique, equally applicable to both systems – "as if in a mirror."

We stood in front of the mirror with an engraving from the Aztec calendar. We had drawn a spiral through the signs of the *Tonalamatl*, beginning with Ce-Cipactli ("One Alligator"), the first of twenty origi-

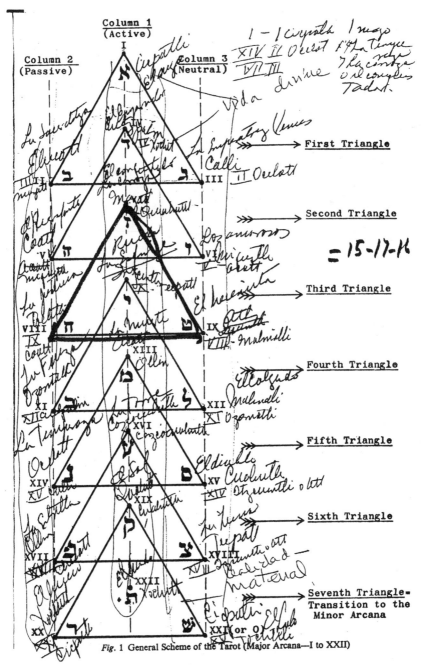

Fig. 1 General Scheme of the Tarot (Major Arcana—I to XXII)

Initial calculations by Dr. Rivera and Dr. Iturbe in pursuit of the correlation between the Tarot and the Tonalamatl. (Original figure from Mouni Sadhu, The Tarot published by Wilshire, Los Angeles, 1962).

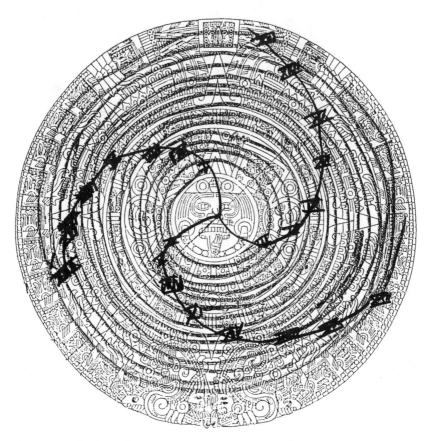

An attempt by Dr. Rivera and Dr. Iturbe to find the correspondence between the Tarot and the Tonalamatl by using an engraving from the Aztec calendar and overlaying the signs of the Tonalamatl and Tarot in a spiral formation on it.

nal signs, and proceeded in order to Ce-Tochtli ("One Rabbit"), the last sign. We then applied a corresponding spiral, also in its proper order, from the tarot, beginning with The Magician, the first sign, and ending with The World, the twenty-second. Nothing happened.

Then, when we realized we had to invert the order, all we had to do was reverse the spiral in the *Tonalamatl* while maintaining the original order in the tarot. The parallels thus drew themselves. We only had to make the necessary adjustments for interpretation.

Both spirals contain the key to humankind's relation to the Cosmos. The swing in the tarot is to the left: humans searching within themselves. In the *Tonalamatl*, the swing is to the right: humankind's

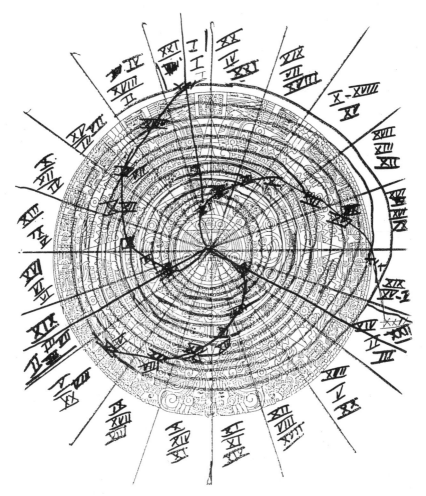

The same Aztec engraving with the signs of the Tonalamatl and Tarot laid out so that the parallels between the two became evident when held to a mirror.

encounter with the Universe. The notion is equally developed in the Maya *Popol-Vuh*, in which humans are described as a cosmic creation deposited on Earth by the authors of all things, at a solemn moment of quietude and emptiness, "even before clouds," when there was nothing but profound silence and the waters of the sea, where "they," our parents, the Creators, deposited Cipactli, an alligator (dragon); and the cosmic egg was hatched on the land.

The two spirals, despite their opposite directions, are still the same; they complement each other, within the aphorism "What lies above, lies below."

At this point we decided we had completed the first phase of our study. Beyond this we needed additional text, more explicit but also more lavish and extended, to describe Nahuatl mythology through the semiotic expression of the gods, the Lords of the night and the day, revealed in the twenty-two cards in the Bourbon Codex and also in the corresponding texts of the Borgia and other codices, wherever they were termed *Tonalamatl*, or "augurs." To the same degree we needed not only the parallels but a description of the emblems of the Chaldeans and the Egyptians, an interpretation of the tarot with all its symbolism, and then to proceed to the comparison between the two decks.

One after the other, the lamatl and the cards coincided. To describe this we required more data, a text more appealing than our succinct notes; we needed broader information. Who better than Carol Miller could accomplish this? She had invested more than four decades in the study of the mythology of pre-Columbian Mesoamerica and had already sought out its convergence with the Ancient World.

"The daily fact of her intellectual life," as she puts it, for a woman who had traveled as much or more, and as intensely or more, than ourselves, actually revolved around parallel mythology, cultural coincidence, Mesoamerican wisdom, semiotic language, as well as art, aesthetics, and behavior patterns. We were well aware of her capacity for work, her amazing discipline, and her agile pen, all of which were well applied to this work that she ingeniously titled, *The Winged Prophet from Hermes to Quetzalcoatl*.

Thus came to light a book that is the product of long years of research and endless revision. It is an amalgamation of points of view, a new approach to old thoughts, a different basis for analysis on a subject never before explored—the parallel between the tarot of Hermes Trismegistus and the *Tonalamatl* of Quetzalcoatl.

None of this has anything to do with "fortune telling." We are concerned exclusively with the philosophical aspects of two of the world's most profound sources of wisdom. We mean to define and interpret these, while we establish their parallel symbolism and explore the essence of the occult relation between Asia and America.

NOTE TO THE READER

Though we have gone to great lengths in the attempt to standardize the spelling of Mesoamerican terms and to correlate images for the pleasure of better visualizing the descriptions of the cards in the *Tonalamatl*, discrepancies will necessarily occur.

In part this is due to the wide range of sources in the pre-Columbian world, and to the vastly different peoples who adapted customs from another culture until they had made them part of their personal heritage and mystique. The Japanese did it as they integrated customs inherited from China or Korea while the Koreans and the Thais assimilated what they had received from China and India, as Buddhism migrated across South and East Asia. Islam coursed from the Atlantic Coast of North Africa all the way to the Indonesian archipelago, the Indian Ocean and China. Hinduism flooded the subcontinent into Sri Lanka and east into Bali. But these cultures remain part of the academic frame of reference in the Western world and the Mesoamerican people—despite their geographic proximity—do not. They are seen as foreboding, rather primitive, and more "exotic" than if they had sprung from Venus or Mars; and are probably just as remote.

So if a transposition from one Codex to another seems irrelevant or if variations in spelling seem confusing, bear with us. The material itself is astonishing and the world it unlocks is not only a treasure house of wisdom, ingenuous charm and visual delight, but it is also the secret to personal fulfillment, adaptability in the everyday world and understanding of one's fellows: in short, the key to happiness, to the replacement of the "self" with tolerance, perhaps the road to maturity and godliness.

THE WINGED PROPHET

PROPHET

From Hermes to Quetzalcoatl

DIVINATION AND THE GODS: THE MEXICAN DEITIES AND WESTERN TAROT

BY CAROL MILLER

The divinatory arts, according to most authors concerned in recent times with the tarot, owe their very existence to Hermes Trismegistus. This Master of Divine Wisdom was responsible for gathering and synthesizing the ancestral knowledge contained in the so-called *golden tablets* inherited from Persia and Sumeria.

As the Thrice-Great scribe of Egypt, known as Thot, Hermes Trismegistus was also associated with the Greek god Cronus, whose counsel he was said to have kept. He was thus confused with the Hermes of mythology and therefore identified with the messenger of the gods.

For this reason the tarot was believed to contain information, possibly secret or at the very least "classified," that constituted a revelation of the deities' intentions, along with an insight into their wishes, as well as clues to their conduct and machinations.

The gods, not just in Greece, but everywhere humans lived, loved, schemed and died, were notoriously willful—or so they seemed—by virtue of their mischief and misadventures, as related in the myths and teachings of the priests. These same gods, therefore, seemed equally equipped and prepared to send information by "messenger." They were also able to manipulate these "messages." This added substance to the notion that gods and goddesses controlled the means and the content of their dictates regarding the conduct considered to be in the best interest of mortals.

The oldest of all known tarots is the Egyptian, still in use today. A traveler, perhaps, or an esoteric philosopher, curiously representative of the ideal of "the gods' messenger," carried it to Europe, where it took root during the Middle Ages. The Visconti Tarot in Italy and the Marseilles Tarot in France are considered the two oldest of those still in existence.

While the tarot disseminated its Hermetic discipline in Europe, northern Africa and western Asia, cultures in the Americas were developing their own divinatory arts. These were documented by means of a codex or illustrated manuscript, in which fantasy drawings and symbolic pictographs related the stories and legends of these peoples' histories, origins, faiths and customs. An important element in this collection of data and interpretation concerned itself with the ancient art of predicting the future.

The Mayas of Mesoamerica called their codices the "Books of Destiny" or the *Tzolkin Augurs*, precisely because of their emphasis on sorting out the emblems that would foretell things to come. These almanacs predated their Aztec counterparts, termed the "accounting of days" or *Tonalamatl*. Such a wealth of data was jealously preserved on pages confected of a material considered durable and resistant,

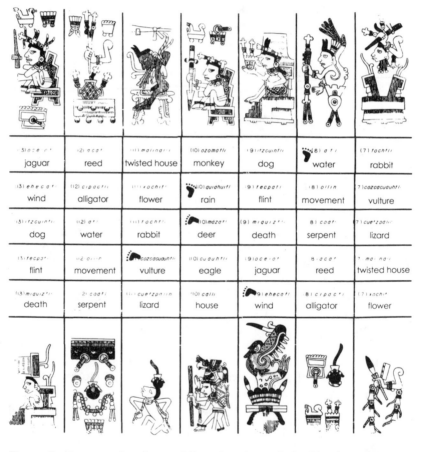

Figure 1. An example of assembling the signs of the Tonalamatl on an almanac page. (This and all other illustrations of the codice are reproduced from Eduard Seler's Commentarios al Códice Borgia *published by Fondo de Cultura Economica, Mexico City, 1963. Used by kind permission of the publisher.)*

also readily available, which turned out to be specially treated deer-skin.

Disciples of the Tonalamatl, for our purposes, were peoples affiliated with the Aztecs, called Nahua (or Nahoa), a term associated with their linguistic group. The Aztec nation was in fact composed of seven different tribes. Their fame today is based on their reputation for bloodletting and sacrifice, or for conquest and subjugation and in fact, they were an aggressive and therefore dominant group. However, some of the peoples they vanquished, and with whom they eventually integrated were notably intellectual, distinguished by phil-

osophical, mathematical and scientific achievements envied wherever their name was pronounced. The enduring debate, as to the greater antiquity of the Mayas or Olmecs, is of no consequence, since most of the authors listed in the bibliography assume a still-earlier influence as the substance of these cultural accomplishments. A number of them, for example, belabor the notion, explored in the esoteric depths of the Bourbon Codex, that Mesoamerican divinatory arts actually originated on the vanished continent, real or imaginary, of Atlantis. Guadalupe Rivera notes that the *Nahuatl* ("atl" meaning "water") god *Atlanteotl* who, like Atlas was one of the four sons of the Titan Iapetus, was condemned to stand forever on the edge of the world, bearing upon his shoulders the vault of the heavens.

Nevertheless, both the Mayas and the Nahuas considered the sublime character of their divinatory arts to originate in the supreme god Tonacatecuhtli and his wife, Tonacacihuatl, inhabitants of the Thirteenth Heaven, a kind of Aztec Nirvana, reserved for the most highly enlightened. According to tradition, the Goddess Mother created the divinatory arts with her talent and the God Father applied them, by means of his wisdom.

In fact, a number of those accordian-pleated books that make up the codices describe in great detail the creation of the divinatory arts and the knowledge of their application. The oldest, a Maya codex called the "Dresden," after the German city in which it has been housed since the conquest, is considered the prototype for others of these remarkable documents—all of which are named for the European libraries in which they are deposited: the Vatican, the Telleriano-Remensis, the Laud, Copi, Borgia, and the Bourbon. Among these, the Vatican Codex has been most dissected in the pursuit of mystic knowledge, by a priest named de los Ríos. The Borgia has been extensively analyzed by the German, Eduard Seler, and the Bourbon remained for a time the province of R.P. Fabregá. A Frenchman, Leonard André-Bonnet, eventually dedicated his anthropological studies to the Bourbon as well and attributed its creative genius to the *Atlantes*, inhabitants of Atlantis whom he considered without a doubt the founders of the Mesoamerican cultures, the philosophical mentors of the Olmecs.

In the Aztec world, the gods whether native or imported specialized in appearing among men. In fact, live humans often personified the gods on Earth. The dead were further added onto the considerations of the living, as they presumably reverberated from their supernatural worlds. Mesoamerican people not only believed in their gods, they painted and sculpted them, often transporting the materials from great distances. They interpreted them with astonishing skill and creative flair. They projected them onto their rites. They maintained them with offerings of food. They killed them by means of the sacrifice of the gods' representatives on Earth. Then they reinforced them by incorporating them into the supernatural world, which shared the considerations of the living.

All of this was accomplished by means of an exuberant and inexhaustible infinity of ceremonies that related humankind to their gods. Scarcely any human activity escaped some sort of corresponding ritual, a complex series of activities that demanded the participation of large numbers of people and the employment of considerable material resources, not only in the invocation of the deities but in the reaffirmation of a religiosity manifest in every social experience—in the fact of society itself.

The anthropomorphic view of the deities, the faith in the dead as a bond with the world of the divinities, and the exorbitant proliferation of ceremonies relating gods and humans permitted the erection and fortification of a structure and a social organization of ever-increasing dimensions, fundamentally elevated on the pervading concerns of the time: war, religion, and trade. The three were intertwined and definitely interrelated, though the philosophy of empire was never fomented in the Roman but rather the contemporary American or the Victorian British sense. It was not a concept of total conquest so much as the establishing of outposts to guarantee a successful commercial exchange.

Both the polytheism and the ceremonialism of the ancient Mexicans were confirmed in the representation of the gods as different natural elements, or as diverse groups, or as human activities. The gods existed to further verify the various astral bodies, such as the Sun and Moon, Venus, the stars, or the Milky Way. There were gods of the Earth, rain, wind, water, fire. There were gods of plants and food products important to human beings, such as corn, maguey, salt, the ritual alcoholic beverage called pulque, and certain medicinal herbs. There were gods for the daytime and the night. Most important, however, was the fact of the gods as a concept—an attitude toward living and conduct—not only on grand occasions but on the least significant ones. They permeated every aspect of life, day by day and one minute at a time.

The gods are therefore proudly patron of every national or hegemonic unit, of each city, neighborhood, priest, or warrior. The people in the palaces had their god and so did the unmarried, in their community bachelor houses. Gods patronized childbirth, sickness, lust, hunting, war, trade, weaving, gem-cutting, gold-smithing, architecture, manufacturing, and design.

At times the gods were lumped into a unit, or the reverse—human activity was collected into areas corresponding to a certain

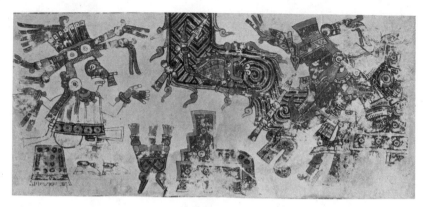

Figure 2. Tlahuizcalpantecuhtli, God of the planet Venus, seen as the Morning Star. He is shown with Xiuhtecuhtli, God of Fire, and in this case, the inspiration of war.

god. Sometimes the patron of a trade or craft could apply his divinity to the guild of that craft, along with the neighborhood or town consigned to the same activity. Or the god of a natural element could be related to the craft in which that element served as raw material. For example, among the water deities were to be found the gods of water-bearers, fishermen, and salt miners, as well as the growers of the reeds from the swamps used in the weaving of mats.

Often a god was associated with the author or initiator of an activity. The goddess of childbirth was considered the first woman to bring forth a baby. The goddess of sustenance was the first woman to make the unleavened corn cakes, staples of the Mexican diet, called tortillas. The fisher god was the first to invent nets and lines.

National gods appeared at times as ancestral leaders, such as the warrior gods who patronized the Mexicas, Tlaxcaltecas, and Tecpanecas. Most gods were seen in human form and with a human personality, a quality shared with the Greeks. Others took an animal form and were seen in a fashion similar to that of the Egyptians, who perceived in many animals the qualities to which humans were encouraged to aspire—qualities the enlightened person would eventually assume for her or himself. In this sense no form of life was termed "lowly," for all of creation was considered equally sublime and, therefore, as instructive as it was admirable. The mythic dragon—common to all cultures—was seen in Mesoamerica as the Plumed Serpent, a complex deity of many forms and attributes, derived as elsewhere on earth from the lizard, snake, crocodile, or salamander. Often human and animal forms were synthesized, again, like the Egyptians, or were combined with one another, or "disguised," in order to seem interchangeable.

Just as in the strata of Mexican society, where social levels or occupations were indicated by the garments used or the singular adornments applied for symbolic or decorative purposes, each of the gods similarly wore its characteristic clothing or emblems: mantles or tunics with indicative decoration; facial or body paint; hairdos; head-dresses; the bearing of specific implements or artifacts; weapons or tools relative to its trade, occupation, or jurisdiction.

All of this gave way to the complex representation or identification of the gods in the idols, paintings, murals, codices, and temple inscriptions, or in the figures of the priests who personified the various gods in their services.

The gods frequently appeared in pairs, as man and woman, or in counterposed images, or in family units of philosophically or symbolically associated groups. They were rarely seen in genealogical lineage though this also occurred, especially where the Supreme Gods and their offspring—semiotic or biological—were concerned, not unlike the case of the Greeks or Polynesians.

The quality of society was also represented in the divine world. Leaders were seen with their servants and subjects, among gods as well as mortals. The most easily recognized examples refer to the God of the Underworld in his dominion of the dead; the God of Rain, Lord of the "paradise" called *Tlalocan*, with his multitudes of lesser rain gods; or the Sun, assisted daily in his ascent by the souls of dead warriors.

But in general, the gods were served principally by the souls of humans who died in a fashion consistent with that god's activity and who, therefore, were integrated into the god's court. Thus, the dead were simultaneously mortals and gods. To this day, despite the superimposition of Catholicism, the people of Mexico celebrate their festival of the dead, provide the deceased with renewed sustenance and remind the departed soul of the faithfulness and constancy of those he left behind. The passing from worldly existence to the supernatural strata is seen as a transition similar to the bridging of social levels in the worldly plane—to be accomplished by talent and applied effort within the framework and the dictates of the rigid Mesoamerican social organization, especially the Aztec, one of the most imputable.

Among the goddesses, as among earthly women, the principal divisions are related to their ages. The old goddess Toci is patroness of midwives and herbal medicine. Xochiquetzalli (or Xochiquetzal) is the young and beautiful goddess, associated with the maidenhead and the bridal bed. Tlazolteotl is the goddess of carnal experience,

Figure 3. Mictlantecuhtli, Lord of the Nether-World of the Dead. From the Códice Borgia.

with filth and sin, and considered more the province of the mature woman.

Often teams of gods appear, seen as fraternal groups, each of whose members represents his own endowments. These units are often pictured as groups of four, a persistent number related, as in the tarot, to the quadrant—the figure associated in Near Eastern philosophies with the Temple of Solomon. In the same fashion, the Aztecs saw the universe, or macrocosm, as a square oriented toward the light. For them, as for the Mayas before them, a human being signified the microcosm—the symbolic agent of the natural world. This was represented schematically by the square within the circle, or the circle within the square: the Himalayan *mandala*.

Figure 4. An example of a tantric or Himalayan mandala.

Four is the number and four is the key—the Tetragram, which for the Hermetics indicated the four letters that represented the god they could never call upon, for, unlike the more pragmatic Mesoamericans, they might never utter his name. Four are the cardinal points: north, south, east, and west; and four are the elements: earth, air, fire, and water.

The number four, then, pointed the way to the mysteries of the Cosmos, suggested in the fundamental figures which occur again and again, as much in the codices as in the sanctuaries of Egypt—the circle, cross, triangle, and square, upon which every other figure is based.

Four are the seasons of the year, the representation of the universe: air is spring, fire is summer, water is fall, and earth is winter. The ancients insisted that polarity corresponds to these indications. Fire represents the heart and breast, air the legs we move on, water our right side—symbolically the principle which liberates or dis-

Figure 5. A Mesoamerican Mandala depicting phase two of the Journey of the planet Venus through the Underworld. In the east or the nether regions the heart of Quetzalcoatl (as Ce-Acatl) is transformed into the Morning Star.

solves, and earth our left side — that which is bound or coagulated. In the moral sense, fire served to indicate imagination and will; air, our thoughts; water, our emotions and feelings; earth, our practical sense, our perception and potential for action.

If these precepts coincided and likened the Hermetic to the Meso-american principles, both further shared the concept of harmony as the basis for a productive life. Harmony in the tarot is indicated by a square, the four contributing elements, completed by the apex of a triangle or pyramid. Thus, the totality of nature is encompassed in a single figure, the microcosm and the macrocosm, the will that impels humankind ever upward, in the pursuit of the Fifth Essence, or Quin-

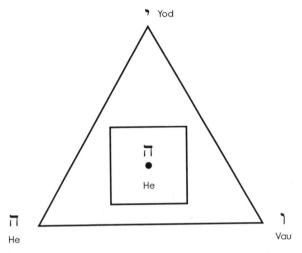

Figure 6. The square in the triangle, with annotations and calculations by Dr. Rivera and Dr. Iturbe. Redrawn from Mouni Sadhu, The Tarot.

tessence, the principle encompassed in "intelligence," the philosophical mercury of the occultists in the projection of particles into matter onto awareness.

In the same fashion, the Mexican gods not only indicated the ideal in relation to conduct, the aspiration of will or the structure of society. They were also conditioned by calendrical indications, thus emphasizing their jurisdiction over specific parts of the world or periods of time. In this manner the gods could govern singly, jointly, or during successive periods in the exercise of their functions.

A god, then, might appear in a multiplicity of aspects and obligations, to such an extent that often gods or groups of gods overlapped or became confused in their relationships. Like a Cubist painting, they were simultaneously the top, bottom, sides, inner and outer concepts; themselves and their diametrical opposite; their will and the violation of it; their purpose and the obstacle to achieving it.

In certain myths, the Sun, the Moon, and the Earth are in themselves deities. The astral body suggests their form or represents the form acquired by the deity. In other myths, the deity appears as the spirit which inhabits an object, as in the case of the God of the Hill, Tepeyolotl, in whose very name is implied the heart or spirit of the hill.

In other cases, a natural force represents the product of a god's activity. The god of wind wears a pointed, triangular mask through which he blows in order to affect the movement of the air. The rush of breezes and the gusty wind preceding the rain are produced by a crowd of little, lesser gods, who sweep with their brooms to open a passage for the water gods, who are actually manifested as rain.

The gods are represented as icons or idols. Their priests and the victims sacrificed in their name also take their form, until they, themselves, become that god. Yet while they *are* the god, they are not. They are his symbol, his expression, his representative and emissary, his concessionaire, standard-bearer, even consignee. The victims of his sacrifice become his minor and lesser aides—gods and servants of a god. Those sacrificed to the rain god, Tlaloc, therefore, become lesser rain gods; warriors sacrificed to the Sun pass into his service.

Certain activities of a deity, or varying aspects and manifestations, may be related to different periods of his existence. Huitzilopochtli, the god-monarch of the ancient Mexicas, a local application of the Quetzalcoatl myth may be considered one of the four Creator Gods born to the Supreme Pair, though he generally appears as a national or regional god, who protects and guides his own people.

The great and ubiquitous Quetzalcoatl, on the other hand, pillar among the four Creator Gods, was also God of the Wind, as well as the priest-king of myth and legend. He reigned at the Toltec capital of Tula, northeast of the Valley of Mexico and today's Mexico City. He was patron of priests and craftsmen. In fact, he "invented," according to legend, most crafts, including metallurgy, among many arts and skills. Like others of the gods, he modified both his position and his activities; that is, the myth tended to mutate in relation to the transition that occurred in his people and their condition, as they evolved and thrived, or declined and faded. But during their height they were more than just prominent. They were magnificent. And Quetzalcoatl was assigned the credit.

It was only fitting then, that the mystique be transposed to Huitzilopochtli, in his corresponding role among the Mexicas, as they superceded the Toltecs and rose to political preeminence.

The Mesoamerican pantheon emphasizes the interrelation of ideas, as they become regional concepts, in terms of the creation of the world, with all its projected forms. The cosmogonic myths assign the principal gods the role of creator, or created, with specific reference to their residence or activity. This serves as a basis for their classification within the conceptual range of the ancient peoples. Though the versions of the myths still extant are fragmentary, their intellectual dimension, their coherence, and their majesty are clearly discernible, even taking into account their complexity and the multiplicity—even ambivalence—of certain of their groupings and interpretations.

These cultures were lavish, opulent, and grandiose. So were their myths and, therefore, their gods. They were passionate, intense, articulate, yet in the same proportion they were severe, truculent, and disciplined. Far from arbitrary, despite their luxury of implication, they were clearly attuned to the nature of the people they governed, both product and consequence—the source and the projection, a cause and its effect.

The point of departure common to all the otherwise diverse and even culturally antagonistic peoples of Mesoamerica was conceived as a pair of gods, the Creators who inhabited the upper heavens—the Thirteenth Heaven—about whose origin nothing is really very well known. It should be mentioned that all knowledge of myth and function, and all interpretation of the codices, has come to us through the writings and observations of the 16th century of conquering non-natives, usually Spanish priests, who relied for translation on their converts at the monasteries. These were not entirely trustworthy sources, in part because of their sense of humor, intended to confound their masters. Furthermore, many among the "masters," like Fray Diego de Landa in the south, set out to destroy all native books and records while preserving his own version of local customs. If cultures with no written testimony can be considered "primitive," it was their invaders who conspired to consign an arbitrary "ignorance" to posterity.

The Creator Gods supreme in the Thirteenth Heaven were called *Tonacatecuhtli*, "Lord of Our Flesh," that is, sustenance; and *Tonacacihuatl*, "Mother of Our Flesh." The couple in another context, with that astonishing gift for mutation and assimilation, was also called *Ometecuhtli*, "Lord Bone" or "Lord God," described conceptually as "Two" or "Half of a Whole"—the sacred status applied equally to the mortal couple—and *Omecihuatl*, "Mother God" or "Two." Their heaven was called *Omeyocan*, "The Place of God" or "The Place of the Two."

The divine couple produced four offspring, among them *Quetzalcoatl*, "The Serpent with Plumes of Quetzal," an allusion to the iridescent green bird of the tropical jungles. The smallest was *Huitzilopochtli*, "The Left-Handed Hummingbird," alliteration of Quetzalcoatl projected onto an expanded pantheon, in the form of another iridescent winged creature.

Eldest among the progeny was *Tlatlauhqui Tezcatlipoca*, "Smoke of the Red Mirror" or "Tezcatlipoca the Red." After him came *Yayauhqui Tezcatlipoca*, "Smoke of the Black Mirror," or "Tezcatlipoca the Black." The mirrors referred to were confected of pyrite, though they were symbolically associated with obsidian.

These principal, and therefore complex, deities of the Mexican pantheon, in one form or another, vary from region to region and moment to moment in history. They appear in all divine legends, historical recounting, and Mesoamerican myths along the coast,

Figure 7. Quetzalcoatl, the Serpent with the Plumes of Quezal, depicted as the penitent of Tula (top) and the God of Wind (bottom). From the Códice Borgia.

down the Pacific slopes of Guatemala and deep into Central America. They were warrior leaders or they were patrons of the most important tribes. They were as provocative as they were demanding. They were intransigent and implacable. Yet they were also incredibly and unexpectedly flexible, probably as a result of their mutable and perfectly adaptable forms.

Tezcatlipoca the Black, for example was, according to the legend, the greatest and the worst, who ruled and dominated his brothers. He was everywhere, says the myth, even in another's thoughts. He knew the secrets in every heart. He motivated every act. It was only by great effort and the exercise of will—also a divine action—that those he victimized or subjugated were able to circumvent his complete domination. He was also called *Moyocoyani*, "The Almighty," the ubiquitous god who never lets anyone escape him. Apart from his role as a Creator God he was also patron of young warriors. As such he was called *Yeotl* (pronounced Yeah-oh-tull), meaning "warrior," or *Telpochtli*, "The Young." In historical legend he appears as one of those responsible for the fall of Tula. Later he became the patron of another great city called Tetzcoco.

Tezcatlipoca, the Red, was identified with Xipe Totec, "Our Lord Sheathed in Skin," feted in the month Tlacaxipehualiztli, when the greatest number of captives was sacrificed. As Tezcatlipoca, the Red, he served as patron of one of the most important groups in the city of Chalco, known as the tribe of the Nonoaloas Tlacochcalcas. He was also identified with the god Mixcoatl or Camaxtli, and through him with tribes from regions in the modern states of Puebla and Tlazcala.

Quetzalcoatl, the third child and a really glorious blend of ideals and virtues, appears to have synthesized a combination of deities who differed originally from the eventual composite. In one form, he was the God Creator, son of the Divine Pair. In another, he was Ehecatl, "The Wind," described in the calendar or Tonalamatl as Chicnahui Ehecatl, "The 9 Wind." As patron of the priests, as well as of craftsmen, he was also Lord of Tula, Ce-Acatl Topiltzin, Toltec regent by tradition, until he was made Lord of Cholula, a neighboring city to the south, where his followers established themselves after Black Tezcatlipoca's treacherous plotting brought about the disgrace of Quetzalcoatl and the downfall of Tula.

The last child, Huitzilopochtli, according to the creation myth, received the name "Lord Bone" (or was the earthly presence of Ometecuhtli, also "Lord Bone",) but was also known as *Maquizcoatl*, "The Two-Headed Serpent," a far cry from "Left-Handed Hummingbird." Tradition assigns him his regal role as patron of the Mexicas. During-their diaspora he led them from defeat and disgrace to triumph and supremacy, offering instruction and guidance, while he indicated the signs to look for along the way, symbols of their manifest destiny.[1]

According to the myth, he was born in Coatepec, near Tula. His mother, Coatlicue, "Skirt of Snakes," conceived him, in one version, when she took to her breast a bundle of feathers found while she swept; in another version, the feathers had been placed there by the evil and wily Tezcatlipoca the Black.

Huitzilopochtli was born fully armed. He defeated the four hundred *Huitznahua*, his brothers, who had wanted to destroy his mother because of her strangely inexplicable pregnancy.

The creation of the rest of the world and all the other gods was the work of these four children of the Thirteenth Heaven. They additionally formed nine—some say even more—heavens, and as many underworlds, crossed by a nine-flowing river, like the Styx. The Earth was mentioned as the first of the heavens and underworlds. These Creator Gods were also responsible for the gods or the beings destined to inhabit each level. According to one version, "everything was made and created without the accounting of the passing of a single year. As stated in the codices, it was all done together and with the absence of any difference in time."

They created the water and in it an animal, Cipactli, sometimes compared with an alligator and, on other occasions, as in the Borgia Codex with a swordfish, from whom the Earth was formed. The Earth itself was called Tlaltecuhtli, "Lord or Madam Earth," or Tonan Tlaltecuhtli, "Our Mother the Lady Earth," and it shared the shape of the monster from which it was created. The Earth was also personified in the gods associated with fertility.

The four Creators, or, as some claimed, Huitzilopochtli and Quetzalcoatl alone, further created fire, governed by the god Xiuhtecutli, "Lord of the Year," or "Lord Turquoise." Fire was considered the province of the celestial regions, one of which was called Ilhuicac Mamalhuazocan, "The Fire-Forgers' Heaven," which was the name of a constellation. The Xiuhcoatl, those rattlesnakes of fire, also lived in Heaven. But fire, in addition, resided in the center of the Earth, in Tlalxicco, "The Earth's Navel." Fire was further termed Huehueteotl, "The Old God"; Ixcozauhqui or "Yellowface," and Cuezaltzin,

---

[1]One sign was an eagle sitting on a cactus (known as a prickly-pear) with a snake in its mouth. This symbol is now the emblem of Mexico and adorns the national flag.

"Flame." From fire, the gods made a half-sun, "which, because it was not whole, shined not a lot but a little."[2]

Another of the heavens was consigned to the Rain God, and was called Tlalocan, "The Place of the Gods of Water." Tlaloc was created to rule there, accompanied by his wife, Chalchiuhtlicue, "Skirts of Jade," the Goddess of Water.

To reign in the lowest of the nether regions, the Mexica hell called Mictlan, "The Place of the Dead," the gods created Mictlantecuhtli, "Lord of Hell," and his wife Mictecacihuatl, "The Infernal Woman."

The gods also created the first man and woman, called Cipactonal, "Day of the Cipactli," and Oxomoco, an untranslatable name, probably of origins other than Nahua. The former was charged with the task of working the land, the latter with weaving. She was also given kernels of corn to use in her predictions in a fashion not unlike that applied to the Chinese oracle called the I Ching. The couple further devised a calendar.

To this first couple a son was born, Piltzintecuhtli, "Lord Child," and, in order for him to eventually marry, the gods created a woman from the hair of the Goddess Supreme. This woman was called Xochiquetzal (or Xochiquetzalli) "The Plumed Flower," or "Quetzal Flower," a name applied as much to Piltzintecuhtli's wife as to the Creatress herself.

Since the Half-Sun they had created gave off very little light, the gods decided to create a better sun, to shine all over the world. Here the myths vary, as in fact several suns were formed, each destined to warm a different part of the earth at a different time, conceived in terms similar to the Four Ages of the Greeks.

One of the most complete versions tells of Tezcatlipoca the Black who turned himself into a sun, while the other gods created a race of giants, so huge and so strong they could uproot trees with their bare hands. The giants lived on acorns and according to certain myths built the most grandiose and monumental of the ancient cities, vast Teotihuacan, a landscape of temples in "The City of the Gods," and perhaps, as stated in other versions, they also built the Pyramid at Cholula.

In time, Quetzalcoatl, as a result of one of his many and persistent quarrels with Tezcatlipoca, the smoking or obsidian mirror, struck the sun with his staff and tossed it into the water. The Sun-

---

[2]Bernardino de Sahagún, *Historia General de las cosas de Nueva España*, Book 7, chapter 1 (Mexico: Editorial Porrua, 1979), p. 431. This book is a 16th century compilation of the language and customs by a Franciscan friar. With annotations and indexing by Angel Maria Garibay K. Available in English as *Florentine Codex: General History of the Things of New Spain*, translated by Arthur J. Anderson and Charles E. Dibble (Salt Lake City, UT: University of Utah Press, 1982.

Tezcatlipoca decided to turn into a "tiger," the Mesoamerican term for the native jaguar, the deity Ocelotl. In this form he killed the giants. The event took place on "Day 4 Tiger," which then gave its name to this sun and to the corresponding era.

After that Quetzalcoatl turned himself into another sun and reigned during a period in which men lived on pine nuts. This period ended when Tezcatlipoca the Black, in the form of a jaguar, tumbled Quetzalcoatl out of the sky with a swipe of his claws. At that moment, however, a southwesterly storm began to rage, with its angry wind blowing from the sea, and in retaliation for Tezcatlipoca's mean gesture destroyed everything in its path. It swept away the people as well, except for a few who turned into monkeys. All of this transpired on "Day 4 Wind."

The next sun was Tlaloc, the Rain God, in whose time mankind lived on the seeds of an aquatic plant called *acicintli*, "water corn." The era ended when Quetzalcoatl made, as described in the codices, fire to rain from heaven, on "Day 4 Rain." People were then changed into birds. Quetzalcoatl named Chalchiuhtlicue, Tlaloc's wife, as the new sun. During this period people ate teocentli, "divine corn," a kind of wild maize. Eventually, however, this era's population was changed into a breed of fish, as a result of a deluge. According to the legend rain fell so heavily from the skies that all was swept in its path, until that period ended on "Day 4 Water."

The sky was seriously damaged during all of this. When it fell, the four Creator Gods built four roads through the center of the Earth, while the many-faceted Tezcatlipoca and his rival Quetzalcoatl created trees to use as levers, to raise the sky again.

The world, then, had to be reconstructed and a new race of people created. The versions vary as to the process but all of them coincide about the creation of a new sun, the one that shines on us today. Meanwhile, a number of people managed to survive the deluge by setting out in a canoe, on paradoxical Tezcatlipoca's advice. After the rain stopped, they returned to land. At the sight of so many fish, they prepared a feast, but Black Tezcatlipoca, enraged at their using fire without his permission, punished the man who had kindled the flames. He changed him into a dog, Chántico, "In the Home," who became the god of the hearth.

According to another myth, Mixcoatl, one of Black Tezcatlipoca's many names, created fire by means of a *mamalhuaztli* or fire-forge. In another, humankind was created anew by Quetzalcoatl, who for this purpose descended into hell to recover human bones. On his journey back to the surface of the Earth, he was startled by a covey of quail. The bones fell from his hands and were smashed to pieces. They had to be ground, then kneaded with the blood of the gods and offered by the deities as a favor to poor Quetzalcoatl, in order to repopulate the world.

Other myths have to do with the creation or discovery of corn. One tells that the various parts of the body of the dragon who created the Earth were used to devise the plants that served as mankind's sustenance.

In another myth the corn god, Cinteotl, was born after the deluge and was the son of Piltzintecuhtli and Xochiquetzalli. Another says that corn was hidden in the Tonacatepetl – "The Hill of Our Flesh" or "The Hill of Sustenance" – and was discovered by an ant or gopher, and it was given to humankind as a gift from the noble and bountiful Quetzalcoatl.

The world at that time was lit only by occasional fires, so according to the myth as described by Sahagún, the four gods decided to create "a sun to illuminate the Earth" but which "will eat hearts and drink blood," and for this reason, "there must be wars, in order to obtain the hearts and the blood."

In one interpretation, the god who became the Sun is considered to be a son of Quetzalcoatl, while the Moon god was the son of Tlaloc and Chalchiuhtlicue. The gods in another case decided to die in order to assist the Sun in its first appearance. They were killed, in fact, by Ehecatl, "The Wind," who had to chase one of them, Xolotl, "The Page," the god of duplicity who disguised himself as corn or maguey, until he was caught, hidden in the water in the form of Axolotl, the capricious salamander. During this period, it was said that in the contemporary era there would be misery and crime, and according to the myths, people will lose respect for their vows; neither justice nor virtue will reign.

This same Sun shone on the Aztecs at the time of the Spanish Conquest in 1521. The belief prevails, however, that it must end on some "Day 4 Movement," when earthquakes will destroy it and the stars, Tzitzimime, will come down to earth, having by this time turned into monsters sent to devour indiscriminately all people.

The most reliable sources of references concerning both human and divine enterprise appeared in the codices. If the interpretation of these documents has left considerable margin for doubt or discrepancy, the codices themselves hold every clue to all we know, and much more, for the ancient Mexicans were methodical, imaginative, orderly, and creative, yet precise.

Their almanac, the *Tonalamatl*, was made up of twenty major cards, or slates, called *lamatl*, just as the original tarot, and later added information concerning two additional entities, to form a total of twenty-two, again, exactly as had occurred with the major arcana of the tarot. Each card determined the destiny of the child born within the corresponding period of thirteen days and represented, in effect, his or her sign of the zodiac.

The divinatory exercises of the priests served to assemble and interpret the total of twenty-two lamatl, or arcana, with regard to the child and in relation to each other, by a process as meticulous and esoteric as the Hermetic traditions of the tarot, in order to suggest, guide, or assign a course for the channeling of that personal destiny. The complete *Tonalamatl* encompassed a period of 260 days, the exact number in the Aztec year.

The accounting of the 260 days was called the *Tonalpohualli* and was linked astronomically with the planetary system, related to the solar year of 365 days, and with the synodic period of Venus, amounting to 584 days. This correspondence comprised the astronomic century of 104 years, in the following manner: 104 years amounted to 37,778 days, during which 64 Venusian cycles transpired; that is, 104 cycles or solar years and 146 Tonalpohualli, or lunar cycles.

This relationship was projected on the cosmic plane by the passing of ten astronomical centuries of 104 years each. Therefore, 104 years represents the conjunction of our planetary system with the great star Aldebaran. The Tonalpohualli, or accounting of 260 days, is further identified with an astronomical phenomenon projected on Earth. In a period of 52 solar cycles or 73 lunar cycles of 260 days each, the Sun moves from the northernmost point of the sacred cities of Mesoamerica to their southernmost point.

For this reason most, if not all, of the sacred cities were oriented on a north-south axis. At Copan, in Honduras, the Sun begins to move from north to south on August 13 and returns to its starting point 260 days later, on April 30 of the following year. In the same fashion, in Mexico-Tenochtitlan, the Sun moved toward the southern axis on March 17 and returned to its starting point on the northern axis on December 2.

The pre-Columbian divinatory arts thus implied a broad sensibility where the cosmos was concerned, stemming directly from the Sun as supreme regent. Yet the Moon was also "divine," since its synodic cycle complemented the same period of 260 days. A number of other god-regents, however, appear in the cards of the various codices. The Vatican, Telleriano-Remensis, and the Bourbon coincide on the presence of multiple series of gods: 1) the god whose name preceded that of the day; 2) the twelve lords of the day which correspond to the thirteen constellations in the Nahua Zodiac; and 3) the nine lords of the night; that is, the nine planets traditionally known to the Mayas and Nahuas.

The priest, wizard, or soothsayer in order to interpret the Tonalpohualli, with regard to the birth of a new being, had to take into account the influence of temporal space, as well as the god of the day of the child's birth, for whom the child was named. In addition, the priest had to consider the cosmic influence of the constellation and the planet-regent, along with the position of the Sun and the Moon, in relation to the period of 260 days.

The Tonalpohualli was, therefore, a system of combined astrology and astronomy, used to determine the influence of the cosmos in the life of any individual. It appears complete in the Bourbon Codex, with all the various series of gods described. These appear in the lower part of the card, or lamatl, and down along the right-hand margin.

The Aubin Codex, called the Aubin *Tonalamatl*, is the only known codex used strictly as a *Tonalamatl*. The pages, or lamatl, which we refer to as cards, are in fact a poor copy of the Bourbon, yet like its superior matrix, offer the total gamut of elements and factors utilized in the divinatory arts as projected on astrological judgments.

Others of the codices present only three of the factors encompassed by the Bourbon and are confined exclusively to the regent gods of the corresponding thirteen-day period, with the gods of the names and numerals related to each of the thirteen days. They fail to include the lords of the day or of the night. Nonetheless, for the purposes of this book, we are concerned principally with the symbolism assigned to each of the gods-regent and the similarity between these and the symbolism of the original twenty major arcana in the tarot, along with the two cards added later, which correspond precisely to the final two arcana eventually designed to amplify the tarot, bringing its philosophy full circle—back to the Magician, where it begins.

Both decks are attributed directly to the gods and both served to define the conduct considered by the gods to best serve humankind's highest aspirations, even ascent to a dimension as godlike as one might dare to dream, by means of a device termed *god's own language*, projected onto the realm of mortal men and women.

ARCANUM I

MYTHOLOGY OF THE MAGICIAN

The cards in the tarot deck are called *arcana*, meaning "mysteries," referring to the "secrets" in Hermetism as described in the *arcanum*, the Latin word for "trump." These secrets, however, are not dark truths at all, and contrary to popular misconception, have never been withheld from mortal men and women. They have been shielded, protected, even guarded, but never withheld. They are openly available to any thinking, positive, and conscientious being, for there is nothing mysterious in the definition of human purpose, nor in the application of intelligence toward a higher than ordinary goal.

Knowledge of these laws or principles offers an enormous potential for mortal awareness for purposes other than the vanities normally indulged in by society. Yet precisely as a result of humankind's incapacity or unwillingness to grow, or to fully penetrate an analysis intended for the glorification of the magnificent in the higher realm of existence—the essence of life itself—the fundamentals of Hermetism have been protected, like a precious elixir, for they are far more valuable than jewels or gold.

These principles were conceived as a guide toward personal rather than collective fulfillment and were generally revealed through symbols, to be captured and applied only by the receptive. An invaluable memorial to Egyptian symbolism has, therefore, been conferred on modern society by means of this semiotic language, expressed basically in its three areas of singular syntaxis: color, geometric figures, and numbers. Each card in the tarot, as is the case of the corresponding Mesoamerican *Tonalamatl*, is related to the evolution of mental contemplation as expressed in this graphic alphabet, to be deciphered and read, or interpreted like any other language.

The first arcanum is represented by Aleph, a Hebrew letter symbolizing "Unity," referring to a real or imaginary cosmic point at which all the events, ideas, actions, forms of life, art, music, poetry, in fact every person and every thought, every force and every illusion in the entire universe must eventually come together. This point is a beginning, a depository, but it is also a finality, the convergence of the infinite at a theoretical pinpoint, where past, present, and future blend, forming a single, perfect presence or concept.

This arcanum, called "The Magician," or the *Divina Essentia*, represents humankind in direct contact with Heaven and Divine Wisdom, wearing the crown of the Infinite. In most tarots, the figure is associated with Hermes, the young Greek messenger of the gods, though a number of versions confirm a connection with the Vedic Sarameya, derived from Sarama, god of the storm or of the dawn. The Hermetic syndrome is further related to a Greek word that conveys an idea of movement, though earlier interpretations suggest the word for "rock" or "stone," and the verb which means "to protect."

Subtleties of the Hermes legend indicate that this figure was either a god of the twilight or of the wind, as in the case of the Ehecatl manifestation of Quetzalcoatl. He was known "to make the sky clear." He probably originated as an ancient Pelasgian divinity of Thracian beginnings, associated with clouds. He was particularly honored by the mythical shepherds of Arcadia—divine park and playground of the deities. It was his mission to watch over their flocks and protect their huts, an assignment which led to the Greek custom of placing his more or less folkloric image at the doors of their dwellings.

The Dorian invasion lessened Hermes' prestige, replacing him with Apollo Nomius, while the primitive Hermes of the shepherds and of animal fertility took on another character. Hermes remained the god of travelers, and in a natural extension of this role, he was also charged with conducting the souls of the dead to the underworld. He was also the god of commerce and profit, licit or otherwise, and of gamblers and games of chance. Since buying and selling require discussion and negotiation, and the art of the trader is encompassed in the overcoming of the buyer's resistance, all by means of subtle and persuasive words, Hermes became the god of eloquence, *Logios*, and was thus confused later with the Egyptian image of Hermes Trismegistus.

To these various functions, however, Hermes added his specifically assigned role as Zeus' messenger, and as such is described by Homer, qualified with the epithet *Diactoros*, meaning "emissary" or "messenger." He came to earth repeatedly with orders from the King of the gods and undertook the most delicate missions. In Hesiod, Hermes was the god who brought the impressions and sentiments inspired by Zeus himself into the hearts of men and women. As an indefatigable runner, he was honored by athletes. Described as Agonios, "he who presides over contests," his statue was placed at the entrance to the stadium in Olympia, home of the celebrated games. He was credited with the invention of pugilism and racing. And, if in earlier times he had been represented as a mature man with a thick, long beard, and hair bound with a fillet, falling in curls to his shoulders, he was later idealized as a lithe and graceful young gymnast, an *ephebe* with a nervous, taut body, short, crisp hair, fine features, a curiously alert expression, a winged hat and sandals, and a winged staff called a *caduceus*.

This son of Zeus and Maia was born in the depths of a cave on Mount Cyllene in Arcadia. On the very day of his birth, Hermes revealed his mischievous character by stealing the cattle previously confided to Apollo's care. He sneaked furtively from his cradle and climbed the mountains of Pieria, where the divine herd had been sent to graze. The infant god separated fifty lowing heifers, which he drove before him under the cover of the night to the banks of the Alpheus. He made them walk backwards so their hoofmarks should not betray the direction they had taken. He himself had cautiously placed enormous sandals of tamarisk and myrtle twigs on his delicate feet. Before shutting up the heifers in a cavern, he picked out two of the fattest and, having ingeniously produced fire by rubbing laurel twigs together, he roasted them, dividing the flesh into twelve equal portions in honor of the twelve great gods.

Afterward, says the legend, he regained the heights of Cyllene, artfully entered his cave through the keyhole, like vapor or a breath of autumn, and crawled back into his cradle like any other naughty child—as if nothing happened.

Apollo detected the absence of the heifers on the following day. He went straight to Hermes, who denied all knowledge of the theft. Apollo, feeling betrayed, was furious. He gathered up the infant Hermes and carried him at once to Zeus, their father, who only laughed at the baby's audacity. Still, Zeus loved Apollo as well and instructed Hermes to return the heifers, stabled at sandy Pylus, near the ford of the Alpheus, in the tall stables beyond the fields.

The reconciliation of the two gods was eventually blessed, according to Robert Graves in his treatment of the Greek myths, when Hermes devised an ingenious musical instrument, using a tortoise shell, stretched oxhide and seven strings fashioned from sheep gut. Apollo was still outraged over the theft of his cattle but at the delightful sound of the divine music, which penetrated his senses, a sweet desire, says the tale, took possession of him. Hermes made Apollo a gift of the lyre he had just invented and Apollo, in turn, rewarded Hermes with a bright whip or a golden wand, a prototype of the caduceus, and entrusted him with the care of the celestial herd. With this, Apollo became the patron of music and Hermes the protector of flocks and herds; and according to the myth their friendship was never broken.[1]

---

[1]Robert Graves, *The Greek Myths* (New York & London: Penguin Books, 1955. Revised and reprinted 1990, Viking Penguin).

Hermes was engaging, ingratiating, and ingenious. He pacified even the jealous and vindictive Hera. He was the only one of Zeus' illegitimate children to find her favor and she even suckled him. He was bright and helpful. During the war against the giants, he put on the helmet of Hades, which made him invisible, and killed Hippolytus. He freed Zeus when the King was a prisoner of the monster Typhoeus, and restored his father's strength by replacing the nerves and tendons which the giant had cut. He protected Zeus during his father's amorous adventures, using every imaginable ruse; and became the King's messenger, having been granted winged sandals in order to cross more rapidly "the celestial spaces, and be borne over the watery sea or the vast earth like a breath of wind."[2]

Hermes' protection was extended to heroes. When Perseus faltered, Hermes restored his courage. He accompanied Herakles (Hercules) in his descent into the Underworld. He went with Orpheus on his search for Eurydice. He gave Odysseus a magic plant that made him immune to the enchantments of Circe. He helped Priam bring Hector's body back inside the walls of Troy. He rescued Aloadae and recovered the golden dog, Panareus, stolen from Zeus by Tantalus. When Tantalus cut his own son into pieces and served him as a feast for the gods, Hermes reassembled the pieces and restored the young man to life according to instructions given him by Zeus. He loved Persephone, Hecate, and Aphrodite. He pursued the nymphs in the forest and produced numerous progeny. He was a benefactor of humankind, a shrewd negotiator, and a master of melodious speech. He could lead the souls of the dead back to the world of light. He was quick-witted, amusing, thoroughly enchanting, and utterly fascinating.

Hermes appears on the arcanum with a jovial gesture, suggesting the triumph inherent in a clever wit and swift action, applied in combination with his divine powers. In the Roman pantheon, he was called Mercury, in recognition of his agility, and his association with doctors and the art of healing, a consideration granted in response to his natural faculty for transmitting divine knowledge into the human—or material—realm.

During the Middle Ages, the image of Hermes was replaced by a juggler or harlequin on the card that later became the joker in the modern deck, in addition to representing the principle of the trump card used in the game of bridge. Its power was indicated in its natural gift for reassembling the cosmic elements implicit in the symbols of

---

[2]Felix Guirand, ed., *New Larousse Encyclopedia of Mythology*, translated by Richard Aldington and Delano Ames (London: Hamlyn House, 1969), p. 124. Originally published in French as *Larousse Mythologie Générale* (Paris: Librarie Larousse, 1959).

the arcana, until they could be applied at the observer's interest or convenience.

This is a powerful and benevolent card. The Magician is fully aware of his youth and dominion over life itself, his potential for fulfillment, and the powers of the superior, or evolved, spirit, which neutralize extremes until a reconciliation has been accomplished, in the balance and harmony which permit the highest accomplishments of the creative mind.

CARD DESCRIPTION

le Bateleur ♐

A young man is shown on the card, dressed in a magician's tunic, though his garments vary according to the style and period of the deck. The traditional cards showed him dressed in a multi-colored robe, with ornaments of gold. A symbol of the Infinite, a figure eight on its side, appears in some decks above his head. He may wear a golden crown but more frequently he appears with a diadem or circlet of gold around his head. A similar belt encircles his waist.

For the Egyptians, The Magician represented eternal life. On all Egyptian or Greek talismans he appears with a serpent in his right hand, symbolizing eternal wisdom and, in his left, the Medieval magic wand, a scepter which refers to the caduceus of the messenger, Hermes. If The Magician appears as a juggler his clothing is festive and colorful. The cap he wears instead of the circlet or crown is intended as a sign of eternity.

He normally stands behind a table that appears in the form of a cube, with three objects on its surface, which may, in turn, be either covered or bare: a cup, a sword, and a coin, symbolizing the Trinity-in-Unity, considered successively as the active archetype, the activity of humanity seen as a male figure, and nature's activity in itself. This concept is translated as Spirit, in relation to Energy, thrust on Matter; or as the inter-relation of ideas, forms, and material objects.

The young man appears on the card in a standing position, to emphasize his active role, while his arms are deliberately placed in a twofold position, suggesting his binary nature; that is, the combination of two opposite poles or planes, as in the metaphysical juxtaposition of Essence and Substance—two balanced opposites, synthesized in Spirit and Matter along a direct axis.

CARD SYMBOLISM

The magician in the card holds a magic wand in his raised right hand to symbolize resourcefulness. Yet the lowered left hand indicates the duality of his condition, confirmed in the straight line along the axis of his extended arms. The binary is further emphasized in his artifacts, implements and adornments, represented in the cup, the sword, the coin, and the scepter—all references to the suits in the original, or medieval decks of cards, of the sort still termed today as "Spanish" decks.

The wand or scepter depicts fire, the initiation of all evolution, the father, virility, and male energy. The cup indicates water and physical life, divination, maternity, and female receptivity. The sword refers to air, a spirit that penetrates the material in order to create humankind, the intellectuality in decision and the definition of the alternatives that permit action. Yet the cross on the sword's hilt in the Wirth deck suggests the union of the masculine and feminine principles.

The coin and the golden ornaments in this arcanum represent the Earth, where life begins, the cavern from which humankind emerged—and in which the baby Hermes was cradled—a starting point, from which to synthesize the various principles in the card until Unity is achieved.

This arcanum stresses the binary condition of humankind's initial position, the binaries similarly encountered in the card's other references: awareness and fulfillment, good and evil, light and shadow, heat and cold.

When two binaries merge, the introduction of a third factor creates a unit, an important concept in Hermetism. When the binaries are neutralized, another fundamental concept, called a balance, is achieved, which permits the potential for harmony, which is the resolution, in fact, of awareness-fulfillment.

Not all binaries are easily neutralized. In philosophy, the binary essence-substance may be resolved in the term "nature." Yet spirit-matter must be resolved as "the soul," life-death as "projection onto the astral," good-evil as "the deed."

In the same sense, the resolution of light and shadow may be seen in half-shadow, essentially the same phenomenon achieved when heat and cold are neutralized in a modification of the existing temperature. The opposition of the sexes, however, is only neutralized in the appearance of a third element, a child, until the three entities are reassembled in a unit as "the family."

The Magician in the first arcanum is intended as a point of departure, the beginning of discrimination and selective thinking, the initiation of an interpenetration of the three planes—mental, astral, and physical—in which humans must distinguish among their mental (*mens*), their Astral or Astrosome (the soul) and their Corpus (physical body), until the idea of unity and activity have been properly and effectively contained.

The first arcanum symbolizes a course of action, in which all beings are in harmony and are returning to that unity, which is their true aim, expressed in the Vedantic idea of the *Atman*, that "unity comprises unity, for everything is contained in everything."[3]

---

[3]Keith Crim, ed., *The Perennial Dictionary of World Religions* (San Francisco: HarperCollins, 1989), p. 792. See especially Vedic Hinduism.

LAMATL I

MYTHOLOGY OF CE-CIPACTLI (THE ALLIGATOR)

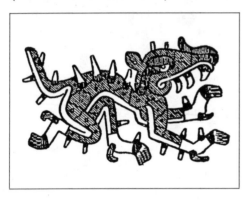

The name of the first lamatl or arcanum in the Meso-american almanac called the *Tonalamatl* refers to Ce-Cipactli, the first of the twenty glyphs indicating the corresponding thirteen-day period in the Tonalpo-hualli, oriented toward the east and the rising Sun, with Tonacatecuhtli as its patron.

In the Aztec calendar, known as the Stone of the Sun, Cipactli appears as the first figure in the left-central upper section, depicted as a human head framed with a spiked aureola, signifying the rays of the Sun. This head, atop the monster body of the mythological alligator-whirlwind, symbolizes the Earth seen as the Mother—all that is fertile, receptive, fruitful, imposing, and abundant—ultimately a blend of the male and female principles.

According to the Borgia Codex, Cipactli was the first being created by the gods, similarly conceived by the Babylonians, Egyptians, and Hebrews, who saw the Earth in the form of a primordial entity from which all divinities, the races of men, and the forces of nature emanated.

Both the Mayas and the Nahuas visualized the Earth as fundamental matter, resting on Cipactli. This world-as-a-reptile forms a juncture with Kakhmu and Lakhamu, a pair of monstrous serpents in Assyrian mythology, elementary beings who gave birth to Ahshar, the male principle, and to Kishar, the female. These represented, respectively, the celestial and terrestrial worlds, not unlike Uranus and Gaia in Greek mythology.

In a further Assyrian parallel, Tiamat personified the sea and represented the feminine element which gave birth to the world. She symbolized the blind forces of primitive chaos against which the intelligent Creator Gods had to struggle for survival, as occurred in the case of Indra, the Aryan warrior god of Nature, the Sun itself, a Tonacate-cuhtli of the Indus Valley. His victory over the dragon Vritra, the Enveloper or the Obstructor, ended with the liberation of the water, which he released, "like penned-up cows," and "to this end he splits mountains, and sends the torrents rushing towards the sea." Indra's achievement determined the fecundity of nature. By "breaking the clouds," he returned the Sun and the dawn to the world. "As he supplies both light and water he appears not only as the god of war but as the principle of fertility."[4]

The Mesoamerican monster Cipactli is also related to fertility and to the fruitfulness of the Earth, as he carries corn on his back, the essence of abundance. Like Tonacatecuhtli, "Lord of Our Flesh," the Father and King of the heavens, God-Regent of this sign, he symbolized the principle of movement which caused the Sun to shine, the waters and winds to circulate, and motivated "the splendor of the Supreme Spirit who plunges into the heart of the universe and irradiates even the secret souls of men, for our flesh is made of corn."[5]

Tonacatecuhtli was shown on a throne of red and yellow ears of corn. Additional ears of corn made up the diadem, like an aureola radiating from behind his back. A coiled serpent of fire, Xiuhtecuhtli, forms his headdress. Quetzal feathers complement his adornments, which are principally formed of cornshucks and leaves, precious and divine, to be worshipped beyond any material wealth.

His wife, Tonacacihuatl, is another version of Xochiquetzal, the young and beautiful goddess of the supple and the graceful, also known as her exact opposite and antithesis, Chicomecoatl, "Seven Serpent," who caused sterility, want, and misery.

In the Vatican Codex, the Divine Pair, as Tonacatecuhtli and Tona-cacihuatl, preside jointly over this thirteen-day period in order to supervise each day, with its number, its day-patron, and its night-patron, who collectively determined the influences on the newborn in this sign. The thirteen days, in turn, combined the nine lords and twenty gods for each of the days in the solar calendar. In this manner each day was different and could never be confused with any other. At the end of a thirteen-day period, Day One would begin again, but with a different name and Lord.

Tonacatecuhtli, Lord of Our Flesh, or "The First Man," was considered the first being ever to inhabit this world, an anthropomorphized Cipactli. He harnessed the wind and divided the waters of Heaven and

---

[4]Felix Guirand, ed., New Larousse Encyclopedia of Mythology, translated by Richard Aldington and Delano Ames (London: Hamlyn House, 1969), p. 326.
[5]Eduard Seler, Comentarios al Códice Borgia, Vol. 1 (Mexico: Fondo de Cultura Económica, 1963), p. 160.

Earth, which at first "was in an uproar and confused, until he put things where they can now be seen." He was humankind and abundance, "he who offers and wears a crown, called as well Seven Flowers because he governed the principalities of the world." He had no temple nor were sacrifices carried out in his name, "for he had no want of them nor did he wish it." His greater majesty, it was said, dignified him to the full extent of his necessities. "He had no need of a sanctuary even in the case of the demons taking it for his own leaving of it, for they would not."[6]

His dominion distinguished this sign with three astrological influences, in particular, all of them having to do with the spells and superstition personified in Chicomecoatl, as the diametrically opposed concept of fruitfulness and abundance: the apocalypse rampant.

Tonacatecuhtli and Tonacacihuatl, being "the first man and woman," were further known as Huehue, or "Old." They wore a knife or blade between them, to indicate the death process inevitable from the moment life begins in conception.

LAMATL DESCRIPTION

This lamatl, governed by the Creator Gods Tonacatecuhtli and his wife Tonacacihuatl, Lords of Sustenance, was additionally illustrated with the gods who, for one or another reason, are associated with the primary couple, in varying forms depending on the codex.

The two Supreme Beings generally appear with their son Quetzalcoatl, the benevolent spirit who bestowed the sacred corn on humankind. They are also shown with Xochiquetzal, the young and joyful Goddess Mother. Occasionally they are accompanied by another of their sons, Tezcatlipoca the Black, adorned with the signs of the days, five above his head, five on each leg and five beneath his feet.

---

[6]Eduard Seler, *Comentarios al Códice Borgia*, Vol. 1, p. 65.

Figure 8. Tonacatecuhtli, lord of sustenance and procreation. To his right is the first or divine couple. From the Códice Borgia.

Tonacatecuhtli, Lord and Creator of the World, who formed the Heavens and the Earth, was said to have invented the four cardinal points and the four blessed elements, and these accompanied him as an integral part of his representation in the codices, symbolized in the instruments of the priests and magicians or wizards.

The staff in his hand, or reed wand, called *acatl*, indicated fire. The cup or chalice used to collect the sacramental beverage represented water. The flint knife, called *tecpatl*, a sacrificial instrument often indicated by a maguey thorn, symbolized air. The bag of copal, the incense used by the priests as one of the most highly prized of religious artifacts, indicated the riches of the Earth, worldly and spiritual, implicit in

Figure 9. Yayauhqui Tezcatlipoca, the Black Tezcatlipoca, with the twenty signs of the days. From the Códice Borgia.

the pursuit of the sacred devotions. The sign of a cross was normally drawn on the bag, as an emblem of the priests of Quetzalcoatl.[7]

The Creator Gods were further depicted with sumptuous breast-plates, bracelets, jeweled crowns whose precious gems were complemented by leaves and kernels of corn, symbolizing the faculties of the Supreme Beings. This was a largesse he shared or withdrew at will in his dealings with mortal humankind. Tonacatecuhtli's crown was further decorated with ears of corn, a representation of material wealth: the flesh of the first beings was said to have been formed of corn.

As Citallantonali, another name for Tonacatecuhtli, he appears as a nocturnal warrior god in the heavens, strolling along the highway of the Milky Way. His arrows and knives further indicate war and penitence.

Xochiquetzalli's (Xochiquetzal) crown of flower pistils indicates the cosmos, a paradise of love and a bounty of flowers and beauty. The quetzal plumes indicate her worth. She is seated on a thronelike chair decorated with turquoise. She is often accompanied by Xochipilli, the lithe young god of spring, her mate and her twin. They are seen as

[7]This cross encouraged 19th-century Mormons in the notion of Quetzalcoatl being in the depository of the soul of Christ, transmigrated when Jesus died in Jerusalem.

newlyweds in a garden of eternal joy and fruitfulness, the counterpart, actually equilibrium, of the apocalyptic Chicomecoatl.

LAMATL SYMBOLISM

This lamatl emphasizes the faculty of the Creator Gods to transmit their sense of order, to transform the world and its elements, and to project onto mortal humans the concept of purpose and fulfillment implicit in the struggle of the Earth to overcome its initial condition of chaos and confusion.

This wealth of alternatives, encompassed in sustenance and pro-creation, dictates an imperative for survival. Yet survival alone is insuf-ficient, according to the Divine Pair, who impose on their children a further and more precisely stipulated mandate: to live with devotion, humility, rectitude, and respect for the gods.

The Mesoamerican world was rich in symbols and each was applied in a multiplicity of forms, its variants dependent on its context, until a whole language evolved, an intricate tapestry of emblems and implications, an inextricable entanglement in a semiotic jungle.

This vast domain requires a methodical exploration, beginning with the earliest clan totemism and continuing through the mythologi-cal dynasties into the most highly evolved networks of philosophical and theological analysis.

The ferocious and the gross achieved a perfect balance within the androgynous male-female equilibrium. The lovely and the sumptuous were carefully incorporated into the reprehensible until everything in the imaginable world had been contained, rather than denied, and modulated instead of obstructed. There was no "evil" except in its application. There was no "wrong" except in the deformation of "right." Everything was relative, everything was admissible. Every-thing endured, within the mutable nature of life itself, so nothing ever changed.

PARALLEL SYMBOLISM

Both The Magician in the tarot and Cipactli in the *Tonalamatl* describe the intercommunication between gods and men, the message implicit in the Divine Word as transmitted to humankind.

This arcanum and its corresponding lamatl stress a starting point, an initiation of method and purpose parallel to the initiation of the earthly process, giving order to chaos and direction to worldly behavior. Both underline the symbolism inherent in the four elements, with their impact on philosophical progression. And both emphasize the dictates of a primary power on the society of humankind.

Each figure on its respective card bears the crown of wisdom and cosmic awareness, considered the domain of those Supreme Beings who are not only endowed with the key to the Infinite. They are also willing to transmit their knowledge by means of lesser gods, wizards, or priests, in order to regulate the necessary rectitude, coherence of conduct, or disposition to action which provide humankind with its fundamental alternatives, the foundation on which a productive life may be elevated.

These younger gods, lively and fruitful, serve as the intermediaries between the mortal and the Divine. As the offspring of the kings of Heaven, they are permitted to judge or to regulate their powers in relation to an individual and his or her worthiness. Their protection is, therefore, also relative yet they have almost unlimited access to both penitence and plenty.

Hermes, as much as Quetzalcoatl, or the androgynous synthesis of Xochipilli-Xochiquetzal, are gifted in the alchemy of the elements. While they proffer abundance they may also permit the proliferation of famine and suffering.

Yet the gods only reflect the people who conceived them. Divine Knowledge and Cosmic Awareness remain the province of the mortal being, permanently confronted with life's dilemma and juncture: the light of fulfillment or the darkness of the ignominious act, the Sun on this "green jewel in the universe" or the unending gloom of the underworld.

ARCANUM II

MYTHOLOGY OF THE PRIESTESS

The arcanum in the tarot called "The Priestess" refers directly to the Vestal Virgins in Rome and the Cybeles in Greece, but even before them, to the Mother Earth Cult in Crete. This cult was later consecrated in Artemis, or Diana, presumed by Roman times to represent the hunt. Initially, however, Artemis was also the patroness of young girls and the maidenly arts and, especially, the sovereignty of the female deity before the conversion to a male figure, undoubtedly for bellicose purposes, when the cult was subtly transformed throughout the Aegean.

The figure also refers to the Egyptian priestesses who served Isis: Goddess of the Moon, wife and sister of Osiris, who constituted half the divine foursome (the others were Seth and his wife Nephthys), brought forth from the union of Geb and Nut — Earth and Sky; in turn the products of the heavenly twins — Air and Moisture — called Shu and Tefnut, born when Atum-Ra, the self-created Sun, rose from the Ocean, Nun.

The second arcanum is further identified with Hera, celebrated Queen of Olympus, daughter of the Titan Rhea, herself a daughter of Gaia, the Earth. When Gaia by her iron will took Uranus, the Heavens, to be, according to the myth, her mate and her companion in all things, their union was corrupted by Uranus himself, who despised his children and swallowed them whole, until the youngest, Cronus, had his revenge. He attacked his father in the marriage bed and as the tale continues, cuts off his male members, and throws them into the sea, where foam bubbled up from each drop of blood; and Aphrodite emerged.

Yet Cronus did to his children what his father had done to him until Rhea plotted retaliation through her own youngest child. A cruel, yet monumental, pageant of tragedy and betrayal, unfortunate but hardly unique, was projected across the course of Western civilization. Curiously, a similar tale which will be told later, occurs in the Mexican codices, and was probably enacted long before the existence of Hellas.

Meanwhile, however, when Zeus finally made sister Hera his queen and wife, their domestic conflict, though less repugnant than Gaia's and Uranus', still conformed to a pattern that persists in semiology, the myths of all cultures, even in modern psychology, while Hera, by her wit and perseverance, maintained her position as the grandest of the goddesses on Olympus. She represented fecundity and all of nature's abundance, incarnate in Woman. During the ascendance of Rome, she was called Juno and was identified with Jupiter, the Father of the Gods.

In certain tarots of the Middle Ages, the figure became "The Papesse," a term applied as a substitute for "The Priestess." The arcanum was identified with Pope Joan, the vicaress who sat on the throne of St. Peter until she was found to be pregnant. Though the resulting scandal cost dearly—her life, in fact—she certainly personified at least a good part of the symbolism traditionally associated with the tarot's second figure.

Afterward, this arcanum suggested a disquieting duality, in which masculine and feminine assumed a perceptible ambivalence, and this in turn assigned specific characteristics to the arcanum, both an access to the knowledge in the occult and a power deemed sacred, an amalgam derived from an exalted hierarchical position and the peculiar power assigned to feminine nature, bound to the Earth but expressed in the birth of an unwanted child.

CARD DESCRIPTION

The tarots of the Middle Ages showed The Papesse or The Priestess seated on a square throne, framed by two columns, plants, or trees. Her garments served to conceal her imminent maternity while they indicated her rank. In various traditional decks she wore a large cross at her breast. This was often shown as the Egyptian "ankh," a cross signifying the gift of life—representing the wealth of the Nile—while it refers to the symbols of the occult.

She carried in her right hand a book containing the knowledge of the occult sciences, thus suggesting the other name by which this arcanum is known: "Gnosis" or "Knowledge" or "The Portal of the Sanctuary."

Medieval Italian cards included the Papal crown, while other cards made a point of showing The Priestess covered with the veil and carrying the crown of Isis: binary values symbolizing the vital and fertile energy of sacred knowledge and her dexterity in the discipline of the occult.

CARD SYMBOLISM

This arcanum is conceived as the totality of humankind's highest achievements, accomplished by means of fulfillment in both thought and desire. Biological fertility is balanced with rationale; that is, logic and emotion are blended, as the path toward reason. In effect, this arcana represents the integration of the unconscious and the conscious, or instinct and reason in the quest for an integration of the total being in human experience.

LAMATL II

MYTHOLOGY OF CE-OCELOTL (THE JAGUAR)

The lamatl or arcanum called Ce-Ocelotl marked the beginning of the second thirteen-day period indicated in the *Tonalamatl* or almanac. Its graphic representation, the mottled head of the magnificent Mesoamerican jaguar, now almost extinct, emphasized the place in Toltec, Aztec, Maya, and Olmec mythology held by this singular feline, the American hemisphere equivalent to the Asian tiger or African leopard.

Called Balam by the Mayas, the name of this exalted deity was specifically assigned to the jaguar, though it was translated into Spanish by priests and scribes during the conquest of the New World as "tiger." Despite its phonetic reference in the Nahuatl language to the ocelot—another smaller and more tame spotted cat of Mesoamerica— the term was also applied to the jaguar priesthood, the cult associated with a ferocious and authoritarian figure.

Two descriptions of the cult's origins appear in the versions of the famous augurial testimonies, *The Book of the Chilam Balam* and *Book of the Jaguar People,* one written in the Yucatecan town of Chumayel and the other in the nearby town of Mani. Each name accompanies its respective document, considered to be at least ten centuries old. Described with precision and fidelity according to the Spanish invaders, and considered to be only sketchy and fragmentary according to Maya scholars, the documents nonetheless were frequently consulted by the priests or soothsayers in the surrounding area.

As a result, the ancient Mayas endowed the jaguar with magical powers, an idea absorbed into their culture after first inheriting the notion from their contact with Olmec priests. The hypothesis and therefore the symbolism, were supported by the physical similarity of the Olmecs to a feline species. In fact, the Olmecs considered themselves descendants of the mythological "tiger people," though a number of studies establish the term as a euphemism for a sect of hermaphrodites.

This lamatl refers specifically to the priestesses of the Goddess Tlazolteotl and to the God Quetzalcoatl, deities of forgiveness. Public confessions were performed before a priestess of Tlazolteotl, part of whose name—"teo," substantiated in "teotl" or "deity"—would suggest a curious bond with the Greeks.

The Priestess was considered the intermediary between the people and Tlazolteotl, who would pardon sins and indicate to humankind the way of penitence for transgressions committed against the moral code, while Quetzalcoatl—the Plumed Serpent— presided over ceremonies describing a modest personal penance or "sacrifice."

The two gods seem to indicate a reference to Isis and Osiris, as Tlazolteotl is established as originating in the lower regions, the Huastec, of the Gulf of Mexico. This is an area deemed sacred in the Olmec pantheon, as birthplace of the mighty jaguar god, in which he reigned supreme.

The priests of Tlazolteotl additionally performed the tasks required by the newborn: baptism and the determination through augurial consultation of the baby's astrological sign and ascendant, in accordance with the divinatory contents of the twenty-two arcanum, or lamatl, in the *Tonalamatl* deck.

The second lamatl establishes Quetzalcoatl as its regent, and bears the image of one of his most highly exalted priests. This was the god, according to legend, who taught mortals the use of the sacred calendars, the application of mathematics, and who, very particularly, instructed his priests in the esoteric knowledge contained in each of the lamatl.

LAMATL DESCRIPTION

The card shows Quetzalcoatl as the son of the Primary Gods, that is, of God Father and God Mother, referring to the Sun and the Moon, in actual fact, at times the Sun and in other instances the Moon. He reigns in the City of the Peaceful Waters at the legendary ceremonial site at Tula.

Most of the codices show the figure seated before a temple, or House of Penitence, where a kneeling mortal asks his blessing and forgiveness. Other codices show him wearing the conical cap of jaguar skin, a characteristic of the oldest deities, those called the Huastec gods, indicating the area at the northeastern extreme of the Mexican Gulf Coast lowlands, in the geographical designation ascribed by Mesoamerica.

The image is often accompanied by a further detail in the kneeling penitent, whose sacrifice has caused his tongue to bleed. The Goddess, Tlazolteotl, is represented by her characteristic garments.

LAMATL SYMBOLISM

This lamatl is dedicated to the relationship between priests and laypeople, and of humankind's need for those priests, for a figure physically similar to oneself, endowed genetically or professionally with the gift or skill necessary in order to negotiate contact with the gods. The Ce-Ocelotl is further dedicated to the preservation of the divinatory arts and the calculation of time in the calendar—that is, the prediction of the future and instruction in the esoteric wisdom of Mesoamerica.

In the binary world, Tlazolteotl indicates mystery and forgiveness, the mystique of one who sinned and, when repentant, was converted. Quetzalcoatl, in turn, represents the blameless priest, in whom the unrevealed secrets of the baptism are confided.

This symbolism was described in the legends of the first generations of Olmecs, or by the Olmec wanderers who settled along the shores of the Gulf of Mexico following their expulsion—possibly by volcanic eruption—from a Central American Eden. Such symbolism encompassed both human suffering and divine benevolence, as described in the two figures from the Huastec pantheon. These are said to derive directly from the remote myths of the cult of the jaguar priest.

The priest-deity was considered to be the product of the union between a goddess and a mythological animal, in this case the formidable sacred jaguar. He is therefore, according to the legend, born a hermaphrodite, but the whole story follows the patterns of Zeus' adventures in the Greek myths and a divine figure's penchant for mortal womankind. Or are we confronted with a Mesoamerican temptation of Christ?

PARALLEL SYMBOLISM

The second arcanum and the second lamatl are both characterized by the binary symbolism in their principal figure, The Priestess in the tarot and Quetzalcoatl as a priest of the deity Tlazolteotl, Goddess of Sin and Redemption.

In the tarot, The Priestess wears the male symbol of the papacy, the maximum ecclesiastical hierarchy, while her passive and feminine condition is translated in her throne and her concealed fecundity. If two columns between which she is framed appear on the card, they represent the symbols of the Sun and Moon; that is, the mental and physical forces of nature.

This sexual duality is implied in the figure of Quetzalcoatl, in relation to the same cosmic bodies. The feminine condition is encompassed in the priestesses of the Goddess Tlazolteotl. The conjunction refers to the sexual encounter between Tlazolteotl and an ocelot or jaguar here on Earth, which generated the first Quetzalcoatl, originally the Darkling God. His personality will remain an enigma for as long a time as a detailed study requires, though most of the clues have long since been obscured by time, the Spanish Conquest, oil drilling, and simple misinterpretation of the fanciful artistic vision and creative imagination of the Olmecs, who were one of the earliest peoples to advance to a culturally significant plateau, at least three thousand and possibly five to eight thousand years before Christ.

The Quetzalcoatl myth was commonly misunderstood, even before the arrival of the Spaniards. The name—and its counterparts in the various pre-Hispanic languages of a number of different cultural nuclei—was assigned to several of the successive apparitions of this figure across the centuries, beginning in the anthropomorphic ver-

Figure 10. The God-Priest Quetzalcoatl, the god of the wind and enlightenment. From the Códice Borgia.

sions of the Olmecs and continuing through Quetzalcoatl's supposed disappearance. His messianic reappearance, according to the codices, took the form of a shining personage, fair of skin and hair, in whose eyes it was said, was revealed the transparency of the skies.

When Cortez arrived, in 1521, on horseback and in armor, with eyes of a sparkling blue color, trailed by a band of followers generally interpreted as fair, by comparison with the "darkling" natives, the Mexicans were convinced that a myth and a legend had become tangible. And, while they were less gullible than folklore would suggest, the renegade from remote Extremadura in rural Spain was infinitely more wily.

So if the Aztec downfall had been written into the divinatory lore of the Mesoamerican peoples, it was also written that a new race, and

Figure 11. Ocelotl, symbol of the Jaguar, god of caves and of sinners seeking penitence. From the Códice Borgia.

with it a new destiny, would be formed in a union, called *mestizo* — a mixture of European and native blood — that followed almost mystically the tale implied in the second lamatl. This time Cortez would be the jaguar and a clever girl from the southern state of Tabasco, as witty and gifted as she was beautiful (probably descended from the Olmecs) would be his Tlazolteotl.

Malintzin, or La Malinche, or just Marina — her Latin name — would be damned as a traitor to her people by later *mestizos*. They called her a slut with a gift for languages symbolizing the fallen woman — victim of conquest but also of convenience. Yet history, curiously, readjusted the myth. Today she is not seen as a product of just expediency, but as a visionary, who saw in the foreign captain a weapon for the revenge of her people, who had been outraged by their Aztec neighbors. She also fell in love and was redeemed by her devotion to her lover. Great pride may arise where there was once shame in the recognition of the talent and political acumen in these two people — Cortez and Malintzin — the personification of Ce-Ocelotl. The implication that their mentor, Quetzalcoatl, is God in the monotheistic sense, or the central figure in the Trinity, or even its very embodiment, is further supported independently of any archaeological or historical evidence already cited in the fact that the priesthood in the Mesoamerican pantheon wore the cap of jaguar skin, a symbol of power among the priests of the Huastec, where the one God—Father, Son and Spirit—was said to have been born.

In both the tarot and the *Tonalamatl*, the Priestess in the second arcanum and Quetzalcoatl seen with the priests of Tlazolteotl review the contents of the sacred books, revealing the key they are known to possess, the clue to the wisdom of occultism and magic, illustrated by an amulet hung about each of their necks. The Priestess wears the ankh, key to the mysteries of Isis. Quetzalcoatl wears a pectoral known as the Gem of the Wind, distinguished by a spiral design indicating the concept of evolution in relation to eternity, movement in mutation.

The parallel identity of the priestesses of Isis and Tlazolteotl is further reflected in the coincidental occupation of both in the initiatory cults of magic, fertility, and transformation; in their power of forgiveness; and in the implicit redemption in their promise of another, better, life after death.

ARCANUM III

MYTHOLOGY OF THE EMPRESS

This arcanum originates in the idea of creation, closely connected with the element of love or, more precisely, a strong attraction. Universal gravitation, clemency, the associations of love both common and cosmic are all seen as aspects of the magnetism of Venus Urania, Venus of the astronomical universe, often referred to as Phisis (Nature) or The Empress.

This *Divina Natura* is conceived as the irresistible loveliness and the desirability of Aphrodite – or Venus – brought forth from the foam of the sea after Cronus wreaks terrible vengeance on Uranus, his father. She is seen as the attraction of earthly elements to each other.

If Venus is described as Mother of the Universe, the Sun would then be the Father. She is shown crowned with twelve stars, later seen as the twelve signs of the zodiac – though originally, in Egypt, only eight signs were recognized – and she is accompanied by the Sun and the Moon, those children of Hyperion, the Titan.

The principle of birth on the physical plane is closely connected with different phases of solar energy, as received by the Earth. These phases are determined by the position of the Sun in a particular sign of the zodiac; thus, in occultism, the zodiac is considered a strong indicator of the physical plane and its properties.

> A woman clothed with the sun, and the moon under her feet, and upon her head a crown of twelve stars: and she being with child cried, travailing in birth, and pained to be delivered (Revelation 12:1,2).

The mystery of life, the struggle to be born, the miracle of reproduction, reveal a pervading devotion in this arcanum, with the Sun as the center of attraction, or planetary love, in our solar system. The Sun is also considered to embody the idea of emanated life, that is, of all creation.

Venus, however, the great and expansive Phisis, reigns with her love over all that has been or ever will be born, and dominates all influences under any circumstances, suggesting that love implies a victory over all obstacles, and guarantees the durability of creative emanation.

The arcanum further proposes that nothing is created; everything is born, indicating that the process of birth results from the natural consequence of any union between active and passive principles. In the further awareness of fusion, occurring when active penetrates, or impregnates, or is integrated with passive, this union may be seen as the underlying philosophy of power, the relationship of mass and energy, the secret of life itself.

Divina Natura consists of a universal substance; in effect, the synthesis achieved in the integration of love, as creative emanation, primarily of a singular energy (including heat, sound, and density), from which all existing objects are only assembled in varying forms. These forms are perceived through the five physical senses and are classed in relation to each, yet all five are sensitive as well to certain kinds of molecular movement, usually termed vibrations of ether, light, air, water, and Earth itself, which is subject to the movement of atoms.

Ether is movement in all directions. Light is movement in straight lines. Air is a whirling movement. Water is balanced movement. Earth is arresting movement. Apart from its private qualities, each element—here we have five instead of the traditional four of the ancient world—possesses the qualities of the senses as secondary characteristics, revealed as sound, color, shape, taste, and scent. Furthermore, each of the kinetic forms is represented in the human mind. Therefore, according to The Empress, everything can correspond to anything else under certain conditions.

CARD DESCRIPTION

The cards representing The Empress often show her seated on a cubic stone, in turn poised on a globe. The cube is covered with eyes like a Nepalese temple, and a figure is revealed, a cat, the clairvoyant animal, symbol of universal power.

The Empress is crowned with the twelve stars of the zodiac and carries a shield in her right hand, showing either an imperial eagle or two crossed handles. The eagle can symbolize the Sun, or the solar figure might appear under the right foot. A scepter in her left hand reveals either the sign of Venus (creation) or the Magic Sword of Paracelsus, an instrument designed to dominate or even dispel harmful concentrations of (invisible) forces.

The sword is shown as a trident (representing the ternary) and is to be interpreted by triangular concepts, for example: 1) archetype, man, nature; 2) past, present, future; or 3) fate, destiny, karma. These are intended to suggest the mental and even metaphysical character of the absolute right of humankind to all three planes of existence.

At times the third arcanum is seen with wings instead of "clothed with the sun," to project the ascension of *Isis Terrestris* (Earthly Isis), or *Isis Coelestis* (Celestial Isis), which gives the figure an angelical appearance. In addition, she wears robes which flow around her imminent motherhood, implying a long and healthy pregnancy, in contrast to the covert and tormented maternity of The Priestess.

A waning moon shows under The Empress' left foot, indicating the sublunar world, the lowest realm of creation, a subtle allusion to cosmic fecundity and divine nature in the Earth's dimension.

CARD SYMBOLISM

The Empress is considered the revelation, that is, the recipient of the generative power of nature. Meanwhile the Sun is seen as an ostentatious figure, the center of attraction in our solar system. It embodies the vital power in the fertility process and the fecundation of the

Earth, from which all of life and eternal creation emanate, representing, furthermore, the harmony in nature in its broadest sense, given to humankind by means of spiritual creativity or reasonable understanding.

Love is symbolized by Venus Urania. She is seen as a fruitful love, bound to the procreativity of the family and geneological extension. The Kabbalah sees this figure as exalted feminity, the double mystery, a compendium of the two preceding cards.

LAMATL III

MYTHOLOGY OF CE-MAZATL (THE DEER)

The figure which initiates the third thirteen-day cycle of the *Tonalamatl* is Mazatl, the deer, who represents the human animal on his or her course through worldly existence, in the sense that he may be free, or be "hunted to death."

One of his regents is Tepeyolotli, or Tepeyolotl, a jaguar god, but in this case identified with the god of the caves, with the night, and the underworld, everything surly, dark, gloomy or fraught with unexpected—or perhaps long predicted—danger.

His other regent is Tlazolteotl, the transfigured lunar goddess, fundamental Earth goddess, goddess of destiny and manifest will, who appears as her own priestess, offering her newborn babe to the deities while she takes it into her service.

This lamatl validates the priestesses of Tlazolteotl, as the medium by which humans may express their sins to the benevolent gods. The figure embraces the very essence of the Goddess Tlazolteotl herself, who appears not only symbolically as in the previous lamatl, but pictured as a full body, seen robust and magnificent, an Amazon warrior. She offers humankind, to whom she gave life, to the gods, as the fulfillment of "the perfect sacrifice" referred to before; it is an expression of survival as much as redemption.

Yet, in this context, Tlazolteotl is also projected as salvation: she offers her sacrifice in the name of her flock, who are the devout, the repentant, but in the sense of a beginning rather than an end. These are the children she has saved, flesh of her flesh, a creation from her womb held out humbly to the gods, who are as contrite as herself. Her redemption is a purification, to permit humans to go forward once again, in search of their greater glory. This implication of acceptance is perhaps the key to Mesoamerican well-being. There is no guilt in the Judaic-Christian sense, in the appeal for pardon, only a tacit recognition of misconduct or transgression, to be purged but never carried as a lifelong burden.

Tlazolteotl is represented as the Moon Goddess, adorned with a nose ring in the shape of a golden half-moon. Her clothing is blue, the color of the sky, so embroidered, so richly embellished that she is called "the lady of the apron of stars." The goddesses of the Aztec territories evoked her image in their lunar devotions by means of similar skirts.

In the typically Maya codices, such as the Dresden, this goddess is identified with Xochiquetzal, deity of the planet Venus, the nocturnal Venus, accompanied by images suggesting the underworld. She is a nighttime goddess, who joins the gods of the caves in the darkness, and flirts with shadows, though she herself burns brightly, as constant as a nearby star, before she dims or vanishes. She is feminine, capricious, even willful.

Like other goddesses associated with Earth, she wears a girdle of ribbons and shells that clacks and rattles, proper symbol for the Mother of the Gods. In this advocation, she appears closely joined to a "Small Baby God," called Piltzintecuhtli, her own son, whom she carries as an offering to the god Tepeyolotli, here represented with the symbol of the solar disc at his feet.

The "child god," once grown, becomes Quetzalcoatl, a god and at the same time a priest, who teaches his theories and ways and the secrets for making the best use of material wealth, the inherent wisdom of the cosmic universe and the esoteric knowledge in the *Tonalamatl*, as described in the previous arcanum.

LAMATL DESCRIPTION

The god, Tepeyolotli, appears seated, on a chair or throne heavily adorned with symbols of the nocturnal world. He is dressed for battle, in a suit of jaguar skin, or he is, in fact, the jaguar Ocelotl, symbol of "The Tiger Knights," an order of war par excellence, but equally representing the magicians and governors of the heavens and the universe, indicated in the "yaoytl" or shield. The goddess, Tlazolteotl, as Tlaelcuani is adorned with streamers of shells and attributes of jaguar skin, a reminder of her Huastec origins. In certain Codices she takes her small son by his hair, proffering him to his blessing and the confrontation with his destiny, at the hands of the solar god, the principal divinity. The scene, despite its Mexican overtones, the symbols and opulence, could easily be that other encounter they seem to describe: a mother presenting her son to his father.[1]

LAMATL SYMBOLISM

This lamatl represents a conjunction of the cosmic elements: the Sun, Moon, and stars, as the text and foundation for human life on Earth, that fragile planetary body which depends for its existence—its verdure and eloquence—on the cosmic order encompassed in the other planets of the solar system.

The figure signifies the closeness of humanity, embodied in Piltzintecuhtli as "The Child God" Quetzalcoatl, seen as an identification with the supreme values of the universe: the fruitfulness of the Earth which feeds and showers its blessings on humankind; a cosmic government or interplanetary system which determines our conduct and status on the Earth, and our dependence for life itself, within this galaxy.

---

[1]According to the earliest suppositions regarding paternity among the hunting packs of humanoids, the female, it was said, obviously knew if the child was hers. The male, on the other hand, had to take her word. So love was invented.

Figure 12. Tlaelcuani, the sinner and Cuítlatl, excrement and sin, pose above Ocelotl, the Jaguar, symbol of Tepeyollotli, god of the caves. He faces his house or calli. *From the* Códice Borgia.

PARALLEL SYMBOLISM

These two arcana, in both the tarot and the *Tonalamatl*, represent fruitful and generative love. The Venus Urania or Cosmic Mother is seen in her material apparition, as the Queen of Heaven who gives birth to a son, a mortal man who will in turn be responsible for the vigilance of the principle of Cosmic Fulfillment on the Eternal Journey, thus endowing him with the potential for divinity latent in all of us, by virtue of conduct, and coherence, or purpose and devotion to the natural order.

The Empress, whose power is more vital than spiritual, rules over men and women in her forceful, even aggressive femininity. The

Figure 13. Tlazoléotl, lunar goddess of filth and sin depicted with Tepeyollotli, the heart of the mountain, and the Jaguar, god of caves. From the Códice Borgia.

eagle she bears, either on her shield or scepter, indicates that her strength may reach as far as the distant galaxies. Yet it also emphasizes the birth process as an inherent factor in her constitution, a natural consequence of the union of active and passive entities, to be sought and nurtured in the atavistic imperative designed to perpetuate the species. A careful balance, however, had to be maintained, between procreation and sin, as much in Egypt or Medieval Europe during the initial dictates of the tarot as in ancient Mesoamerica, as a precaution against population explosion and the resulting drain on available resources.

Tlazolteotl, the American Venus, had no need to insinuate her cosmic reach. She wore her skirt of stars as an implicit identification with the Cosmos, her place of origin. She appears in the *Tonalamatl*, furthermore, in battle garb, offering the new being she has just produced to the Jaguar God, presenting her offspring as much for baptism as for acceptance in the continuity of the human family on Earth, to be introduced into the ways of universal knowledge. Tepeyolotli, as God, portrays the supreme power in magic and esoteric wisdom.

Both female figures are related to the Cosmos by virtue of the semiology in their ambivalence. The Empress appears, in certain cards, framed by a halo of twelve stars, representing her dominion over the zodiac and the strength of the Sun as broadcast to Earth according to the hour and the sign. Yet she embodies, specifically, the birth, the being given life by a fertile Venus, bound to the Moon—that is, matter at its most elementary level of creation, the total opposite of the Sun.

This arcanum repeats a message, the fact that in reality nothing in the universe is created but rather springs from something else and will be encompassed in three factors: the engendered, the progenitor, and the product. There must always be, even at the molecular level, a father-active, a mother-passive, and the androgynous, the child-neutral.

In this third sign of the *Tonalamatl*, the deity Tepeyolotli appears in his advocation as the oldest of the gods, Lord of the Night. He is associated with the revelation of the all-encompassing Tezcatlipoca, Lord God, neither black nor red, whole nor fragmented, Supreme Father of all Other Gods, Giver of Life, author of the mandates invoked in prayer, before the priestesses of the Goddess Tlazolteotl, when the penitent—ourselves—confessed his carnal sins, and Tezcatlipoca was merciful.

The Goddess then granted forgiveness and the priest imposed the penitence, complied with on the day deemed apt, as determined by the *Tonalamatl*, here seen as the Book of Judicial Astrology. Children at birth were presented to the priests, who would then indicate the child's destiny, in accordance with the zodiacal dictates in the tome, as related in the lamatl or arcanum corresponding to the baby's day of birth.

This all-seeing, all-powerful father figure, this benevolent authoritarian, was also characterized in Yoaltecutli, called "Lord of the Night" after one of the stars identified in "Orion's Belt." The constellation was called *Cabrillas* by the Mexicans, a term meaning both "Pleiades" and "Little Goats." The name was used indistinctly by way of both designation and affection, as this particular constellation was venerated with special devotion, and, like other facets of life among the Mexicas, treated with a singular brand of sardonic humor in evidence in Mexico to the present day.

Tlazolteotl, like the Venus Urania, was also known by several names. Among others, she was termed Ixcuina, the "lovely lady"— the Goddess of Beauty—and, like the Roman Venus or the tarot's Empress, lured men into carnal sin, despite the fact—or perhaps because of it—that each of her lovers would eventually repent at her feet and implore her forgiveness. Forgiveness for what? For doubting her purity, of course, or her nobility of purpose.

ARCANUM IIII

MYTHOLOGY OF THE EMPEROR

This card refers directly to Zeus, called Jupiter by Romans and astronomers, in recognition of a personality as vital and abundant as it was opulent and overbearing. He was that remarkable creature, the innate ruler. Zeus reflected all that humans project in a figure of authority: good humor, quick wit, resourcefulness, temper, wile, but above all, the arbitrary imposition of his dictates by virtue of his position, a patriarch never to be questioned.

Zeus was the youngest child born to the Titans Rhea and Cronus. Cronus himself had been the youngest born to Gaia, the Earth, and Uranus, the Heavens, her mate and companion, chosen of her own free will, according to the legend, "to be her equal in all things." No subservient female was she.

Yet Uranus disliked his children, probably with good reason, for they were a monstrous brood—the hideous Cyclopes, Oceanus whose salt streams circled the world, Prometheus' father Iapetus, along with many others. So Uranus attempted to destroy them all, until Cronus plotted a dreadful defense, aided by his mother. He was to swallow, successively, all of his children, until his wife Rhea, desolate, gave him a stone wrapped in swaddling clothes, to replace her smallest child. And if Cronus brought about the world's despair by violating the dictates of harmony with the cosmos, Rhea simply fled with the living baby, stealing away with him to Crete. That craggy island-survivor, home to the fierce and the vengeful, who sing to freedom and compose verses to extol liberty, provided him with a refuge on the slopes of Mount Ida and a nursemaid in the form of Amaltheia, the goat, who fed him rich milk, sweetened with honey, distilled just for him by worshipful bees.

The baby grew among those who knew the mountains and the wrath of storms. His mother came often to him and taught him the arts of seizing power. When time had passed and he had grown to full strength, he attacked and overcame Cronus and bound him in chains. Then he forced him to disgorge all those children he had previously swallowed, including the stone Cronus had believed to be Zeus himself. The stone was set down in Delphi and later was revered and anointed with oil.

Now Zeus and his great brothers and sisters ruled in place of Cronus. The new leader also freed those other monster creatures, children of Gaia and Uranus, who had been imprisoned in the deep places of the Earth. These sons of Heaven were grateful to him and gave him lightning and thunder, weapons by which he could confirm his supremacy in a power struggle continuing long after he became King of Olympus. There were still those old Titans who believed brute force, sheer weight, and size could overcome skill, intelligence, and cunning.

Yet Gaia had provided the Titan Prometheus with a number of weapons, including a great truth: that in the future, victory would be the "province of the mind, of shrewd discipline, as opposed to strength and force. Prometheus therefore supported Zeus until the empire was firmly established and the king's power confirmed.

The monsters who had refused to submit were destroyed by thunderbolts, or bound and fettered underground to be deprived of light and freedom of movement—to the Greeks a terrible punishment.

Zeus, like many others who have just risen to power, was even fearful of his subordinates and grudging in the largess to be shared with mortals, a fact that led to conflict with a former collaborator, Prometheus. The remaining gods, however, accepted the duties their Lord had assigned them, leaving Zeus the absolute master of light, of the heavens and lightning. He could provide rain and thunder at will. He was a purifying god, an absolute monarch given to strict duty and respect, the One God, the Cosmos Incarnate. In Rome he was Thundering Jupiter, Protector of the City. In Assyria—in a variation on the Mongol patriarch with his falcon poised for the kill—Jupiter appeared on a talisman, the world under his feet and a crow perched on his forearm. Possession of the talisman was associated with great and far-reaching power.

CARD DESCRIPTION

The card shows The Emperor seated, often on a stone cube, in which case each side forms a square, causing the figure to represent one of the geometrical symbols of the fourth arcanum. The stone signifies the Masonic emblem of constant and arduous initiatory labor. Novices aspiring to admission in the order were taught how knowledge of the rock could transform apparently inanimate matter into a polished cube, that is, perfect form. Authority appears in an outer form which has been prepared in advance. From this foundation or vantage point, the *auctoritis* seated on such a cube could potentially dominate cosmic wisdom.

The Emperor's clothing and triple crown suggest a power that permeates the three planes of existence. In his right hand he holds the scepter bearing Jupiter's emblem. In effect, this position of authority obliges an awareness of all three planes in each realm and is translated into the creation of individual beings and whole groups—earthly humanity.

The best and most precise tarot decks display The Emperor's hands in relation to his head and shoulders in such a manner as to form an ascending triangle, with the head as the apex. This is counterposed with the position of his legs, which are crossed, the right over the left, thus forming another triangle whose vertex points downward. The Imperial Eagle is drawn where The Emperor is seated, a cross identified by a hierophant—a talisman or pendant associated with the sacred mysteries—hanging from its neck. In his left hand, The Emperor holds the world, over which he reigns with eternal majesty.

CARD SYMBOLISM

This arcanum is characterized by the dominion of masculine vigor, as opposed to the feminine force of The Empress. The accompanying eagle represents the need for creative thought at its most elevated level, the "high flight" of thought, a striving for perfection. Far from mere ambition, this is seen as the aspiration toward what is described as the perfect form of things, within the established framework of a recognized state of being.

The perpendicular stem of the cross, with which the imperial bird-of-prey is adorned, symbolizes the channels that permit the flow of a current, expressed in the horizontal arms of the cross: positive and negative, masculine and feminine, the world and the underworld; in effect, the duality, and thus the dilemma, of existence.

Also known as the *Petra Cubica*, this arcanum advocates not only a concept but its realization, not only an idea but its pursuit, in the mental, astral, and physical phases, projected onto the theosophical ternary of form, authority and adaptation.

The total that is the sum approaches the basic principle of Hermetic philosophy, the quaternary, or tetragrammaton, a general formula applied to each dynamic process in the universe. Expressed in Gnostic terms, the total can be seen as the active, or male, and expansive principle, vivified in the passive, or attractive, therefore female, principle. From the union arises, or is born, the third, the androgynous neutral element, which borrows and transmits what it borrowed into the next cycle. When the pattern is fulfilled we are permitted to contemplate the First Family, or a finished cycle of manifestation.

What concerns us here, however, is the cubic stone, its symbol of power, and of the agent that governs over the human community, seen as temporal, logical, analytical and yet which presupposes not only authority but adaptation, a mutating perception of power.

These are the indispensable qualities of the leader, made tangible in the concept of authority itself, personified in Jupiter, Emperor Supreme of the Roman Pantheon, or the great Zeus, wily and imperious, representing all foibles and concerns joined in the overwhelming monumentality of the figure atop Olympus.

LAMATL IV

MYTHOLOGY OF CE-TOCHTLI (THE RABBIT)

The fourth lamatl in the almanac of the divinatory arts was a dynamic arcanum, mutating and vigorous, governed by two different gods.

The first was Xiuhtecuhtli, God of Fire, a dual concept, as is fire itself. It was seen in the Promethean sense, as a gift from Heaven, a source of power, of comfort, a benefit in the service of mankind. But it was also tacitly perceived as an uncontrollable horror, god in anger or out of control.

The second element in this lamatl was Xipe Totec, God of the Moon, the Moon seen here in the male sense, as an active force, chariot of the tides, author of the cycles in women, and the harvest. This god was also considered the Giver of the Mandates. In certain codices, he was known as Itzapaltotec, the God of the Sacrifice.

Fire was a means by which the Mesoamerican peoples offered their gods something of themselves in their daily prayers. The kindling of the hearth represented the first advocation presented to the corresponding god, who would receive a portion of the family's food and drink. For example, a spray of pulque—"honey water" fermented from the liquid in the heart of the maguey—was frequently dashed on the flames to bring them to life. During festivities, special receptacles containing food were placed near the fire, or a portion of the meal intended for the guests was set aside, near the hearth.

Always, at the beginning of the day's labor, gentle words of gratitude would be expressed, in recognition of the fire's goodness, its unrelenting disposition to cook meals, warm the house, boil the water, serve in domestic tasks, and in heating medicinal baths or the baths of purification called Temazcalli. Furthermore, the faithful flames provided light to see by after nightfall.

Xipe Totec was a god of the sacrifice by the time he reached the Aztec pantheon but he was originally the God of Spring, revealed in various ways but always without his skin. As Itzapaltotec he was represented as a flint knife, and as such was conceived as fire, for the flint served to kindle the flames.

Xipe Totec was possibly Zapotec in origin, and can be seen on the *urnas* or funerary vases of Oaxaca as a mask of human skin, with two long black lines drawn down both sides of his nose. Despite his sinister aspect, however, he was far from a god of terror. As befitting a god of spring he was shown, like a snake, with new skin, after a long process of rebirth. When Xipe Totec's figure, or the figure of the priest in his service, was covered with a departed soul's skin, he was considered to symbolize the fact of the person's renaissance.

Eventually this process of renewal was conceived in more puritanical terms, according to precise and absolute dictates which punished drunkenness, adultery, homosexuality, prostitution, and foul language, but even greater sins were pride, self-pity, and private initiative—all deemed negative with regard to the common good.

Nobles were more obliged than warriors, freed men, or slaves to the impeccable upholding of the code. They were also expected to show mercy, compassion, and abstinence, in duties designed to lead and guide ordinary citizens in a life of austerity and hard work. Any noble considered oppressive toward his people or who was accused of vice and abusiveness was punished, according to the rules of Itzapaltotec, which honored this god in morning prayers before subjection to a ceremony known in Greece and Rome as the gladiatorial sacrifices. The offending noble would then be called upon to defend his life before a challenging group of warriors.

In this fashion not only authority was maintained, and the mandates honored, but also the essence of art and culture was preserved in the magnificent cities of Mesoamerica—cities of music, botanical gardens filled with exotic plants, exquisite craftsmanship wrought in gold, feathers, fine cloth, and precious stones (the work of artisans contracted and supported by the state), and zoological gardens containing every species of fauna in Mexico and beyond.

LAMATL DESCRIPTION

This arcanum in the *Tonalamatl* is illustrated in most codices with two figures, usually representing the gods Xiuhtecuhtli and Itzapaltotec or Xipe Totec, though often the figures refer to the more colorful Chántico and the dazzling Quetzalcoatl, who will be described later.

Xiuhtecuhtli and Xipe Totec, the master and the donor, respectively, of fire, both wear attributes related to this fundamental element. The clothing of Xiuhtecuhtli refers specifically to his more aristocratic origin, exemplified in the breastplate decorated with turquoise, identifying him as a firstborn god, older than the apparition of the Sun and the Moon, more powerful and authoritarian.

Xipe Totec, on the other hand, is clothed in the skin of the "unfortunate," presumably syphilitic god, Nanahuatzin, who threw himself into the fire in order to become the Sun and restore light to the world. Nanahuatzin was Quetzalcoatl's twin. Together they became the Sun and afterward the evening star, revered as Totec, until Quetzalcoatl evolved in another dimension and Nanahuatzin was consigned, depending on the people and the period, to a lunar status. Xipe Totec's conical cap refers to Quetzalcoatl and his Huastec origins.

The vessel represented in the lamatl contains gold and jade, thus portraying the "precious recipient" of woman, blessed and adorned, the passive seen as enormously lovely and desirable.

LAMATL SYMBOLISM

The gods represented here symbolize the age of darkness on Earth, when fire existed as a safeguard to protect people from predators, to dispel the terror, real or imagined, prevalent in every shadow, tree stump, cave, or well. This fire received the sacrifice of gratitude as people demonstrated, as tangibly as they could, their appreciation for so exalted a gift.

Yet the fire served a cultural purpose as well, as it developed into a source of inspiration and well-being, and this provided a nucleus for telling stories and relating experiences that would grow and flourish from one generation to the next, contributing to civilization of great dimension and vast scope.

Xiuhtecuhtli was an ancient fire god, who embodied the forces of nature, those overwhelming and seemingly omnipotent displays of raw energy that so baffled early humans—lightning and the rays of the Sun—while Xipe Totec exemplified the sacrifice, in honor of the god who illuminated humankind's existence.

Figure 14. Xiuhtecuhtli, the master of fire. From the Códice Borgia.

The flint knife representing Itzapaltotec or Xipe Totec suggests the symbol of Tecpatl in the Aztec calendar, honoring those "Children of the Sun" who considered themselves a "Chosen People," impelled to survive like others before them, and thrive in their Manifest Destiny.

The vessel shown in the Borgia Codex is a lunar symbol, complementing the binary character of the lamatl by representing Xiuhtecuhtli as the Sun and Xipe Totec as the Moon, projected on the dichotomy of Nanahuatzin, who lost his solar brilliance when he was converted to the Moon, that nocturnal companion of the gods.

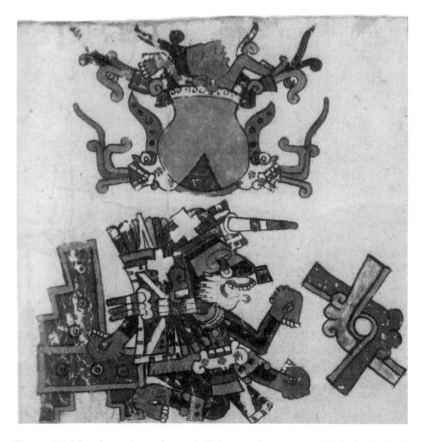

Figure 15. Nanahuatzin as the syphilitic, another aspect of Xolotl. He is the god associated with twin births or the appearance of the deformed. From the Códice Borgia.

PARALLEL SYMBOLISM

The Hellenic deity alluded to in this arcanum in the Roman representation of Jupiter, was the son of two primary gods. His marriage to Hera produced the second generation of lesser gods.

Jupiter, as Roman king of the gods, symbolized the strength of the Fire Creator, and his possession of lightning and thunder guaranteed dominion over his home in the celestial mansions, seat of his imperial power. He ruled over Earth and the heavens. He was the maximum governing entity and Lord Supreme of Fire. Seated on his cubic stone he also symbolized that dimension of human attainment presuming its domination over Nature. The eagle on his shield, or engraved on the stone, links him directly with the Sun, whose strength and cosmic power he enjoys.

The eagle, in some decks, wears the Cross of Life or the Egyptian ankh, which identifies his figure with the powers of the priesthood, and their position in diametrical opposition to the malefice of the gods of death.

This consecrates the eagle's importance, as Master of Earthly Power and Dominion, complementing his honored task as a Lord of the Celestial Fire and the Heavenly Hearth, where the embers are jealously guarded.

For if these embers were bestowed on mortal man or woman, or the flames were kindled, the earthlings—according to Zeus—would have access to civilization, and would then be equal to, and rivals of, the gods themselves. The Emperor, therefore, takes great care to guard his divine powers, which can be translated into real and effective action, the strength of the priesthood and rigid control over humankind's patterns, goals, and behavior.

The goddess Chántico, whose name means "on the hearth," ruled over a temple called Teglame, considered a collective home, a kind of community center. This Fire Goddess, like the Eagle of the *Petra Cubica*, presided over the homely hearth, but she was considered especially devoted to those fires singled out for her everyday homage among Mesoamerican families.

She appears on the lamatl with lavish apparel adorned with symbols of the Heavenly Warrior, similar to The Emperor's armor. She is principally distinguished, however, by a red and white staff and the apparatus of war or the gladiatorial sacrifice, but is also decorated with flowers, as the Celestial Hearth would be, on which the sacrificed and those killed in battle are laid to rest.

Her position on the lamatl lies opposite Quetzalcoatl, who is normally seen here protected by a golden kiosk. He boasts lavish jewels and a stunning display of wealth, to be interpreted as power. He sits on a cubic throne, in the same fashion as The Emperor, yet his garments are so rich he seems far more than a king, priest, or prophet. His breastplate portrays an artful assembling of symbols in a circle, not unlike the composition of the elements at Stonehenge: water (precious rain, gift from the heavens) intertwined with a rattlesnake that bites its own tail, in the manner of a Chinese dragon or certain representations of Sobek, the Egyptian crocodile god.

Like the Lord of Heaven or an empirical Zeus in his golden pavilion on Olympus, Quetzalcoatl reigns in his paradise, Tlalocan—the "Place of Tlaloc," the Rain God—and carries in his hands the flowering branch borne by the dead when they appear before him, their Master, in search of judgment.

In the Bourbon Codex, a god or goddess—the figure is ambivalent—is accompanied by the sign of a planet, which projects a cosmic dimension on the arcanum. There are also references to the characters associated with the deities of death, more specifically the "nocturnal sun," the Midnight Sun, in effect, though the Mexicans below the Tropic of Cancer were very far, indeed, from the Nordic phenomenon.

The relationship of these emblems and figures to the description of Xiuhtecuhtli and Xipe Totec depends on the codex and the geographical area or cultural group referred to. It depends, too, on the interpretation, in the corresponding documentation. Mexico was far older and much richer in culture and references than archaeology (through scientific dating techniques) has been prepared to concede. Yet we are most concerned here with the symbols involved.

Both the tarot—in its multiple versions—and the almanacs called *Tonalamatl*, emphasize the quality of high thought and action, whatever the picture on the card. Yet every deck is different.

The fourth arcanum in both describes, in almost identical terms, a recognition of the forces of nature as the artifice of majesty. And they magnify the blessedness of humility and gratitude before a power beyond comprehension.

Furthermore, both stress our presumed limitations and the jealous conservation of weapons or privileges deemed delicate or dangerous in uninitiated hands. Perhaps, for this reason, both demand exemplary conduct from mortals. But most significant, though stated very subtly, is the inference of noblesse oblige: an ordinary citizen, even lesser gods, may judge the actions of leaders and rulers, expecting as much from an emperor as Zeus demands of himself. Power, though absolute, like moral rectitude, honor, obedience, reliability, truth, glory, and beauty, may all be questioned, subjected to revision, and renewed, like any other contract.

ARCANUM V

MYTHOLOGY OF THE HIEROPHANT

The Hierophant refers to still another manifestation of Jupiter—the wisdom and benevolence of all the universe—who pardons sins through the word of his priests and the sacrifice of penitence. Such is expressed in the concept of the fifth arcanum, *Magister Arcanorum*, or "The Great Teacher," indicating the enlightened will as an active authority, so precise that the card's hieroglyph represents the act of *breathing*, that is, the mechanic of living, the vehicle for achieving the spiritual initiation considered essential in the redirecting of human weaknesses.

The talisman in the Babylonian book of magic, *Picatrix*, shows a god on a throne, called in the Kabballah "The Throne of Merkbad," an association with the ship or vessel from another realm, described by Ezekiel.

In the Middle Ages, when tarots of earlier periods converged in Europe, the figure was redefined as The Pope, thus indicating a supreme religious dignitary, by then embodied in the Roman Catholic Church, with all its mystic heritage gathered across Central and Western Asia, Egypt, and the Near East. The reference, of course, though symbolized in the blessing, the binary of The Horns of Isis, the Silence of the Initiate, the two columns of Jakin and Boaz, and a gesture expressing Will, is still not God—the Radiant Beginning—but mortal. Though we cannot discern the nature of the chair, he is seated and therefore tending to the passive yet powerful. He is male, active and triumphant, Master of Magic, with the gift of Light to dispel the forces of Darkness, thus turning them toward goodness.

The Breath of Life associated with The Pope suggests a dependence on the vital processes of the organism, regeneration (the opposite of "degeneration") as a path toward redemption, a cycle defined as the solar renewal of spring, ideally ascending along the chain of circumstances toward the Infinite, that which is androgynous and inaccessible, the universal self, the absolute.

The Jupiter concept was seen in Egypt as Horus, the Falcon, an ancient sky deity who soared protectively across the heavens, surveying all. He became so identified with the Pharaoh that he was the first of the King's titles. As the God of Lower Egypt, Horus exemplified the earliest anthropomorphic transformations in the original animal deities. Later, all gods were portrayed as humans though they retained their respective animal attributes and characteristics. During the Ptolemaic era, however, a period contemporary to Rome, the return to the zoomorphic form of Horus is clearly visible in the temple at Kom Ombo, along the Nile not far from Luxur, in Upper Egypt.

Horus, like Zeus (Jupiter) or Quetzalcoatl, fought for and won his supremacy after a long battle involving his own kin and the monumental forces of Nature, conceived as living beings. Ra, the self-created Sun, rose from the Ocean, Nun, in order to develop his family. Yet these presumably divine origins only served, as they did in Greece, to heighten humankind's projection of their own foibles onto deified personalities, as when Osiris, the god-king of the underworld responsible for resurrection, confronted his evil brother Seth, who then slew Osiris and dispersed the dismembered parts of the body. In a cruel gesture, Seth even buried the head at Osiris' own temple at Abydos. Osiris' faithful wife and sister, Isis, Goddess of the Nile, Heaven, and Earth and Patroness of Philae, roamed the world — Egypt — until she found and reassembled the parts. Her son, Horus, then destroyed Seth and assumed command on Earth.

The Falcon God formed part of the nine-god complex of Heliopolis, which defended Ra against the continuous attempts of the serpent Apophis to swallow him. Ra survived, of course, and later, as Amon-Ra, was reconfirmed as father of all the gods, including the Pharaoh, who was considered not only a single deity but really many gods incarnate in a single body. As Son of Ra, the Pharaoh was directly descended from the Creator, the Sun, and a human mother, a procedure translated to Zeus in Greece when the King of the Gods disguised himself as a bull or swan, or appeared in any of a number of other roles in order to engender various demi-gods.

Horus, as a descendant of the Cosmic Creator and Supreme Being, functioned very much like any other pantheonic authority figure that has accepted a human soul. In effect, he must acknowledge the realm of the female principle, which then proceeds to fill this realm with existence, as a concept; in other words, the synthesis of that which is learned. All of this contributes to the necessary development of *auctoritas*, the key to ethical rulership.

CARD DESCRIPTION

The Hierophant (or The Pope) is seen with his triple crown, symbol of the three universal forces or, more commonly, crowned with the two horns of Isis, a full Moon between them, signifying her dominion over the Earth and Heavens and her condition as Moon Goddess with the full moon gleaming on the Nile.

His right hand is extended in the blessing of the two penitents who kneel before him, their backs facing us. He carries a scepter in his left hand, the cross at the top at a level higher than his head, suggesting enlightened willpower as an active authority. Like The Priestess in the second arcanum, he sits between two columns, a binary representation neutralized, in this case, by the man's figure.

The two kneeling figures, one dressed in dark robes, the other in light, suggest the triumph of the pentagram, or The Great Sign of the Microcosm, the world in miniature, a magic symbol, the potential for undeterred evolution.

The Pope, by his blessing, has turned negative to positive. This Master of Magic has used wisely the temporary ignorance of the two penitents and their resulting weakness in order to redirect their potential. Since they have shown themselves to be receptive to The Teacher's guidance, they are implicitly assigned the possibility of karmic redemption, or a liberation much sooner than would otherwise have seemed feasible.

CARD SYMBOLISM

The fifth arcanum encompasses the teaching of traditional knowledge, a channeling of religion as derived from the esoteric secrets of the Book of Thot and the Kabbalah.

The Pope expresses the interpretation of the material world, the blending of active and fecundating principles—Cosmic Awareness—with elements from which the human body is constructed. These are focused in ethical dominion, to prepare for the possibility of the Great

Action, or the alchemy of quintessentia—the fourfold realization of matter plus the fifth element—seen as the Kingdom of Nature.

The arcanum symbolizes the manifestation of entities on the planes beyond the physical, where the metaphysical compendium dominates the astral mechanism. In simpler terms it uses the positive to vanquish the negative, by means of the power of awareness. This constitutes an impetus which impels the finest vibrations, the replacement of anxiety with a total faith in destiny, a sense of the rightness of all things, the harmony within.

LAMATL V

MYTHOLOGY OF CE-EHECATL (THE WIND)

 The symbol of Ehecatl, God of the Wind—an embellished Quetzalcoatl, covered with a mask in the form of a beaked bird—indicates the beginning of the thirteen-day period of the lamatl Ce-Ehecatl. This representation was once identified with Kukulcán, the Maya God of the Wind, and was converted by the Nahuas into Ehecatl-Quetzalcoatl, the Ultimate, the Absolute, the Illuminated Being consecrated in myth and legend. His exploits were interwoven with those of his devoted hierophant, the priest Ce-Acatl, described more extensively in the twentieth lamatl.

Quetzalcoatl was venerated simultaneously as a priest and a king, a monarch god who was also his own papal nuncio. He was known to have challenged the evil sorcerer-priest Tezcatlipoca the Black to a series of battles. Tezcatlipoca, in this manifestation called "Smoking Mirror," was distinguished by a right foot which gleamed like a looking glass. He constituted a counterposition to Quetzalcoatl, thus completing the binary good and evil, like the light and dark penitents in the tarot, or their respective symbols, indicated in The Hierophant.

At Tula, says the story, "Smoking Mirror" sent a collection of demons to Quetzalcoatl. Disguised as innocent old men, they were assigned the task of tempting their Lord. They tried to incite him by describing the glories of the fermented "honey water" called *pulque* and Quetzalcoatl had almost resisted their appeal, until he stuck his finger in the bubbling beverage and licked the pulque off his finger. He was soon quite drunk, and in this state was seduced by a woman sent precisely for this purpose.

Upon awakening, as he recovered his normally alert and righteous state, Quetzalcoatl, aghast at having broken both his vows, of abstinence and continence, and ashamed by additional mischief provoked by his enemy, became so angry he burned his palaces, buried his treasures in the nearby mountains, and prepared to leave this land.

He was so devastated by sadness, and revulsion at his weakness, that he changed the profitable cacao plants—literally money that grew on trees—into hostile prickly pear and sent the songbirds from his realm. The Franciscan priest Sahagún, a Spanish colonial historian, narrates the legendary journey into exile, across mountains and deserts. When Quetzalcoatl finally reached the snowy pass over the sentinel peaks of Popocatepetl and Ixtaccihuatl—the entrance into the Valley of the Mexicas—he was further confounded when his escort, an assemblage of the blind and the deformed, died of the cold. He then decided to perform Herculean tasks by way of penitence and for a time even went into retirement in the great pyramid at Cholula.

Did Quetzalcoatl really exist? His image, and the tales of his tribulations, appear in every Mesoamerican culture. He was a leader, a teacher, the enlightened, the ennobled. At Cholula it was said he wove a raft of living serpents and charted his course across the heavens toward the south. As he lived in the cities of the Maya the myths mingled with history. Yet historians, both then and now, confirm the appearance of the guide and priest Kukulcán—Plumed Serpent—among the Mayas about a decade after Quetzalcoatl's abdication and exile. And the impact of the Toltec culture on Mayapán, Chichén Itzá, and other Maya centers has been documented since long before the Spanish Conquest.

The God Regent assigned to the fifth arcanum in the *Tonalamatl* to complement the suffering and burdened image of Quetzalcoatl is a feminine figure designated as Chántico or Cuaxolotl, a goddess associated with the Sun and fire but also with the Earth and fertility. She is always indicated by the use of a bright yellow color and therefore termed an astral figure, though she was a nocturnal goddess. Her image was normally kept in a dark house, protected by deep shadows, symbolizing the night at its darkest, before the appearance of the heavenly bodies, that is, before the dawn of the Sun, of humankind, and of nature.

This version of Chántico is associated with the Huastec pantheon and through it with the mythic land where the gods were born, "The Land of the Red and the Black"—that classic esoteric color scheme. Her face is shown painted with tar and she is dressed in red. The goddess is often represented with animal tusks. This identifies her with the earliest Olmec concept of the gods incarnate in the spotted felines of the jungle and the priests, called Jaguar Men, responsible for the cults of those gods.

Like the gods around the islands and canals of Xochimilco, a traditional garden spot near present-day Mexico City, famous for its flowery abundance, Chántico was specifically associated with the fertility of the Earth and the powers of Heaven, that rain of fire defined as thunder and lightning. Chántico is considered part of the formation of the Earth during the Dark Night of Chaos, when family life began, and the bellowing gods of might, who hurtled fire across the sky or opened corridors in those downpours of rain, were gradually seen in the more tender terms of a female, a gentle goddess of the hearth, to serve in the preparation of meals, homely tasks, and times of quiet and reflection, when culture was defined. Good and evil were ultimately personified in Quetzalcoatl and his priests, the projection in a single figure longing for moral and ethical evolution, the essence of human residence on Earth or in society, the subtle perception of excellence in the juxtaposition of positive and negative.

LAMATL DESCRIPTION

Chántico, Goddess of Fire, appears in the Bourbon Codex seated on a square throne. She wears a crown of eagle feathers and is thus associated with the sun. Her adornments of gold and rich jewels verify her hierarchical significance, but imply as well the golden light of the Sun and the riches bestowed on the Earth by solar largesse.

She is pictured facing a house, which indicates origin, a specific birthplace, a home where the Sacred Laws and their mysteries were also born. Kings and priests customarily withdrew to such a house for the purpose of meditation, sacrifice, and a communion with the gods.

Chántico appears on the card accompanied by the child god Piltzintecuhtli, with his king's attributes. He is a priest accompanied by legions of other priests. The most exalted among them are those related to the sun or the rain of fire from heaven, represented by a flint knife or Tecpatl, which serves to extract fire from the Earth, or by a vessel designed for incense, or for the kindling of the sacred fire.

Figure 16. Chántico or Cuaxolotl, goddess of fire. From the Códice Borgia.

In other codices Chántico is accompanied by Quetzalcoatl, not as a child but as a full-grown man, attired in the vestments of the High Priest, carrying in his hand, like The Hierophant, the symbol of light and power.

LAMATL SYMBOLISM

Chántico, as Goddess of Fire, represents not just flames and fireworks but also the fiery core of the Earth and flashing meteors in the cosmic sky. Eternal fires. A restless heaven and lonely people. A man lighting his hearth to single out his home, a woman preparing the meals, a child bewitched by the red and gold, a clairvoyant at his meditation in the depths of the coals.

Chántico also embodies self-sacrifice, discipline implicit in the love of excellence. She encompasses penitence within the home, domesticity, the cherishing of self-control that makes possible the stability of the family, the cornerstone of the community and the foundation of civilization. All of this is seen as an ethical maturity, which leads directly to the inner harmony that may aspire to a place among the gods. The Western mind might lean toward a notion of duty or regimented obedience, but the Mesoamerican idea, far more Eastern than Occidental, places the responsibility on the individual for his or her despair or fulfillment.

The symbol of a fine cord, which often forms part of her dress, further associates Chántico with the "sacrifice," that is, with penitence, that sublimated act, part of the quest for a higher awareness.

The conch and the small seashells in clusters around her are used to indicate her identification with the cosmic gods. She is, in fact, both a solar and a lunar figure, bound to the sublime but simultaneously earthly, not unlike the Greek or Egyptian concepts of their deities.

Her son, Quetzalcoatl, carries the symbols of the rays of the Sun. He carries them for her. He bears them, in fact, in recognition of her. She, in turn, carries the flintstone instrument in her own hand, raised high, the implement used to conjure Divine Fire.

PARALLEL SYMBOLISM

The fifth arcanum is perceived as the spiritual complement of the fourth. Like its predecessor, the card relates to Zeus, or Jupiter, as the bearer of fire, of authority in relation to the primal ethic.

The hearth, in turn, is related to daily life and earthly existence. At the same time, it symbolizes the presence of the gods and contact—even intimacy—with them.

The priests of the ancient Occidental world, so called, as much as those in the Mesoamerican cultures, were responsible for the keeping of the Divine Fire, which served to feed the hearths of humankind. These priests related their wisdom to an esoteric transmission of knowledge to their people. The secrets of the universe or the origins of the planet were considered areas of selective information, identified with power, the quintessence of religious awareness, projected onto the mundane world of the humble. Ordinary people are not ignorant, however, only less well-informed. The priests were obliged by their calling, therefore, to guard their secrets—in actual fact a precious treasure, to be channeled into teaching while they meted out punishments and penitence, divination, or the instruction of aspiring adepts.

All this was symbolized with great precision. The Hierophant, for example, wears a serpent like a belt around his waist, implying eternity with wisdom, just as Xiuhtecuhtli, the God of Fire, carries Xiuhcoatl, serpent of fire, on his back, in order to emphasize his cosmic wisdom and infinite power.

Two wrong-doers kneel before the Hierophant, begging forgiveness for their trespasses and in order to obtain it, they are prepared for the sacrifice implicit in penitence, viewed in Christian culture as "repentance." Itztapeltotec faces Xiuhtecuhtli in the same manner. The former is the lunar deity who strips away the skin of the penitent while covering himself with a conical cap alive with valuable seashells, a desirable item in Mesoamerica. By means of these lunar symbols he becomes, in fact, a consequence of sacrifice, both the means and the act—skin-piercing flint, skin-searing fire, pain, blood. Like the Hierophant who indicates a course of action through the Breath of Life, the Mesoamerican deity, in effect, practices what he preaches. He becomes the very thing he portrays.

And when the youthful Nanahuatzin throws himself into the sacred fire, to be transformed into the Moon, he reinforces the reference to the Moon Goddess Isis, whose double horns decorate The Hierophant's crown.

Both arcana stress the quest for fulfillment and righteousness, the path of ethical authority, an emphasis which encompasses the most specific values of the community, while it defines the conduct of the individual in terms of his family nucleus. Both arcana further state that only by means of enlightened individuals can a society surpass itself in brighter, more worthy and more durable achievements.

The struggles of Zeus and Quetzalcoatl then, would seem to be translated in the personal actions of ordinary citizens, who require the gods' example in order to perfect their views of their own position in the universe.

ARCANUM VI

MYTHOLOGY OF THE LOVERS

This card refers to a chilling morality tale, one of the most enduring in all of Western history. The story begins on Olympus, in the persistent domestic squabbles between Zeus and Hera—his eternal infidelities, her unending jealousy—until finally, furious and disheartened, Hera challenges two of her family—colleagues and rivals—to a test.

Having convinced Athena and Aphrodite to accompany her, the three goddesses travel on the wind across the Aegean to the gentle slopes of a graceful hill, where a lovely boy tends his flock above a serene and verdant countryside. He is the shepherd-prince Paris, one of the nineteen children of the King and Queen of Illium, or Troy, the most exalted and prosperous city in the Near East. It can be seen, shimmering in the distance, beyond the joining of the two sacred rivers, rising like a golden crown on the hill of Hisarlik.

And there the ingenuous boy, about to bite into his succulent red apple, notices the three gleaming figures of the goddesses in their white garb, among the orchards and the tall grass. He is taken aback. Then Hera speaks to him, to calm his fears, explaining they have come to consult him, in the manner of a test.

Then Aphrodite, according to the tale, implores him to tell them which is the fairest, and to bestow on her his red apple, that emblem of discord and downfall forever implied.

Paris was terrified. At his hesitation, the story says, the energetic goddesses increased their pleas. Hera promised him power, for power was considered the gift all men desire. Athena replied that power was useless without wisdom.

At this point Aphrodite reflected on her own argument. She knew that Hera had concocted this farce because she was jealous of Thetis, the river-goddess daughter of Ocean, to whose child, Achilles, Zeus had offered immortality in the waters of the sacred stream. Zeus may have weakened before Thetis' pleas, or he might have been Achilles' father. In any case, the insistent maiden has demonstrated some hold over the King of the Gods, resulting in Hera's fury; but her scenes of jealous rage had only earned her a quick reproach from the authoritarian master.

Aphrodite also knew that Athena would support her own chosen one, Odysseus, in the inevitable battle, soon to come. This would endanger Aphrodite's son and protegé, Aeneas. On the other hand, if Illium were destroyed, Aeneas would be free to migrate with a small band of survivors to another land and to distinguish himself for all time, at a distant point in southern Italy, by founding the city one day to be called Rome.

She then appealed to Paris with the greatest gift of all, she said, the one most truly desired by all men, in the undying love of the most beautiful woman on earth. As she spoke she called to another of her sons, the capricious Eros (Cupid), who quickly struck Paris with one of his magic arrows. Paris silently handed the apple to Aphrodite and in so doing unleashed the terrible Trojan War. The willfulness of the gods had in a single and apparently senseless gesture, been projected on unsuspecting humankind, and the war would drag on for ten years, uniting the Hellenic states under Achaean leadership. Yet the price for political expediency involved a sequence of tragedies that affected generations to come.

The sixth arcanum of the tarot is represented in the hieroglyph signifying the eye and the ear, those organs which permit contact with the world at large. A young man appears on the card, being tempted from both sides. On the one hand he sees a modestly clad young woman, indicating the path of Right at the crossing, his evolutionary triangle, his innate virtue.

The way of vice, the negative or involutionary triangle, is represented by another young, but beautifully clad, woman, as an emblem of evil and temptation. She tries to pull the man toward her but the Genie, hovering blindfolded over the three figures, directs a punitive arrow at her.

The arcanum is considered a bifurcation, or crossing of the paths, the idea of choice or decision. The pentacle is built on the Seal of Solomon, or Solomon's Star, which indicates the sign of the macrocosm. Each choice is a reflection of the other, until the idea of all outer worlds and conditions (the macrocosm) is impressed on the human (the microcosm), that infinitesimal reflection of the whole. The entire principle of the arcanum is elevated on this interrelation of analogy and reflection.

CARD DESCRIPTION

This card has experienced innumerable transformations, from the first talisman of the Patrix to those 19th-century decks that indicate the influence of the Rosicrucians or the impact of the esoteric popes and Court de Gébelin, who altered their respective tarots.

A number of values come into play with this card and many codes of conduct are examined. Fidelity was less prized in the Aegean world, for example, than hospitality and the refinements of diplomacy, and both were violated when Paris ran off with the wife of his host Menelaus in Sparta. Passion might therefore be sanctioned, but the sin of arrogance was indeed serious. The card is thus designed to extol conjugal felicity, under the auspices of a protective angel, representing the spiritual subtleties of romantic commitment, the joining of two halves of the same being in search of perfect harmony.

To the Rosicrucians the first woman, considered the positive emblem, suggests a moment of transition, the path toward divine knowledge, indicating Eve at a similar juncture. This is reinforced in the symbol of the apple and the temptations of forbidden sensations. Why forbidden? Because they disrupted the structure of a household and family, the key to a stable society.

The young man in the center of the card is seen to be very immature. His decision will be made while he still has time to experience or remedy the consequences. This is projected in the Hermetic code of ancient Egypt as the Law of Analogy, that is, free choice, which permits at every crossroad in human experience, the dual possibility either for good or evil. As such, however, it can be delicate or gross, true or false, temporary or eternal, active or passive. The second arcanum offers Gnosis, or knowledge of the ways given for free choice. The fourth arcanum presents the authority which indicates the right of free choice. The sixth arcanum, meanwhile, reminds us that by exciting the imagination, individual initiative can be either inspired or distorted, further defining the potential for another choice: productive action or nonproductive indulgence. This is the eternal dilemma in the quest for a kind of harmony, seen here as serenity or inner peace.

CARD SYMBOLISM

The human predicament is interpreted at the turning point, in a situation destined to affect both romantic life and the stability of marriage, in fact the substance of integrity, when confronted with the temptations of uncommitted, that is, fragmented or fictitious love. The way to harmonious love, says the sixth arcanum, is by means of ecstasy. The Hindus anoint the lingam with milk and all cultures, in one or another sense, worship the phallus, but only, says this card, in the pursuit of redemption, through incarnation. The ultimate ecstasy, then, is no more than the final fulfillment of being. The analogy confirms the symbolic counterpoint in subjective imagination; that is, the balance in the direct proportion of the elements. There will always be as much good as evil, positive as negative, and so on, and they will operate in perfect balance. The binaries will eventually be neutralized when humans exercise free choice and therefore accomplish their goal, the achievement of complete harmony, customarily ascribed to the androgynous state of The Absolute.

LAMATL VI

MYTHOLOGY OF CE-CUAUHTLI (THE EAGLE)

The sixth lamatl is governed by two deities, Xochiquetzal and Tezcatlipoca, in varying applications. Remember the mutability of the gods, as they are transposed in time and place. Their subtle variations are extolled until a new deity, or a new form of the former deity, takes on a whole new identity. In this case Tezcatlipoca is seen as an all-encompassing entity, neither red nor black, but rather the counterpart of Quetzalcoatl. He is really the dark side of Quetzalcoatl, the gloom and evil in us all, and as such was the god of sorcerers, the witch doctor's deity, associated with evil and wrong-doing. He was remembered especially because he defeated Quetzalcoatl, prince of heroes, but it is Quetzalcoatl who vanquishes Tezcatlipoca in the end.

Conversely, however, children of the humble classes were educated in a *telpochcalli* or youth hostel, of which Tezcatlipoca was patron. Here they were taught religion and the martial arts. Education was compulsory for pre-Columbian children. Lessons were generally given orally and were memorized precisely as they were heard, with emphasis on history and tradition. Each child born appeared before a registry official who administered every imaginable task in society. Any personal initiative was prohibited, so the public official was responsible for assigning the newborn his or her duties from the outset, in order that the child might be prepared to undertake life's assignment.

Tezcatlipoca is symbolized in the Borgia Codex as the dancing dark or black god, in this indicating both the racial and symbolic nature of his persistent conflict with the fair and enlightened Quetzalcoatl. In the Bourbon Codex, he takes the form of the sacred dog, not an Anubis (conducting the dead) but a remarkable black or dark gray animal from the Pacific tropical lowlands in the Balsas River Valley, completely hairless and with skin warm to the touch, a charming and benevolent dog that served as food, heat, and companionship, a cure for rheumatism or cold feet.

In the Vatican Codex, Tezcatlipoca either black or green, appears disguised as a wild turkey, a native American fowl. The god's various names and forms likened him to Zeus. He often occurred as a flying shadow, a fearsome monster, even a jaguar, though ordinarily he was invisible and impalpable. He was personified in the summer Sun, which ripens the harvest but also brings drought and sterility. He was linked with the Moon as the god of evening. He was invoked, in his different forms, at festivals, some of which consecrated him as god of music and dancing.

The Aztecs feared him more than any other god and offered him blood sacrifices. Every year the most handsome among the kingdom's prisoners was chosen to personify him, and the surrogate Tezcatlipoca was heaped with honors and pleasures for an entire year. Twenty days before the date fixed for his sacrifice, he received four girls as his wives, representations of four goddesses of dual intention, as malevolent as they were pleasurable. Then began a series of festivals and dances, but at the end, on the fatal day, the young "god" was conducted, with great pomp, to the last terrace of the temple, where he was sacrificed, his living heart cut out as an offering by the priest with an obsidian knife.[1]

Yet the dark Tezcatlipoca, like the insidious Zeus, had a romantic heart. According to legend he fell madly in love with Xochiquetzalli (Xochiquetzal), goddess of femininity and purity, worshipped by the Mesoamerican peoples as a deity of flowers and love. Charming and lighthearted, she lived on a mountaintop, surrounded by musicians and dancers, but Tezcatlipoca appeared in one of his guises and stole her from her true husband, the rain god Tlaloc.

Xochiquetzalli, after a time, and blinded by weeping and sorrow, desolate with remorse for her sins, changed into the dark and lascivious goddess Ixcuina. Because of Tezcatlipoca's negative influence, her personality changed completely, until she fused, over the years, into a composite form of what had originally been two separate conceptions, not unlike Helen, Queen of Sparta. Yet Mexican mythology,

---

[1]The "sacrifice" could have been real, as described, or just symbolic. Since the scribes of the Colonial period were guided or swayed by their indigenous sources, testimonies are not entirely reliable.

like the Egyptian, gave rise to symbols as incredibly rich as the myths themselves, launched from the very outset of civilization.

LAMATL DESCRIPTION

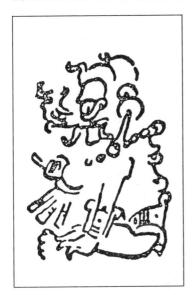

In the Borgia Codex, this lamatl is illustrated with a lovely goddess accompanied by her seducer, one of the black dancers who made up the court of honor in the goddess' dwelling-place in the heavens. This indicates a certain ambivalent association between gloomy and somber Tezcatlipoca and Xochiquetzalli's male twin, Xochipilli, who represents singing and dancing, and to a degree, that juncture, that decision or choice, referred to in the tarot.

The Bourbon Codex shows Tezcatlipoca, in place of the dancer, disguised as a sacred dog, again suggesting the positive-negative counter-point. The evil sorcerer appears in the Vatican Codex as a legendary bird, thus assuming more exalted qualities. As in the case of Zeus, the Absolute, an Illuminated Being despite his earthly conflict, these interweavings of qualities indicate the extent of human projection on even the most illustrious deities, except that the gods never waver nor hesitate in their choice. The duality is contained in the contrapuntal versions that make up the concept, as in the case of the dark Tezcatlipoca, who appears in the lamatl as an alternate to his positive facet, the Great Huitzilopochtli, the Storm God, master of thunder and lightning like Zeus, the Greek King of the Gods, or his Mexican counterpart, with whom he is eventually identified, the magnificent Quetzalcoatl. Huitzilopochtli was born fully attired for battle, dressed in blue armor, like Athena springing from the head of Zeus, with hummingbird feathers decorating his head and left leg and a blue javelin in his left hand, a sign of skill. He was called The Hummingbird of the South, or the *He*, a curious reference to the ancient Hebrew letter applied in the tarot, at the same time as an association with black or green Tezcatlipoca's occasional appearances as a feathered animal.

The goddess in the lamatl is framed by symbols of the indivisible marriage, and of penitence. The indestructible rite serves as the foundation for an inviolable institution. If the violation occurs, however for whatever reason, the lawgivers assign as much responsibility to the woman—though her participation is passive—as to the offending violator. The desirability implicit in the woman's femininity is sufficient provocation, according to the law, and for this reason the lamatl illustrates the penitent's chastisement, accompanied by a couple performing the ritual dictates of sexual union.

Figure 17. Xochiquetzal, often termed Xochiquetalli, goddess of flowers and fresh romantic love. Her twin is Xochipilli, prince of springtime and flowers. From the Códice Borgia.

LAMATL SYMBOLISM

The Mesoamerican peoples were puritanical and severe, far more strict than the Mesopotamians or Egyptians and infinitely more rigid in their moral code than the Greeks. They were unrelenting in their application of justice or their assignment of responsibility. They considered that each citizen, from birth, had been fully informed of the rules and traditions; there were to be no digressions. Xochiquetzalli's and Tezcatlipoca's dubious behavior therefore implied a binary struggle between love conceived as conjugal fidelity and decreed by custom, law, and religion; and love born of sexual desire and concupiscence, a situation that warranted the severest of punishments—social outcast or even death.

Figure 18. Xochipilli, the young god of flowers, procreation and sustenance. From the Códice Borgia.

Xochiquetzalli, in this interpretation, as love's duality, takes on the lusty image of Tlazolteotl, the Mexican Venus of guilty love, carnal pleasure, and scatological filth. She symbolizes the vantage point from which two options are clearly visible: the devoted love of the faithful wife or a lascivious aberration that provokes the wrath of the gods.

The one is seen as obeisance, joy, and fulfillment in the perfect mating of two halves of the same being. The other is repudiated and met with the law's most painful sanction, as described in the lamatl, which shows a ritual ball game in all its solar symbolism, suggesting the Quetzalcoatl-Huitzilopochtli ethic. The game's loser is decapitated, as an offering to Xochiquetzalli and Xochipilli, her twin and son—an Egyptian parallel—expressing the beauty and joyousness in youth and happiness, music and dancing. Yet despite his happy nature, Xochipilli was always depicted with the head of a corpse.

PARALLEL SYMBOLISM

All of life seems to conspire with a series of temptations. Lateral paths attempt to distract us from our chosen course. The sixth arcanum in both the tarot and the Tonalamatl have in common the duality in the choice between right and wrong. They also share the tacit condemnation of the one while extolling the other. There is no margin for rationalization. There is right and there is wrong. Laws, moral codes, and custom supply all we need to know, and having chosen one way we may alter the decision to return to the other.

Important in both cases is the potential for action. The three planes of Hermetism provide the alternative, regardless of society's structure. The individual is ultimately the measure of his or her own morality. The individual is allowed to see himself or herself as one with matter and the absolute, or may choose a life of pleasure and the amusements of a superficial existence.

Venus (Aphrodite) provokes Paris until he succumbs to the temptation of "the undying love of the most beautiful woman in the world." Yet the moment he hands the apple to Venus he unleashes the wrath of the gods, an apocalypse implicit in the symbol of the four concubines delivered to the chambers of the surrogate Tezcatlipoca on the eve of the boy's sacrifice.

Paris betrays everything held sacred in society: honor, his parents, order and discipline, trust, even those precious alternatives to hostility and aggression which are diplomacy and hospitality. Yet more important, he has digressed from the path of rightful conduct and so disdained the inherent enlightenment with which all of humanity is potentially endowed, the path of the mind and of culture, of music and the arts, nobility of purpose in the raising of children. He has renounced the riches of civilization for the ephemeral appetites of the flesh.

In the Ce-Cuahtli, the goddess-regent Xochiquetzalli represents women who are married and pregnant and who rejoice in their fertility. She is the emblem of fulfillment in the labors of the home, of weaving and tilling, because these activities bear fruit, and she invented them as the religion implicit in love's devotion.

Yet she fell under the spell of carnal temptation and left her "religion," the pleasures of home and hearth, for the casual satisfaction in dark Tezcatlipoca's attentions. She turned away from a productive life, of flowers and dancing and the celebration of love's gentleness, to follow the night and magic, the evil in a god who violates the marriage bed.

Xochiquetzalli was deceived, it seems, by Tezcatlipoca's wile, his tiger's garb, and the amulets of love—a diadem of human hearts symbolizing nocturnal desire, "that fragrant flower that opens at midnight." Had she been, however, firm in her decision, no ruse could have offered sufficient temptation and no emblem suggested greater pleasure than her lawful wedlock.

The decision, then, is organic, as implied in the tarot, product of the conviction of the heart and confirmed in the eye and the ear. This is translated in the flowers and music, radiant and glowing, in the symbolism of Quetzalcoatl and Huitzilopochtli, in whose temple the twin flower gods, Xochiquetzalli and Xochipilli, were revered.

Yet Xochipilli, in that exasperating amalgamation of Mesoamerican intent, and fusion of concepts, in fact personifies the positive and benevolent manifestation of dark Tezcatlipoca, the quality in us all that remains forever susceptible to redemption.

ARCANUM VII

MYTHOLOGY OF THE CHARIOT

The seventh arcanum stands for victory, based on the first septenary of the Tarot. The construction is fundamental in a summary thus far: Husband (1) fertilizes wife (2) resulting in the birth of an androgynous child (3) which, properly guided and cared for, attains sufficient authority (4) to find itself on the enlightened plane (5) in the name of the entire family; but there confronts the dilemma of good and evil (6), chooses the Path of Right and gains the victory (7).

The card is exemplified in the hieroglyph of an arrow in direct flight. Once released it soars, straight and true, toward its target. The arcanum is seen as The Chariot of Hermes, rich in symbolism, driven by the daring, those who can be silent and directed.

The conqueror in The Chariot is bound to Mars, or Ares, son of Zeus, chosen to effect Divine Destruction, the counterpart of the Divine Stability in The Hierophant, reflecting Balor of the Irish (a kind of martial Cyclops), and Donar (or Thor) of the Teutons. All of these are terrible male gods of war and battle. Only the Egyptians in the Mediterranean and Indians on the subcontinent of Asia, saw Destruction as a woman. "As the bearer she is also the executioner of life." They knew the lioness to be far more fearsome than the lion.

Sekhmet, rendered in Greek as *Sakhmis*, means "The Powerful," one of the titles of Hathor, the anthropomorphized cow, Egyptian Goddess of Love and Life. The title was granted when, as a lioness, she threw herself on the men who rebelled against Ra, the Sun and Father. Her savagery and fury so exceeded all the Sun God's expectations he feared the extermination of the human race and begged her to cease her carnage. "By thy life," she answered, "when I slay men my heart rejoices."[1]

In order to salvage what remained of humankind, Ra resorted to wile. He spread seven thousand jugs of beer and pomegranate juice, containing a magic potion, across a battlefield. Sekhmet, thirsty and mistaking the red liquid for human blood, drank so rapaciously she fell into a stupor. The human race was saved, but to appease the

---

[1]Felix Guirand, ed., *New Larousse Encyclopedia of Mythology*, translated by Richard Aldington and Delano Ames (London: Hamlyn House, 1959), p. 36.

goddess the Sun, Ra, decreed that on that corresponding day each year there should be brewed in her honor as many jugs of the philter as there were priestesses of the Sun.

The Nordic tribes, however, who saw the God of Thunder as King and War in one, thought they heard the wheels of Donar's chariot on the vault of heaven, and when the thunderbolt struck they said the god had cast his fiery weapon from on high. In the temples, it was to Thor, or Donar—who finally prevailed even over Woden—that the most richly ornaménted altars were consecrated. To place them under his protection, children were given his name.

Court de Gebelin, in his esoteric commentaries, considered this card to honor Osiris, triumphant in the underworld. The talisman, however, invokes the Persian Picatrix in which Mars is seen rising toward Scorpio, revealing the full glory of his powers, his triumph, and his grandeur. The talisman is illustrated with a covered chariot, drawn by lions in full mane, gorgeous and imposing.

The cards of the Middle Ages showed Mars with his sword or whip. The chariot was often drawn by winged horses or sphinxes, prophets grounded, but given to flight. On occasion, in honor of Donar, the sword in the earlier arcanum was replaced by a battle axe. The Gringonneur cards of 1392 favored the Teutonic image.

The conqueror is normally seen in a chariot of cubic form, indicating triumph and awareness, created by the dynamic cycle symbolized on the front of the chariot in the form of Egyptian ornamentation, that includes a sphere with two serpent-like offshoots, supported by outstretched wings, joining the male and female principles.

The picture of the seventh arcanum indicates the synthesis in the pentacles, which are *designed as symbols*, as opposed to action. They may be reversed—which is precisely what Cortés and his band of conquerors did upon their arrival in Mexico—to suggest black magic. This axiology unfolds in the thirst for knowledge, which can be as avid as Sekhmet's thirst for blood.

CARD DESCRIPTION

In many decks the Conqueror rides under a blue canopy, strewn with golden pentagrams, indicating the higher subplanes, so called, and their inhabitants, in the astral world. These pentagrams are stronger than any human power but they also protect and assist humankind. In occasional decks they are seen as the twelve stars or the twelve signs of the zodiac.

The canopy is often supported by four columns, representing the Hermetic virtues: to dare, to be silent, to know, and to try. Between these columns the Victor-Magician performs but always beneath the canopy. He wears a golden crown adorned with three pentagrams, which symbolize his so-called unenforced, free and conscious penetration of the three planes of the world. He is clad in the armor of Knowledge and Victory, which protects him from dangerous and deadly elements—in effect, the elements in disharmony.

On the Conqueror's right shoulder (as if seen in a mirror, that is, on the spectator's right, the Victor's left), we may see a white crescent moon, symbolizing his ability to evolve, the "Solve" of the Androgyne. Above his left shoulder, however, a dark crescent moon tells of his ability to condense these subtle forms and diminish them until they occupy the lower subplanes.

On the armor of the Victor-Magician, he wears the signs with which he can protect himself in the event of attack, seen at three right angles, indicating the correctness of his logic, the arranging of his thoughts in a reasonable manner and his physical keenness and infallibility.

In his right hand he holds a scepter, on which rests a square, which is also a base for an equidistant triangle, meaning that Spirit dominates Form. For this Spirit the globe, or physical plane, is a mere background. In his left hand he carries the sword of victory, his weapon on the physical plane, which becomes his convincing manner of speech—diplomacy and negotiation as opposed to violence—on the higher subplanes of transition.

Two sphinxes pull the Conqueror's Chariot. The left sphinx is black, the right one white. They face each other but they pull in opposite directions as they appear to gallop across the surface of a great globe. Nailheads holding the rims together are visible on the wheels of The Chariot. "And the wheels had height, posture and a terrible appearance, the whole body full of eyes around these four."

CARD SYMBOLISM

The four columns are considered to represent the four elements— Earth, Air, Fire and Water—which threaten the Conqueror, but which equally incite him toward fulfillment. This synthesis appears as the spiritual stimuli of humanity in relation to the planet; and the ideological resistance, the earthly karma that struggles against all obstacles, but presupposes that the obstacles in fact exist.

The two sphinxes are seen as the two poles of the astral vortex, the universal, the whirlwind signifying good and evil in juxtaposition. They scurry across a globe, the quaternary of the "elementary Rota," promising the resolution of the Earth's evolution when the elements find harmony.

The Chariot turns on wheels, but these are seen as vortex-like creatures, which serve for transmission of the astral whirlwind, with the nailheads as their eyes. These represent the cells—substance of life itself—that is, individual beings in any material form that have discovered their autonomy and, with it, the gift of contemplation. This gift is indispensable as a weapon against the seductive forces of evil in the Battle Ultimate—the attempt to reconcile the opposing forces at war within and around us. There can be no definitive victory, no absolute triumph, until total awareness encompasses the sublime ideal, in the consideration that no limitations exist to anything at all, that everything is possible and attainable by the mere thought of it.

LAMATL VII

MYTHOLOGY OF CE-CALLI (THE HOUSE)

The seventh lamatl represents the sign Ce-Calli, the House of Night and Darkness, governed by the Goddess Itzpapalotl and by her companions, the Cihuateteo, female warrior deities who came down to Earth from their private heaven during the feast of the goddess Tititl, celebrated during the winter solstice.

The Cihuateteo were said to be the souls of women who had died in childbirth. They were considered demigods, as the fact of birth was described as a struggle against nature. The woman who died during this battle of opposing forces was considered worthy of distinction similar to that granted other warriors who died in battle.

The souls of such women went into the heavens to the west, an area reserved for them and from which they descended twice a year. The festival was commemorative of dead women in general and was the counterpart of the festival of Xocatlhuetzin, consecrated to male death.

These celebrations were strictly mythological in character, reminders of human integration with the Cosmos. The souls of small children were considered especially sacred in this culture of exuberant expression, with the soul itself, the Mesoamerican astrosome, according to popular belief, located in the area of the head. A dead child was therefore invaded by the magnanimous gods of the Sun: Heat and Abundance—in effect, Jupiter and Juno—called Tonacatecuhtli and Tonacacihuatl, and its soul transposed to the realm of those other privileged—women and warriors—who were deities and also teachers.

The Cihuateteo were seen in the night as "bullets of fire," probably comets or shooting stars, and were especially visible, according to mythological historians, in the countryside, or at crossroads, the latter symbolically representing a moral as well as a physical juncture.

At such points the Cihuateteo were seen with particular clarity by those who stopped to study them, to make note of their appearance and pay heed to their indications.

In such cases they were clearly seen as "chariots descending from the sky," driven by sorcerers or warriors desirous of carrying off young children, a version strangely parallel to the Hungarian legend of Attila and his Skyway of Warriors. This pathway appeared in the heavens, it was said, in times of stress or conflict. Attila, they claimed, when he left the Valley of the Magyars, promised to return whenever they called. Twice his brethren were attacked and twice Attila appeared, his horsemen tearing up the plains with their sharp hooves; and the ground trembled under their feet. The third time, however, the Magyars cried for help and pleaded for the return of their avenger, and still the invaders swept over them, until a distant thundering was heard on the horizon. It grew louder and closer until a brilliant highway of stars appeared in the sky and Attila's horsemen could be heard at a gallop across the heavens. They swarmed out of the night and darkness, only the starlight glinting on their shields and swords. They decimated the enemy, who retreated, never to return, and Attila rode away on the Skyway of Warriors. Neither he nor his horsemen were seen again.

Itzapapalotl, referred to as "The Obsidian Butterfly," associates this lamatl with transformation, metamorphosis and evolution. From the lowly larva or molten lava the goddess becomes a butterfly, sublime in its beauty, airy and graceful, bound only to its earthly destiny of ephemeral beauty, an insight into the world beyond but a view quickly obscured by the reality of human limitations yet to be overcome.

She establishes the transfiguration in personal conduct, the implication of redemption, no matter how humble the beginnings and fulfillment, no matter how fleeting. She is linked to triumph and the grandiose, associated with Tonacatecuhtli and Tonacacihuatl, sources of opulence and splendor.

LAMATL DESCRIPTION

The Borgia Codex uniquely represents Itzpapalotl as protectress of the Goddess Tlazolteotl, the Venus of filth and repugnance. As in the case of the Egyptians, who found no form of life too lowly to repudiate and who elevated the scarab to divinity, the Mexicans saw Tlazolteotl as far more than just guilty love, for her presence was an alternative, seen as a pathway to redemption.

The legend claims that a certain Jappan wished to become a favorite of the gods so he left his family and all his possessions—in an allegory, a traveler's tale or a cautionary experience—to live as a hermit in the desert. He discovered a very large rock on which he lived day and night, spending his time at his devotions. The gods wished to test his virtue and commanded the demon Yaotl (Yeotl = the enemy), a warrior god, and another manifestation of Tezcatlipoca, to spy on him and to punish him if he yielded. Yaotl sent him the most beautiful women, who vainly implored he descend from the rock. His indifference annoyed Tlazolteotl, who was determined to seduce him. She appeared before him and he was deeply moved by her beauty.

"I am amazed, brother Jappan," she told him, "by your virtue. I am also touched by your sufferings and wish to console you. How can I reach you more easily?"

The hermit failed to detect the ruse and climbed down in order to assist her to the top of the rock. His virtue succumbed. Yaotl arrived at once and, despite the entreaties to the contrary, cut off his head and changed him into a scorpion. As such, Jappan hid under the stone which had been the scene of his defeat.[2]

The Vatican Codex emphasizes the duality of Tlazolteotl, by representing her as the butterfly itself. The Bourbon Codex shows the goddess disguised as an eagle. In the Tellerian Remensis Codex, the

---

[2]A folktale handed down over the centuries. Also described by Fr. Bernardino de Sahagún in *Historia General de las Cosas de la Nueva España*, Book 1, chapter VII (Mexico: Editorial Porrua, 1979), p. 37.

Figure 19. Itzpapalotl, the Obsidian Butterfly, a goddess that originated in the Chichimec people of Central Mexico. She was seen as Mother Earth and the incarnation of the Cihuateteo, those demigod nymphs who descended to earth for the festivals of the solstice. From the Códice Borgia.

butterfly, Itzpapalotl, is seen as the Goddess of the Earth—again, a dual indication of Aphrodite's carnal essence.

Tlazolteotl's face and body are yellow and her jaw is a skeleton with exposed teeth, a reference to the ubiquitous symbol of the *vagina dentuta*, the destruction and physical chastisement implicit in carnal transgression to the extent of an implication of terror in all sexual contact, even the sanctified concept fostered in Medieval Christianity.

The majority of codices show Itzpapalotl as a drawing on the dwelling called Tlillan, Temple of the Night, a house of nocturnal darkness in which the child god Pilizonteotl (Piltzintecuhtli) is presumed to be sheltered, a Lord of the Night identified with Quetzalcoatl as a child. This reiterates the reference to small souls and young children, ordained for rescue and protection.

A number of codices show Pilizonteotl decapitated. From his body two serpents emerge, moving in opposite directions, just as the image of the Goddess of the Earth, suggesting, simultaneously, lust and fertility—the potential in adults that is still reversible in the child.

LAMATL SYMBOLISM

All these images and symbols have to do with the night and its omens, with the stars and comets that cross the nocturnal heavens, indicating human destiny.

They also suggest a westward orientation, toward the evening sky in which the Sun hides itself and from which the new moon emerges. The west is seen as the land of birth and primal origin, indicating an important apparition, perhaps, or event occurring there, while to the Egyptians, as to the Magas, the west, which swallowed the Sun, was death and the afterlife.

To the Mexicans, the Occidental horizon sheltered the Cihuatlanipa, the land associated with the powerful instincts awakened by the female: the mystery of sexual desire, of beauty, of amorous abandon, and of sin.

The symbol of the "Flowering Tree," seen broken in this lamatl, suggests man's potential for breaking with his manifest destiny, in the dual quest either for enlightenment or for the pathway of destruction, even as far as death.

The morality tale is expounded in Jappan's fate as a scorpion, for his wife, Tlahuitzin, was still alive. Yaotl went to look for her and brought her to the stone where her husband was hidden. He revealed her husband's betrayal and then cut off her head, too. She was transformed into a fire-colored species of scorpion and, as such, joined her husband, in order to produce an entire brood of little many-hued scorpions.

The gods, however, decided that Yaotl had exceeded his authority. They punished him by changing him into a grasshopper. Still, the possibility always existed that through the curative powers of religion or medicine all people could reconstruct their destiny or retract their transgressions, thus taking their lives along another course. For this reason doctors and midwives, as well as priests of the cult of Tlazolteotl, revered "The Obsidian Butterfly," the elegant and bewitching Itzpapalotl.

PARALLEL SYMBOLISM

The Chariot in the seventh arcanum is a cosmic symbol. The Conqueror bears his sceptre of the Sun and wears on his shoulders emblems of the Moon and stars, which crown his carriage like the twelve signs of the zodiac.

His canopy is sustained by four columns, which are translated in the *Tonalamatl*, the Book of Destiny, as the Four Suns in the four successive worlds prior to the present one through which all forms of life were obliged to pass in order to reach their current state—or the four stars assigned to hold up the heavens. In effect, they are the Four Pillars of Hermetic faith.

The two wheels holding up the platform are confirmed in Mexican mythology as the great gods Tonacatecuhtli and Tonacacihuatl, a binary representation which dominates the world and protects humankind on the astral plane. The two sphinxes—or other animal pairs, always suggesting a fantastic or legendary nature—run in opposite directions. They are not unlike the two serpents, fertility and the Earth, questing despite their disorder in a search aimed at integration and fulfillment.

The Conqueror carries his sword, symbol of power, of conquest, and of war, in a parallel with the *Tonalamatl*'s veneration of valor in battle, the warrior's triumph confirmed by a special place in the sky. This further suggests the warrior's celestial origins, thus his right to a heavenly resting-place.

The Chariot is designated as a sacred depository for the secrets of Hermetism. The vehicle seems to guarantee the mortal human's right to a victory over worldly evil, providing he or she finds congruence in conduct.

The Goddess Itzpapalotl, the lamatl's regent, descends from heaven in a vessel or dwelling surrounded by knives and butterflies' wings. She is represented in the garb of flight, a feathered armor with eagle's claws: her appearance on Earth was made tangible only by the sight of four columns or bases suggesting an eagle's talons.

In the culture of the Tarascan tribes in the area known as Michoacan the bird is described as a star, driven by a figure dressed in a suit of feathers, similar to the impression of a bird of prey as it dives out of the sky, or Horus himself, the mighty falcon god, further confirmed in his gifts as the god of medicine. The yellow color associated with the figure emphasizes the resemblance to an astral body.

The Bourbon Codex shows the vessel as part of a house, or terminal, implicit in the name *calli*. The figure, or driver of the vessel, wears a serpent around its neck. In the same composition a tree appears, symbol of Tamoanchan, whose name means "there in the house from which they emerge" referring to the Paradise from which the gods or astral bodies descended, personified in Itzpapalotl, Quetzalcoatl, and even Black Tezcatlipoca, who broke a foot when he fell.

The tree is divided in two. One part is rooted while the other flies toward heaven. Like the Assyrian-Chaldean zodiac, the Mexican zodiac had thirteen branches, with thirteen signs and constellations, confirmed in the *Tonalamatl*, or The Divine Calendar, which divided all life and its events into explicit periods of thirteen days each.

As in the Conqueror's arcanum, the lamatl suggests the coming of the gods to Earth, arriving in their celestial chariot, a Divine Phaeton. The binary is implicit in the earthly as it appears below the Celestial Spirit; and the whole is conducted by a triumphant figure, originating in the cosmic infinite, touching Earth to bring humankind a great gift from the gods: their wisdom, their benevolence and the promise of redemption, the benefits of heaven, and the blessings of stability as a respite to our frantic pursuit of the material.

ARCANUM VIII

MYTHOLOGY OF JUSTICE

The eighth arcanum is represented by Themis, a daughter of Uranus and Gaia belonging to the race of Titans overcome by the Olympians. Themis, however, far from sharing the disgrace of her brothers, was constantly honored on Olympus. In fact, Zeus, at the beginning of his reign, had even chosen her for his wife, when the Moerae (the Fates) took her to the Olympian king from the far-off regions where Uranus dwelled.

Later, when Zeus married Hera, Themis remained at his side to offer counsel and service, which uncharacteristically never offended Hera. For when she arrived at the assembly of the gods, it was from Themis's hand Hera received the cup of nectar.

Themis was helpful and obliging. It was told she had received the infant Zeus from Rhea, his mother, and later she presided over the laborious birth of Apollo and Artemis, the outcast twins born to Leto on Delos, when a jealous Hera had banished her husband's mistress from the realm. She also made Apollo a gift of the oracle at Delphi, which, along with the divinatory arts, she had inherited from Gaia, her mother.

Her province on Earth was extensive, for she was the Goddess of Justice. She was called *Soteira*: she protected the just and punished the guilty. Judges emitted their verdicts in her name. As Goddess of Wisdom she was called *Euboulos*, the Good Counselor, and as such, she presided over assemblies. She maintained order on Olympus among other duties as custodian of the gods' ceremonial feasts, while she served additionally as interpreter of the gods' will, for she had been granted the gift of premonition and oracle. It was she, after the Deluge, for example, who suggested to Deucalion the means of repopulating the world.

Her union with Zeus produced a number of children, including the Moerae (Fates), Eirine (Peace), the seasons (Horae), and Euomia (Wise Legislation). The Hesperides were also said to be her daughters.

She is represented as a woman of grave countenance and austere features, with her attribute, a pair of scales. Her hieroglyph is described as a field, or passive realm. The idea of balance is implied in one of her titles, *Libratio*, which combines with Grace and Charity to create Justice itself. She is *Lex* or Law, and she represents the concept of the metaphysical scales, which in turn provide the idea of both ascent and descent. Referring to the domains of Nature, she is the symbol of the mechanic of purification—that is, a reassembling of the elements toward the ideal of balance and the removal of the karmic stains which trace their path through cause and effect into mental impulse.

The first duty of the Victor of the seventh arcanum lies in the introduction of order, lawfulness, and justice in the conquered realm by means of these balanced principles. The astral plane is then seen to be in harmony with its counterpart, those specific animistic conditions so lavishly displayed in Mexican mythology.

Certain tarots identify Justice and Wisdom with Athena, the goddess born to Zeus and Metis—daughter of Oceanus—the instrument by whom vengeance was administered to Cronus. Metis was chosen to feed Rhea's husband a draught, which forced him to regurgitate the stone he had swallowed in place of Zeus, and with it, those other children swallowed before.

Metis, said Hesiod, knew more things than all the gods and mortals put together. But Gaia and Uranus warned Zeus if he had children with her they would surpass him in power, and dethrone him. He reacted as Uranus and Cronus before him had done. When Metis was about to give birth to Athena, Zeus, in order to forestall the danger, swallowed whole the mother with her unborn baby. He now embodied supreme Wisdom, yet he was tormented by an intolerable headache. To cure him, Hephaestus (though others claim it was Prometheus) split open his skull with a bronze axe and from the gaping wound, shouting a triumphant cry of victory, Athena emerged, fully armed and brandishing a sharp javelin. At the sight, wrote Homer, all the Immortals were "struck with astonishment" and filled with awe. "Great Olympus was profoundly shaken by the dash and impetuosity of the bright-eyed goddess. The earth echoed with a terrible sound, the sea trembled, and its dark waves rose . . ."[1]

In Crete it was said the goddess had been hidden in a cloud and it was by striking this cloud with his head that Zeus had caused Athena to emerge, an event which took place near Knossos beside a stream, the Triton, so she was also called Tritogeneia, or born of Triton.

It was furthermore explained that she was a daughter of Poseidon and of Lake Tritonis. Others said her father was the giant Pallas, whom she had killed because he intended ravishing her. In any case,

---

[1]Felix Guirand, ed., *New Larousse Encyclopedia of Mythology*, translated by Richard Aldington and Delano Ames (London: Hamlyn House, 1969), p. 108.

her birth infuriated Hera, who, in reprisal, gave unassisted birth to the monster Typhon.

Athena became Zeus's unabashed favorite, a preference so marked it aroused jealousy in the other gods. "Thou hast fathered," said Ares to Zeus, "a rash and foolish daughter who only delights in guilty acts."[2]

Some claimed her peaceful, others a warrior goddess, Protectress of Heroes. She was, however, chaste in the extreme, exaggeratedly modest, pitiless in her punishments, unrelenting in her justice. Intransigent and clever, called by Homer "clear-eyed and cunning," she carried out a long dispute with Poseidon which ultimately confirmed her cult and her name on the Acropolis at Athens—and her gift, the olive tree, so durable a treasure it survived not only Poseidon's wile but Xerxes' burning in the Persian Campaign.

Yet she was as benevolent in peace as she was redoubtable in war, and rendered valuable service to humankind. She taught the people of Cyrene the art of taming horses. She devised the harnessing of the first war chariots. She showed Jason's companions how to build the Argo and got Odysseus, her protected one, home from Troy, though it cost her another ten long years, after the decade of war.

Her greatest skills were revealed in the humblest handicrafts. She invented the potter's wheel and made the first vases. She excelled in women's work and devised the art of weaving cloth and embellishing it with wonderful embroidery, though she was jealous of her accomplishments and let no one surpass her in dexterity, as Arachne could testify. She blinded Teiresias for accidentally setting eyes on her, yet softened her punishment with the gift of prophecy. Hephaestus, though crippled in a fall from Heaven in a fight with Zeus, was unbearably smitten, though he found her unattainable, so "scattered his seed on the earth, which shortly afterwards gave birth to a son, Erichthonius."[3]

Athena found and raised the child. She enclosed the infant in a basket which she confided to the daughters of Cecrops, forbidding them to open it. Two of the sisters, however, unable to resist, unfortunately opened the basket and fled in terror at the sight of the infant wrapped in the coils of a serpent, a provocative parallel to the Mesoamerican myths.

---

[2]*New Larousse Encyclopedia of Mythology*, p. 108.
[3]*New Larousse Encyclopedia of Mythology*, p. 108.

CARD DESCRIPTION

On certain cards the figure of Justice is shown with wings, to indicate her divine origins as a winged prophet. On others she is seated between two columns, a canopy—to symbolize protection—joining them. She is always crowned. She carries a sword in her right hand, a balance (scales) in her left. On her breast, a Solar Cross or hierophant-amulet hangs from a chain. The picture often appears as in a mirror. She is usually seated, a gesture of apparent passivity, on a cube-shaped stone which is hidden from sight by the folds in her flowing garments.

The three binaries in the card are all neutralized by third elements. The first consists in the two columns, neutralized by the figure of Themis between them. The Hermetic explanation differs from earlier ones. To wit: if Jakin is the right column, with Themis in the middle, then on the other side there must be Bohaz. That is, in the existence of the astral vortex, or the tourbillon (whirlwind), to which the force expressed in the sword also belongs, the existence of a second force may be anticipated, redirecting and therefore balancing the total construction.

The second binary is formed of the scales in Themis' hand, with herself as the neutralizing element. The composite indicates the law of cause and effect and the necessity of returning, at all times, to balance.

The third binary is described in the concept of strength as opposed to balance, the sword and the scale. In this union they are seen as Justice espoused to Victory. The whole creates the Law of Reaction, the balance between the static and dynamic binaries.

The figure on the card wears a golden band, while another covers her eyes, yet she is far from blind. She is Truth, identified with the justice exercised by King Thot in Egypt, who weighed the souls of the deceased. If the weight of the heart equaled that of the feather symbolizing rectitude, the departed being was allowed to proceed into eternity.

CARD SYMBOLISM

The inner voice of the conscience demands equity in every vital act, in terms of a well-ordered future, law and balance, stability, logic, and discernment.

The Sacred Book of Thot, the Law Giver, was identified with its symbolic Hindu equivalent, *Vairagya*, in the concept of the well-tempered instinct, which responds intuitively to the required counterbalance between astral desire and a non-desire of equal magnitude, without the addition of animistic or personal interest.

The metaphysical Hermes operates on the three planes of existence simultaneously, leaving traces on the arts, letters, and science. The Grand Master of Magic, the patron of initiates and Hermetists, was also known in Egypt as "The Scribe of the Gods." He was represented as a man with the head of an Ibis, the sacred bird. He wore the lunar disc on his forehead.

In the tarot, this arcanum refers to something already accomplished and therefore no longer considered to be active. This explains the "passive" inference in relation to the seated figure, for she represents a degree of decision rather than overt action as such. Yet in the application of the decision lies a potential for concentration so enormous, if not unlimited, that it can convert ripe ideas into forms by reversing or diverting the evil emanations of negative human will.

Here, then, is an elaborate structure of thought by which to conceive Justice, which goes far beyond the simplistic extremes of "crime and punishment" to actually create a retroactive reprisal against the wrongdoer. His or her own power is unleashed in personal detriment by the well-placed power of illuminated and balanced concentration.

LAMATL VIII

MYTHOLOGY OF CE-ATL (THE WATER)

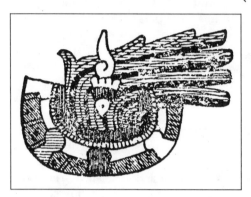

The eighth lamatl, corresponding to the thirteen-day period called Ce-Atl, is defined as the First Water, primordial liquid, seen as life itself, source of birth and fertility.

The God Regent, Yayauhqui Tezcatlipoca, second son of the Supreme Gods, appears here in his advocation as Chalchiuhtotolin, the "precious turkey." He wears the sign of the wild fowl on his temple. Through the bird's eyes, "Smoking Mirror" is capable of occult vision and the perception of all the truth obscured by humans, but revealed in their actions. He can thus grant or deny the benefits and privileges coveted by humankind, the external and therefore visible apparatus verifying the conduct stipulated by the gods.

Black Tezcatlipoca was endowed with the power to offer or withdraw wealth, status, health, and honors, but he simultaneously sowed the discord born of differing criteria, thus invoking the wars that resulted from a violation of the precepts of justice.

Treacherous plottings were a commonplace with him. During an important festival at Tula, he danced and sang a magic song. He was soon imitated by the multitudes who followed him in delight, but he led them onto a bridge which collapsed under their weight. A large number of them were hurled into the river where according to the legend they were changed to stones.

Shortly after that incident, he appeared to the Toltecs to show them a puppet magically dancing on his hand. In their wonder they crowded around, but in the crush a number of them were suffocated. In stating his case before Tonacatecuhtli, his father and the God of the Thirteenth Heaven, a recalcitrant Tezcatlipoca claimed the losses occurred only among the sinful and that he had deliberately propitiated their punishment.

According to one legend, the Aztecs thought that Tezcatlipoca wandered at night in the shape of a "giant," wrapped in an ash-colored veil and carrying his head in his hand. When nervous people or people troubled by a restless conscience saw him it was told they dropped dead on the spot. But a brave person, pure in thought and deed, could theoretically seize him, as long as he held on until sunrise.

Tezcatlipoca would curse and beg to be released. Then he would cajole, offering wealth and invincible power, as long as he was released—like Dracula—before the dawn. If the brave man held on, said the tale, he would receive four thorns—for the four elements—as a pledge of victory from the conquered. The brave man would by then have torn out Black Tezcatlipoca's heart and taken it home wrapped in a cloth. But when he undid the folds of the cloth he would find nothing but white turkey feathers, a thorn, ashes, or an old rag.

Tezcatlipoca was also presumed to be the author of the dishonor of Coatlicue—she whose garment was woven of snakes, who was already the mother of a daughter and a number of sons, called the Centzon-Huitznahuas (The Four Hundred Southerners). One day, it was told, while she prayed, a crown of feathers fell from Heaven onto her breast. Her daughter was furious, believing Tezcatlipoca had violated her mother's honor. She urged the Centzon-Huitznahuas to murder poor Coatlicue to accomplish her immediate purification. But instead Huitzilopochtli, whom the mother carried in her womb, spoke to the girl and calmed her. Huitzilopochtli then sprang into view, fully outfitted in his blue armor, like Athena from the head of Zeus, his gleaming hummingbird feathers in iridescent contrast to his body, like Krishna, painted blue. The blue javelin in his left hand, a heavenly emblem, confirmed his divine skill. He hurled himself on his sister and killed her and then slew the Centzon-Huitznahuas and all who had plotted against his mother.

Yet while Huitzilopochtli was the protector and guide of the Aztecs on their journeys and for them represented honor and justice, Tezcatlipoca was nonetheless considered in the binary as the god of providence, identified with Chalchiuhtotolin, the "precious turkey," representing the waters of life, and joy and song, as this robust bird, originally wild, came to be cultivated in Mesoamerica as the most highly prized of delicacies. Its meat was encouraged, even honored, at the largest and smallest family gatherings, public festivities and religious ceremonies, and precisely for this reason, because of the singular distinction awarded the native turkey, Black, evil, licentious Tezcatlipoca had such easy access to any and all events.

It was said however, that Tezcatlipoca appeared, unexpectedly, even ubiquitously, to restore to people the word of Tonacatecuhtli, but he was also endowed with the authority to decree or inflict punishment on those considered by the gods to be guilty of wrongdoing or sin. Tezcatlipoca, for all his duplicity and conniving, in effect, served as the emissary of Justice on Earth, in the name of the God Supreme.

LAMATL DESCRIPTION

The most important figure in the eighth lamatl of the Borgia Codex, the Chalchiuhtotolin, is dressed in glorious colors and adorned with lavish jewels of "green stone" or "emerald"—the term applied to the exquisitely carved native jadeite—and gold.

A symbol pours from its mouth, indicating the word for the light captured in the claw of the sovereign bird. His autonomy and majesty is seen as clarity and right conduct.

He is accompanied by a central water vessel, from which lead dual containers, symmetrical conductors through which the aqua vitae may or may not pass, depending on the equilibrium maintained in the central, or principal, container.

The Bourbon Codex shows Chalchiuhtotolin facing a container from which pours a foamy liquid, probably pulque—fermented "honey water" and the most favored Mesoamerican beverage. Thus, the figure provides nourishment while it also serves to ferment the corn flour used in the ceremonial bread.

The image of Pilizinteotl (Piltzintecuhtli) also appears, the Child God who maneuvers the serpent by means of his Divine Powers, implying the wisdom and the attributes of Quetzalcoatl.

The House of Darkness appears as well. From its interior a message emerges, portrayed as a flood in balanced contrast, associating the Divine Word to an Arrow. Water vessels overflow with precious liquid. Other vessels contain ritual blood and precious jewels. Two stems are represented with arrows hanging from them, symbols of the exercise of divine justice, as commanded by Tonacatecuhtli and Tonacacihuatl, expressed through their son Tezcatlipoca, The Black, he who lost a foot when he fell from heaven. When the foot was later repaired it was replaced by a round mirror similar to the one he wears on his forehead,

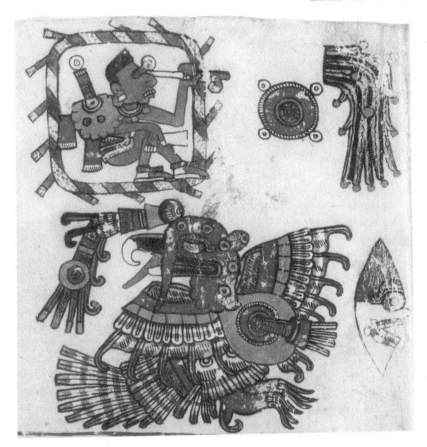

Figure 20. Black Tezcatlipoca as the jade turkey, in his guise as Chalchiuhtotolin, also known as hen-chalchihuitl. From the Códice Borgia.

and accompanied by bells on his ankles. And, while he represents justice and honor, and spreads wealth, he is also the cause of war and disorder.

LAMATL SYMBOLISM

Yayauhqui Tezcatlipoca—as his advocation, Chalchiuhtotolin—symbolizes the plumed messenger of the designs of Providence. This Holy Ghost forms a part of the Trinity, in which Tonacatecuhtli is the Father and Quetzalcoatl the Son.

Chalchiuhtotolin presides over the sacrifice in order to redeem the sins of the penitent. He is the conductor and guide who regulates human behavior and who judges, in the name of the father, the actions of humankind. He administers penitence and sacrifice. He officiates over worldly goods and spiritual tranquility. And, finally, he establishes the nature of justice on Earth, determining those who will remain in the vale of earthly suffering and those who are permitted into the realm of Tonacatecuhtli, in the Thirteenth Heaven, the Aztec Nirvana reserved for the truly enlightened.

The house illustrated in the lamatl contains the symbol of the Divine Word, pierced by an arrow, which represents God's justice as it pours from the vessel of life within. The gods of the house are authorized by the Supreme Father to maintain the equilibrium established in the counterposed images of Quetzalcoatl and Tezcatlipoca, who appear as the juxtaposition of all that life offers: the entire gamut of perception and opportunity, of the positive and negative. The two face each other, patron and civilizer, masters both of life and its intrigues, of the arts of culture or profanity, of the wind and its devastation, of the Creator and the Power of Destruction.

PARALLEL SYMBOLISM

The Justice depicted in the eighth arcanum is more properly seen as the justice authorized by humankind as a neutralizer for its own actions. This justice, in effect, exercised by humans over themselves, is presumed as an extension of the justice symbolized by the Father governing the world through his emissaries, the angels and archangels, winged messengers and prophets.

In both the tarot and the *Tonalamatl*, the central figure is a winged entity which descends from above by God's mandate, to impose Heaven's justice on humankind, in order to provide or withdraw Divine Blessing according to the total estimation of personal conduct. The concept is further implied in the penitence or sacrifice—a person's position and good fortune, or its opposite, seen as reward or denial—and imposed at the whim of the messenger of the gods.

Black Tezcatlipoca, especially as represented in the Ce-Atl, is a parallel to Lucifer, the Angel of Evil, that Devil of the Middle Ages. He is indicated by the form of an eagle or rooster, which is a graphic judgment on the Fallen Angel, a son of God fallen from Heaven and from Heaven's grace and interpreted as a seductive bird of precious plumage.

In both cards the emphasis remains on the equilibrium, the balance of forces designed to maintain a viable restraint on the tendency to both good and evil. Any tipping of the scales to one side or the other, affects the balance of society itself, therefore interfering with nature's functions.

In Greek mythology the transference of the symbol falls on Hephaestus, who in effect interprets Zeus' commands on his forge and through his metallurgical skills. Yet, if conciliatory Quetzalcoatl, the positive force, invented metallurgy for the Mexicans, it was Tezcatlipoca, the treacherous, the dissenter who shared Hephaestus' distinguishing characteristic: Zeus threw Hephaestus from Heaven during a quarrel, causing him to lose a leg.

Just as Tezcatlipoca wears mirrors as part of his attribute, the arcanum in the tarot is seen as if in a mirror, suggesting the reflection of the counterpart, the opposite of what is projected. Yet we are not dealing with opposites. We are faced with juxtaposed versions of the same entity, in perfect balance, therefore in harmony with each other and with the Cosmos.

The cane or reed in Nahuatl mythology occupies the position of the scepter in the tarot. The rod is the symbol of justice, or at least the infliction of a punishment. It is drawn in the hieroglyphs in the shape of an arrow, to represent not just direction but power, supremacy, and the right of judgment. Yet its symbolism lies closer to that of the sword or lance, as an interpretation of victorious battle, the triumph of forces, and, in addition, the unerring course of action straight to its target.

Both Quetzalcoatl and Tezcatlipoca, sons of the divine pair and as such authorized to exercise judgment and punishment, are represented as the arrow or a reed wand, instruments associated with the water in which the cane or reeds grow. Before beginning any trial, civil judges have their symbolic wands or mallets brought to them, just as seen in the arcanum, because justice must be enforced, with a sword if necessary. It is an emblem of decision until such time as reason triumphs and the balance is recovered, and human beings, finally harmonious, enjoy the sublime state implied in the *vases communicantes* of the lamatl or the scales of justice in the tarot—the power of free, creative and egalitarian thought.

ARCANUM VIIII

MYTHOLOGY OF THE HERMIT

The ninth arcanum refers specifically to Hermes Trismegistus – Thrice Great, Thrice Venerated – patron of science and literature, wisdom and invention, identified by the Greeks with Hermes, the Messenger of the Gods.

Earlier, however, the card was associated with the initial principle of the Orphic cosmogonies, which claimed as their authority the apocryphal observations of a priest named Onomacritus. The philosophic and scientific absorptions of the Orphic systems, though attributed to Orpheus, in fact emphasized the abstractions and subtleties in the metaphysical, as opposed to the mythological.

They were founded in Cronus, or Time, from which came Chaos, symbol of the Infinite, and Ether, representing the Finite. Chaos was surrounded by Night, which formed the enveloping cover under which the creative action of Ether was able to organize matter. This eventually assumed the shape of an egg, of which Night formed the shell.

In the center of this gigantic egg, whose upper section formed the vault of the sky, and whose lower section was the Earth, the first being was formed: Phanes, or Light. Thus the arcanum is termed *Lux Occulta*, Self-Initiation in the Hidden Light.

It was Phanes in his union with Night who created Heaven and Earth, and who in this version engendered Zeus. The Orphic doctrines finally converged in their supreme god Dionysus, yet the premise was far more fully developed in Egypt in the form of Thot, or Thoth, the Graeco-Roman name for Djehuti or Zeuhti. Worshipped throughout Egypt as a moon god, he acted as divine spokesman and keeper of the celestial records.

Djehuti simply meant "he of Djehut," the name of the old province in Lower Egypt whose capital, Hermopolis Parva, evidently served as the cradle of Thot's cult before he established a later and more important sanctuary at Hermopolis Magna in Upper Egypt.

According to theologians, Thot represented the true universal Demiurge, the divine ibis (a heron-like bird) that hatched the World Egg at Hermopolis Magna. They taught that he had accomplished the work of creation by the sound of his voice alone, leading to the

Hermetic principle regarding the Will of the Individual as invincible against the elements: harmony achieved through self-awareness: the gently, or softly spoken.

When Thot first awoke in the primordial "Nun" he opened his lips, they said, and from the sound that issued four gods materialized and then four goddesses and for this reason the future Hermopolis was called Khnum, or City of Eight, to honor those who sang, morning and evening, to assure the continuity of the sun in its course.

In the Books of the Pyramids, Thot is sometimes the oldest son of Ra, sometimes the child of Get and Nut, occasionally the brother of Isis, Seth, and Nephthys. Normally, however, he is a vizier and scribe rather than kin to the Osirian family, a collaborator who remained faithful to Osiris even after his murder. Because of the trueness of his voice, which amplified the strength of his magical incantations, it was claimed he was the incontrovertible force in Osiris's resurrection.

He helped Isis purify Osiris's dismembered body, then assisted her in the defense of the child Horus against an onslaught of perils: the poison of a scorpion bite, the curing of a tumor, a dual with Seth. And, after the decision of a tribunal that Seth return his nephew's heritage, he became Horus's vizier as well, and succeeded him to the throne when Horus resigned his earthly dominion. Thot ruled peacefully during 3,226 years, thus fortifying the arcanum's association with longevity and prudence.

Endowed with complete knowledge and absolute wisdom, it was Thot who invented the arts and sciences, arithmetic, surveying, geometry, astronomy, soothsaying, magic, medicine, surgery, music with wind instruments and strings, drawing and, above all, writing—humanity's guarantee of the perpetuity of its doctrines and discoveries.

As inventor of the hieroglyphs, Thot was named "Lord of the Holy Words." As the first of the magicians, he was termed "The Elder." His disciples boasted they had access to the crypt where he had locked up his books of magic and they undertook to decipher and consign to memory those formulas they said commanded all the forces of nature and subdued the very gods themselves. It was this infinite power, attributed to him by his followers, that earned him the name Thot, which the Greeks translated as Hermes Trismegistus, "three times very, very great."

After his long reign on Earth, Thot ascended to the skies, where he undertook various employments. He was the Moon God—or at least the god responsible for guarding the Moon. According to legend, Thot challenged the Moon and won a seventy-second part of its light, from which he created the five intercalary days. As a lunar divinity, Thot measured time, which he divided into months (to the first of which he gave his own name) and into years, which in turn were divided into three seasons, as opposed to four in the temperate zone.

He was the divine administrative force, responsible for all calculations and annotations. He appears at Edfu before the temple trinity, recording the geographical division of the country with its dimensions and resources. At Deir el Bahri, he is shown carrying out a scrupulous inventory of treasures brought to the gods of Egypt by a naval expedition on its return from an exploratory mission in search of the land of Punt.[1]

He was the keeper of the divine archives and patron of history. He noted the succession of the sovereigns and, on the leaves of the sacred tree at Heliopolis, wrote the name of the future Pharaoh whom the queen had just conceived after union with the Lord of the Heavens. On a long palm shoot he also inscribed the happy years of reign accorded by Ra to the King.

He was the herald of the gods as well as clerk and scribe. "Ra has spoken, Thot has written." During the dreadful judgment of the dead before Osiris, Thot appears, weighing the heart. If found not wanting, he proclaimed his verdict while he wrote "not guilty" on the tablets.

---

[1]As described by Eric Flaum in *Discovery: Exploration through the Centuries* (New York: Gallery Books, 1990), p. 10. See especially chapter 1.

CARD DESCRIPTION

Ancient amulets show an old man with a long beard, accompanied by a stag. Together they represent long life and wisdom. The hierograph indicates a roof or its framework, symbolizing protection, defense, and insulation from harmful influences. The arcanum depicts an old man walking, holding in his own right hand (as opposed to the image in a mirror) a lamp containing three lights. The lamp is partially hidden under his wide-hooded cloak, which covers him with its triple folds.

In his left hand, The Hermit holds a long walking stick, which supports his steps. Several knots are visible on the stick. The number varies according to the deck, but is usually either three or seven—cabalistic numbers. The stick itself is associated with the staff of the Egyptian priest, who was originally accompanied by a small vial—his magic—or a vase containing honey. This was a reminder of the offerings to the ibis-headed god, which occurred a few days after the full moon at the beginning of the year, when he was approached by his friends with the words, "Sweet is the truth."

In the Hittite version of the amulet, from nearby Asia Minor, the old man is portrayed in an attitude of supplication, petitioning Heaven for the help of the gods in constructing a life of rectitude, later interpreted as a plea before Thot at the judgment of Osiris.

In the Middle Ages, an old pauper or a beggar appeared on the card. He held himself upright with his staff while he carried an hourglass. Later the ancient timepiece was replaced by a lantern with three wicks. He is shown walking a long and difficult road, but his face reflects the inner peace he perceives beyond his travails.

CARD SYMBOLISM

The Hermit's age indicates not only the knowledge acquired through experience but the disposition to solitude, not just in the sense of physical seclusion but as a condition of receptivity to meditation, the only reliable source of wisdom. His earthly encounters have been tempered by karmic prosperity in the physical world; that is, he *learns* from his experience. His movements suggest that any stagnation or arrested development is unlikely for one who persists in the quest for self-knowledge.

The three wicks of the lamp imply enlightenment on all three planes of existence. The symbol is reinforced in the three knots of the staff and the triple folds of the cloak, called The Cloak of Apollonius of Tyana. In itself it symbolizes isolation or withdrawal from the troubles of the outer, or physical world.

The staff supports the cabalistic character of the three planes, the merging into the realm of nature, where everything will be synthesized in the ability to confront and cope with a method and a goal extending beyond the material phase of existence.

The Hermit signifies the ecstasy of the Prophet, suddenly enlightened by grace, while he projects his inspiration onto a religious ethic in the most profound sense, beyond any material dominion. His example of divination is considered equal to the level achieved by the archetype. Yet the experience implies a commitment. By directing one's own energy onto the astral plane, through and beyond awareness, deep concentration is achieved. The finality of spiritual harmony, according to the Hermit, is more than an aimless journey along an endless road. This arcanum verifies not only the worth of the excursion, but the viability of the goal in the perfected synthesis. One word of caution: once the journey is undertaken there can be no turning back.

LAMATL IX

MYTHOLOGY OF CE-COZCACUAHTLI (THE VULTURE)

The ninth lamatl is represented by Cozcacuahtli, the vulture, a collared buzzard, bird of prey and scavenger, identified with the first of the gods regent: Xolotl, the Sacred Dog.

Like Anpu, the Greek Conductor of Souls, inseparable from Hermes, or the jackal god Anubis, who opened the doors of that other world for the Egyptian dead, Xolotl was assigned the task of transporting a lifeless bulk and delivering it to the underworld, generally laboring by darkness unless accompanied by Tlalchitonatiuh, the Nocturnal Sun.

The arcanum in the tarot refers to esoteric wisdom and the occult sciences that originated among the Assyrians, Babylonians, and Egyptians, and surely the Sumerians and the Aryans before them. The origins of the Mesoamerican symbol, however, remain as vague as the beginning of culture on our own continent.

The lurid tale portrays the place called Anáhuac, derived, it was said, of Atlahuaca, the "territory surrounded by water." This land, or mysterious island, associated by dating techniques with the earliest cultural history of Mesoamerica and going back at least 15,000 years, suggests its birthplace had ties of some sort, cultural or geneological, with Lumuria—possibly Atlantis. This hypothesis has been supported in the disquieting antiquity of an assortment of cultures whose remains could easily extend, according to carbon testing devices, back in time perhaps 30,000 years. In which case, it would be reasonable to assume, a native American hominoid in fact existed and had no need, except for purposes of cultural or commercial exchange, to parade back and forth across the Bering Straits.

The important thing is the lamatl in the Bourbon Codex, which portrays the gods, especially Xolotl and the card's other regent, Tlal-chitonatiuh, on a slip of ground threatened by fierce currents, enclosed by the symbols of the heavens and the cosmos. Were these the shipwrecked? Stranded or abandoned survivors of a disappearing continent, a departing vessel, a cataclysmic upheaval or holocaust?

The water, according to the codices, represents the Chicuna-huapan, the "River that flows nine times," which doubles back on itself nine times or around nine bends or curves, through the under-world; and which Xolotl must cross in order to deliver Tlalchitona-tiuh, the Nocturnal Sun, to the other side. The fact of the river is expressed clearly in the codex, described by means of the hieroglyph *Ilhuicatl*, indicating the "Heavenly Water," yet remains ambiguous. Does this water originate in the heavens or does it come from the gods who lived there?

The Borgia Codex is more specific. It illustrates, by means of coded emblems, the water as representing the Western Sea, where the Sun, on Xolotl's back, plunges in its descent toward the under-world, that secret realm of hidden knowledge and carefully guarded wisdom.

Some of these emblems, nonetheless, would appear to depart from their mystical or mythological application, to assume the sar-casm of a political cartoon, disguised as an esoteric, or even a pro-phetic, vision. In this context Xolotl, obviously not very popular, was pictured as a ruler-deity, who may have really lived. He was described by unflattering names, suggesting a "rapacious monster," which associated him as much to the image of the divine messenger as to the "filth dripping" vulture, carrion still clinging to its beak.

Xolotl was said to have headed the wave of tribes called the Chichimec, from central Mexico, who possessed the bow and arrow, a revolutionary weapon in its time. He and his people, according to the pictographs, conquered one by one the towns on or around the vast lake, the Meztliapan or Lake of the Moon, today known as Tez-coco, that occupied a good part of the Valley of Mexico. The tribe finally settled in a place called Tenayuca.

The ambitious and resourceful Xolotl and his people swarmed unchallenged by the Aztecs, at that time only a small tribe, mostly former serfs and unprepossessing mercenaries of the now-decimated Toltecs, who had established themselves along the southern shore of the lake. The belief was fostered that they had originated in antiquity, on an undisclosed island. The codex illustrates a man in a canoe rowing away from the beach, accompanied by four priests. Each car-ries a bundle of sacred objects on his back.

In one of these hefty parcels the holy men carried the image of Huitzilopochtli, until then an icon virtually unknown in that part of the country. They believed, or were prepared to disseminate the notion, that this new deity was their invincible protector. He was the Sun that "killed" the Moon and Stars the moment he appeared with his powerful light. He was the new and improved storm god, a god of war worshipped in the temple of Great Tenochtitlan (now present-day Mexico City). He wore hummingbird feathers—highly prized goods—fastened to his left leg, to emphasize his left-handedness, an allusion to his iconoclastic nature. His attributes included a serpent of fire and a stick curved in the shape of a snake, indication of everything fertile and productive, all the arts and science. His cult was, in effect, challenging what they considered the now decadent and degraded icon of Quetzalcoatl.

The codices further verified the tradition of a series of "waters," including a flood that occurred in Aztec and Mexica pre-history, with a confusion of languages as part of its aftermath, in a parallel of Biblical history.

The sacred books told of humanity destroyed by a deluge; but one man, they said, Coxcoxtli, and one woman, Xochiquetzal (Xochiquetzalli), had escaped in a boat, in which they reached higher ground on the mountain of Colhuacan (Culhuacan, now a Mexico City suburb). They had many children, according to the tale, who remained mute until a dove in a treetop made them the "gift of tongues," yet these differed so thoroughly that the children failed to understand each other.

Then Xolotl appeared to escort Huitzilopochtli with the light of a "gifted Sun," that had penetrated the secrets of the underworld on its journey. It could therefore reveal and share with the cult's followers, the esoteric arts, a code of ethics, and the miracle of verbal communication, until the people surpassed their predecessors in cultural accomplishments. Xolotl, however, in time, was relegated to an apparently insignificant role as the god of the ball game—an entertainment usually associated with the ruling class and protector of all twins, but especially the symbolic inference of himself as the twin of Quetzalcoatl.

The sign's second regent, Tlalchitonatiuh, or Yohualtonatiuh, represented the Sun of Darkness. According to a myth called the Story of the Four Suns, the gods created four successive worlds, after the initial creation of the Earth. Torrential rains followed and drowned all of humankind except for those few who changed into fish under the First Sun or into chickens and dogs after the rain of fire following the Second Sun. The people of the Third Creation fed on pitch and resin and were either swallowed by an earthquake or devoured by savage and hostile animals. The Sun of Wind and Air shone on the Fourth World, when humans were changed into monkeys and fed on nuts and fruits. The Fifth Sun is our own.

LAMATL DESCRIPTION

The lamatl portrays the figure of Xolotl seated on a red throne, decorated with the jaguar skin associated with the Olmec gods of the Huastec. He is dressed in the garments of Quetzalcoatl as Ehécatl, the God of the Wind. The wind "mask" topped by the conical cap is worn in recognition of his bringing love into the world, by bestirring the maiden Mayahuel. He represents the spirit freed from any material association.

Xolotl is depicted here as Quetzalcoatl's twin and follower, possibly a political convenience, more likely just symbolic. He wears a blue bar in his nose to indicate his role as the god of the dead and the underworld. He is painted black and is shown with the talons of an eagle or the claws of a jaguar. In his hand he carries either the symbol of a ray of lightning bent double, or an ignited flint: the light of the fire that nourishes life originates in either of them.

His headdress flashes with flames and firelight, indicating wisdom to the ancients, for without fire they were cold and hungry, powerless against the elements, lost before the terrors of the night.

The headpiece is like an oversized crown, flamboyant and extravagantly adorned with precious stones, particularly the "green stones" called emeralds, the color of "the green platter" of the Earth, or the iridescent feathers of the quetzal bird. His breastplate describes the wind, another reference to the grandeur—culturally, intellectually and certainly politically—of Quetzalcoatl.

In occasional codices, he appears accompanied by the Nocturnal Sun, Tlalchitonatiuh, whose eyes burn like the flint they symbolize. He is depicted with a lighted cigar in his mouth, to indicate the ubiquitous power of fire, and of flint, which permits its control or conjuring at will. The "night fires" or the "perpetual flame," the paral-

Figure 21. Xólotl, the dog that guides the Sun through the netherworld of the dead, depicted here with tlapapalli, the four colors, another manifestation of Ahuiatéotl, the god of pleasure. From the Códice Borgia.

lel of The Hermit's lamp, mentioned in the *Popol-Vuh*, the Sacred Book of the Creation of the Mayas, refers to the horrors of arrogance and the glory of enlightenment.

"There was little clarity on the face of the earth," noted a Quiché Maya historian in the *Popol Vuh*, sacred books from the Guatemala Highlands. "As yet there was no sun. The heavens and the earth existed, but the sun and moon remained hidden from view. And the vain man said: 'The Sun and the Moon are like those who drowned in the Flood, faded and supernatural. I will be greater now than they, or any other that has been formed or created. I am the Sun. I am brightness and moonlight. Vast is my splendor. For me men will walk and triumph. My eyes are silver, bright as precious stones, as emeralds; my teeth gleam like the finest jewels, like the canopy of heaven. My nose can be seen from afar like the moon, my throne is silver and the earth lights up when I parade before my seat of office.' But he was not the Sun nor did his vision transcend the horizon.

"The vain and foolish man was punished with 'hideous destruction' for the sin of pride and for willfully likening himself to such as the gods."[2]

---

[2]*Popol Vuh, Las Antiguas Historias del Quiché*, translated from the original text with introduction and notes by Adrián Recinos (Mexico City: Fondo de Cultura Económica, 1952), pp. 34–35.

LAMATL SYMBOLISM

Xolotl symbolizes the hidden wisdom that can only be attained in crossing, like the nocturnal Sun or Thot, the Ibis, the sea of knowledge. Prudence and restraint, perfected in the process, can help to overcome the obstacles encountered on the earthly journey.

By taking the Nocturnal Sun on his shoulders, Xolotl helps this unique source of clarity and brilliance to illuminate a world that would otherwise be condemned to darkness and ignorance. Still, the coldest and most impenetrable darkness occurs just before the dawn, symbolized in the vulture, the beast that salvages what it can in order to remain alive. Mankind, therefore, has the option of another course of action—illumination in wisdom and achievement through thought—to lead him for all time out of darkness.

The Creation, related by the Mexicans, largely coincides with the versions of the Egyptians and Chaldeans. It not only describes an experience that seems to have occurred several times in the course of history but interprets the event in a parallel fashion, as a juncture like any other. The question is no longer one of survival, as such, but the terms of the *concept* of survival.

Are we to remain on this Earth at any cost? Or are we to contribute, in passing, a portion of the wisdom inherited from the past, which we would appear obliged to interpret and transmit to the future, hoping to somehow perpetuate an ascending pattern, instead of the maniacal cycle of inevitable decline.

PARALLEL SYMBOLISM

Both the arcanum and the lamatl are described in a venerable figure tested by age as well as experience. Cozcacuahtli, the ancient predator seen as a tired vulture, has exhausted the pathways of night in search of its destiny. The transition offered by death will provide another life, already ordained in Heaven or the underworld.

The Nocturnal Sun is symbolized in the tarot by The Hermit's lamp and in the *Tonalamatl* by Xolotl's flint. The monstrous dog is obliged to light the way of the dead in its passage through the underworld, as vanished souls cross the waters of the sacred river on a seemingly endless journey. Yet the effort is rewarded on the opposite bank, in the clarity of the newborn Sun, in enlightenment and the renewal of the spirit.

In the Vatican Codex, the Nocturnal Sun, or Tlalchitonatiuh, accompanies Xolotl on his labors, as a life-giving image related to fire, to the Earth, and to its fruits, like Coatlicue with her "serpent woven skirts," the mother from whom all things issue. Xolotl, by contrast, is shown as the plodding and usually maligned dog, closer to Hermes, it would seem than to Anpu, yet the association with the benevolent canine redeems his otherwise thankless task. He serves his master as assiduously as Thot served Osiris, and he remains just as devoted to duty. On the other hand, unlike Thot, he keeps no careful logs, nor documents more than the facts accumulated on his behalf in the codices.

The lighted cigar in Tlalchitonatiuh's mouth or the flint carried by Xolotl are like the unquenchable wicks in The Hermit's lamp, illuminating the pathway of the dead as The Hermit lights the way of the living, protecting their followers from the obstacles or impediments of the journey. The Hermit moves along very slowly, feeling his way with his staff. Tlalchitonatiuh moves just as carefully as he sinks into the depths of the Earth; and yet both are looking to shed light—and therefore knowledge—on unknown places.

The Hermit's stick or rod gives him support, like Huitzilopochtli's snakes or the arrows shown in the Bourbon Codex. The emphasis on the symbol of the three planes of existence is fortified in the lamatl: three arrows, three knots on the stick.

Virtue and wisdom, therefore, are not necessarily the inevitable products of age and experience. Yet both the tarot and the *Tonalamatl* emphasize the potential in the application of simple good sense and a modicum of humility, as well as strength and stamina in order to prevail. For even the most extravagant of inherent skills or the most astonishing talent are nothing if not applied with diligence and tenacity. The key is constancy, as opposed to daring.

ARCANUM X

MYTHOLOGY OF THE WHEEL OF FORTUNE

The two-headed Roman god Janus appeared on an ancient talisman to illustrate the persistent vigilance of past and future, the vehicle for the reinforcing of memory and moderation. A similar concept is translated in the image of Cerberus, the monstrous watchdog—counterpart of the Mexican Xolotl—posted at the gate of the Kingdom of Hades, beyond the black poplars and sterile willows of the Grove of Persephone.

With his "fifty heads and voice of bronze," he was born of the love of the giant Typhoeus for Echidna. Cerberus was usually represented, however, with only three of his heads, though the rest of him bristled with serpents—not unlike the skirts of Coatlicue. His mouth dripped black venom, in an image curiously parallel with the carrion dangling from the beak of Cozcacuahtli, the hovering and repulsive vulture of the Aztec underworld.

Cerberus was always to be feared, though he wagged his ears and tail. He could only be appeased with cakes of flour and honey. Hermes would calm him with his beguiling voice or keep him at bay with his caduceus, and Orpheus could charm him with his lyre, but normally his vigilance at the entrance to the nether-world assured that a traveler beyond the Styx would be trapped there. The great river surrounded the underworld with its nine loops, like the Nine-Flowing Chicunahuapan of Mesoamerica, so escape was unlikely.

Cerberus guarded the past, the present, and the future. Only Herakles (Hercules), in the last of his labors, dared to measure his strength and wile against that of the monster but when he finally strangled the beast with his bare hands and carried him up for a moment to Earth, Cerberus infected with his venom a number of herbs that previously had been considered inoffensive. This was both a curse and a blessing. Herakles suffered a temporary rash but afterward, physicians and sorcerers made prudent use of the herbs, both in beneficent remedies and in terrible philters, or potions.

The Kingdom of Hades patrolled by the dog took its name from the ruler of the underworld, derived in turn from a privative prefix of the verb "to see," evoking the idea of mystery. Hades was The Invisible. He was also called Pluto, from the word for "riches"; it was he who received buried treasure and who guarded subterranean minerals. And it was he who was considered to be the god of agricultural prosperity and abundance.

Hades was also called Aidoneus. He was a son of Rhea and the ferocious Cronus who devoured him, as he had swallowed his brothers and sisters. He was fortunately delivered by his brother Zeus, from whom he received as his share of the inheritance the kingdom of the underworld, which he ruled as an absolute master. He only abandoned his domain on two occasions: once to abduct Persephone and once to search for Paean in order to be cured of a wound inflicted by Herakles, who struck him on the shoulder with a sharp-pointed arrow.

And while he delighted in his gloomy domain he could, if he wished, emerge at any time, without being seen, for his helmet made him invisible. He was a good husband to Persephone, though he pursued a nymph in Minthe. Persephone, or possibly her mother Demeter, grew angry at this and turned the unhappy nymph into a plant (mint), which first grew in Triphylia and was ever afterward sacred to Hades.

Hades was very little venerated, though as the Roman Pluto he received considerable homage. Hades was essentially a god of mystery, terror, and the inexorable. Pluto, on the other hand, was regarded as a benevolent deity and his cult was often associated with the agricultural rites of Demeter. To pray to him, said Homer, one struck the ground with bare hands or with rods. A black ram or ewe was his preferred sacrifice. His sacred plants were the cypress and the narcissus.

The tenth arcanum is identified with the human forefinger, the vehicle of the imperative gesture, the outward movement stressing the active power of the microcosm (human) as released from imprisonment in the closed system of the chaos of passivity. The amulets of antiquity therefore referred to Janus, the god of departure and return, and, by extension, the god of all means of communication.

Janus was also the god of "beginnings." As a solar deity he presided over daybreak (*Matutinus Pater*) and was early in Roman culture consecrated as the author of all initiative and, in a general sense, of human initiative. This Italic god, completely Roman in origin, was ascribed the essential role in the creation of the world, called Chaos at the time when fire, air, earth, and water were all a formless mass. When the elements separated into perceptible entities, Chaos took the form of Janus, his two faces representing the confusion of his original state. He was the God of gods, Janus Pater, until he also became the first god of doorways, of public gates through which all roads passed, the key which opens and closes the door, and the stick (*virga*) which porters employed to drive away those who had no right to cross the threshold. His two faces (Janus *bifrons*) allowed him to observe both the exterior and the interior of the house, and the entrance and exit of public buildings.

The card in the tarot is referred to as The Wheel of Fortune, or the Sphinx, a testament connected with the idea of the law, the vigilance of a structure in which, nonetheless, all mental principles and currents flow freely. It is also called The World's Mill, which grinds everything, assimilates everything and prepares everything. It raises one thing while it lowers another, as a true *rota*, leaving nothing immovable except its axle, which suggests the possibility of the existence of illusion, that which is matter. The axle of the visible and sensible world is thus merged with the unlimited dimension of peace in fulfillment.

This arcanum represents the wealth of the underworld, and of the Earth and its enterprises in general, but indicates the vulnerability of riches, the moral chaos in their pursuit, and their loss at the moment of death.

CARD DESCRIPTION

Certain very old cards originated in the legend of King Midas and used his figure as the card's model. They included four additional figures with donkey's ears, symbolizing Midas' kingdom.

During the revival of the tarot in the Middle Ages, a number of Egyptian figures were incorporated into the image, to signify the inconstancy of human existence, the caprice of fortune, the mysteries of life itself and Time, which takes us at will and alters what we had considered our original choice.

The picture in the tenth arcanum shows a Sphinx atop a platform, armed with a sword, in the upper portion of the card. Beneath the platform is a giant wheel, the spokes of which are formed by two perpendicular lines and two diagonal lines, which end in a double caduceus.

The wheel's hub, in certain cards, is engraved with the seal, or hexagram, of Solomon. Two inscriptions, the Great Tetragram and Rota, are interwoven on the wheel itself, to be read from right to left. In the course of its rotation the wheel draws up to the Sphinx on the right side, bearing the figure of Cynocephal-Hermanubis, with a triple caduceus in his right hand, while from the left side the same wheel casts down the body of the crocodile Typhone, with its human head and a trident in its left claw.

In the upper part of an earlier version of the card an angel could be seen, instead of the Sphinx, holding an open book. To his right, opposite him, an eagle held another book in its talons. Two winged animals appeared beneath the wheel, each carrying similar books. All of this has been simplified in later decks.

CARD SYMBOLISM

The whole figure constitutes a closed and finished system which has been subjected to the inner processes implicit in the crown of The Sphinx, called the invariable method. This is projected on the fundamental Hermetic principle: To Dare, To Keep Silent, To Know, To Will.

These precepts presume to lead toward perfection in fulfillment. The whole mill, or wheel, dominated by the platform of this method, elevates certain elements or factors, while it diminishes others. By striving upward, it says, the elements under the sign of Azoth, the great solvent, still retain their dog's head as a symbol of their former, more imperfect state—traces of impulsiveness, darkness, and evil instincts—yet they indicate a potential for the mill of transformation. This mill enlightens us by providing something higher and more implacable, pulling and kneading us, in a painful process, in order, according to Hermetic teachings, to prepare a better dough for a future bread. The bread in the metaphor refers to the Biblical offering, sign of love and giving, a product of positive interaction among certain harmonious ingredients and the gracious intentions and hard work of the doner, a combination capable of disarming even a Cerberus.

The symbols emphasize the angel with a book (mental potential), an eagle (astral potential), and the physical binary of two animals below the wheel, which still have wings, to show they are potentially able to fly higher than their present position at the foot of the whole construction.

This cryptic language implies certain important symbolic proposi-
tions. Foremost is that truth must be lived. It must be exemplified in
the exponent's own conduct, rather than looked upon as something
isolated or distant from him. The card emphasizes that some will find
truth an inexhaustible source of inspiration and knowledge. Others,
it claims, the less imaginative and creative, the less daring and vital,
will disapprove, and so nullify the principle, this reflection of the law
or Hermetic testament in the symbolic mirror, representing hope.

LAMATL X

MYTHOLOGY OF CE-CUETZPALLIN (THE LIZARD)

The concept of a Kingdom of God in any philosophy necessarily implies the existence of harmony and viability of action, within a demarcation of time and space. Its counterpart, sin and corruption, are associated with evil and death, with distorted figures, with nightmares, and terror. The thirteen-day period described as the Ce-Cuetzpallin is represented as a lizard, a naked and miserable, crawling animal, akin to the snake in the parallel of Adam and Eve.

The lizard was specifically represented, according to the codices, by the female womb, of which the animal was a symbol, and for which its body—dried or fresh, chopped, whole, blended with herbs or distilled, boiled into an infusion—was utilized in the curing of uterine ailments. The lizard was also used in potions, for the remedying of "spells" in which "moral and law-abiding men" were "corrupted" in the pursuit of "unlawful and unnatural pleasures inside the houses of condemnation." This was a violation of the codes exercised "outside the confines of the temple of aberration" where normal people lit their fires, dressed their bodies with colored powders as a protection from the elements, celebrated their feasts, tilled their fields, and attended their sacrifice.[1]

The God Regent of the lamatl, Ixtlacoliuhqui, is portrayed as Invisible Temptation, for he is blind, like the cosmic night "from whence he came." He is a Lord of the Heavens, the son of God Creator Tonacatecuhtli and his wife Tonacacihuatl, who "sent the

---

[1]This interpretation has been translated from the Borgia Codex, as are several other passages in this chapter.

fertile spirit and the necessary warmth for mortal parents to engender children." Yet he married Tlazolteotl, the lustful Venus who sups on filth and thirsts for sin. Together they perceived humankind as fallible, mutant, still imperfect beings, as corruptible as they are frightened.

The interpretation according to Sahagún, establishes that this thirteen-day sign produces only hardship and "bad things": false witness, adultery, deformed babies, and war. Ixtlacoliuhqui was the noonday star following a backward course, depicted as twisted fibers of sisal and maguey. He was erroneously described in Sahagún's chronicle, following the conquest, as a god of ice, sent from a heaven both dark and chill. The correct designation has to do with thread and cord and he is, therefore, shown with a spindle. It was said he had wronged by sinning "in a place considered for recreation and pleasure" and had been expelled, stark naked. For this reason he is symbolized by the naked lizard, which "led mankind into blind misery."

In the Borgia Codex, Ixtlacoliuhqui is accompanied by Tezcatlipoca, seen as the sinister god of judgment and a Mesoamerican Testament, a black Tezcatlipoca, shown with a bear's face and brilliant eyes, dead and risen, with a body that gives off the stench of the damned. He is responsible for weighing, like Thot, the souls of the dead to determine their right either to gentle Heaven or that dismal underworld, ruled by Mictlantecuhtli, with his queen and mate Mictecacihuatl. There, beside the Nine Underground Rivers, the faded souls of the mournful dead were condemned to an insubstantial eternity patrolled by Xolotl, the infernal dog.

The rigid Mesoamerican class system required that, even in the afterlife, the dead soul pursue the occupations of his or her worldly existence, within the same context. In this way the severely or especially guilty suffered eternal torture, unless he or she had made full restitution through penitence and sacrifice. The most heavily sanctioned transgressions were committed, according to Black Tezcatlipoca's code, against the gods themselves. The "moral idea" implicit in a balance regarding the human condition was always as flexible, or as reversible, as the human conscience, yet mortals could displease the gods by simply doing as the gods did. Humans could therefore incur divine wrath both by offending the moral law or by attaining too much wealth or happiness, in which case the error consisted in exciting the god's envy.

Given the Aztec social structure and the rigidity of the accompanying classism, it followed, by Tezcatlipocan logic, that unexplained wealth, like euphoria or ambition, was usually illicit, thus punishable to the fullest extent of his divine fury. Thus, in his black manifestation, Tezcatlipoca was considered The Inevitable, an extension of the blind Ixtlacoliuhqui, enforced as a demon image that not only punished, but incited, carnal sin, in order to evoke the punishable.

If the daytime was light and clarity, Black Tezcatlipoca was night and evil; yet even Ixtlacoliuhqui, despite his association with the noon star, was the aberration, the erroneous course, and therefore the path of corruption, even in the heavens.

LAMATL DESCRIPTION

In the Borgia Codex, the two gods are seated facing each other. The black Tezcatlipoca appears on the right, a judgmental god exercising his authority in the name of the God Creator and Divine Justice. Ixtlacoliuhqui sits on the left, his eyes blindfolded. He is invisible: his black mask hides his features. He appears on the throne of the solar gods and wears two wheels on his hat, with the symbol of cosmic movement, the four cardinal points, and a central symbol which indicates the generation of eternal motion, that is the passage of time.

In every codex, Ixtlacoliuhqui wears a curved cap outlined in sharp points, used to indicate the meshing of the gears of a great wheel. He furthermore wears two smaller wheels, which are designed to turn on an axle not unlike those of the Roman war chariots or the chariots used by Alexander against Darius, sharp and deadly which in themselves were a terrible weapon.

The blindfolded god is drawn with lines that indicate transparency or invisibility, in the same fashion as glass or transparent objects are illustrated in the Codices. Ixtlacoliuhqui, as in the case of other Huastec gods, is seated on a throne decorated with a jaguar skin, his conical cap tilted back and pierced by an arrow. The jaguar skin was later seen as a tunic used by the warriors which this god ostensibly made invulnerable to enemy attack.

In the Borgia Codex, the black Tezcatlipoca appears standing on top of the symbol which indicates the cosmic night. In his right hand

Figure 22. Itztlacoliuhqui Ixpuimilli, god of the cold and the stone, and deity of chastisement, shown here with Yayauhqui Tezcatlipoca, the Black Tezcatlipoca, lord of judgment. From the Códice Borgia.

he holds a bundle of arrows and the shield of the gods called *Chilama*; in his left hand he holds the symbol of power.

The "fallen man," in the sense of a sinner, is also depicted. In the Bourbon Codex this is replaced by a drowsing couple, whose soul or aura flows freely around them like a kind of misty flame, which tries to invade other forms and is infused with a brand of energy seen as eternal.

LAMATL SYMBOLISM

In this lamatl the mystery of life's duality is revealed, implying reincarnation and redemption. The invisible quality of the human aura is made to appear as the potential of one being to invade the form of another, as designated by a supreme judge and with regard to the verdict applied to good and evil actions.

The Law of Compensation is fully treated in the graphic implications. Karmic law or cosmic cause are viewed as inevitable, in relation to a pre-established course of action—that is, a destiny, written long before the birth of any individual, which situates him in relation to life's alternatives.

Yet a precise code also implies an alteration of the structure, depending on the individual's awareness, his capacity to see beyond even the blindness of the gods, and his disposition to penitence, a term of trial, as it were, in the underworld, for the purpose of being released in another incarnation or manifestation.

The symbolism of the wheel on Ixtlacoliuhqui's garments refers to the esoteric dimension of the human spirit, which may presumably evolve, decarnate—though it never dies—and be reassembled at a later time as a reborn and revitalized entity, far more admirable than its predecessor and probably invulnerable.

PARALLEL SYMBOLISM

The related symbolism in both the arcanum and the lamatl make common cause in the vagaries of chronology, emphasizing the mutability of the time factor as an alternative, independent of the lifespan itself.

Human conduct, in the tarot as much as in the *Tonalamatl*, operates on a plane beyond the range of human life. Ixtlacoliuhqui, the god regent of the Ce-Cuitzpallin, is the spinner's god, of the cord produced by means of the spindles that form part of his headdress. These symbolize the continuity of human behavior as well as self-determination in relation to the outcome.

Ixtlacoliuhqui was seen as a deity fallen from Heaven as a result of his lost virtue. In his capacity as a sinner, he became the god of the adulterer's sacrifice. His singular mask, which lends his portrait an enigmatic quality, suggests an unsolved mystery, a parallel to the mystery of The Sphinx which governs the arcanum of the Wheel of Fortune. The riddle behind the mask is made to seem invisible, yet like all enigmas, the substance is as permeable as the situation. Only a renewed vision is required, a different light, to bring clarity to the otherwise intentionally obscured. Cerberus, like Black Tezcatlipoca, is never to be challenged. He can easily, however, be outwitted, by the clever application of the most invincible of all weapons: purity of action, virtue, consistency and rightness of purpose, the peculiar harmony of a mandate before which all beings must eventually yield. Yet they may win in the end, decrees the message from both sources, if need be, in another form or incarnation.

The tenth arcanum is related to that Hermetic tradition which offers access to the secrets contained in the seal of Solomon, in the Word of God, by means of the *rota* or wheel, the Mill of Eternal Knowledge. The card encompasses the wisdom in the sacred writings of the Old Testament, the Kabbalah, and the divinatory almanacs, which all concur in the symbolic implications of the crocodile and the serpent, a parallel to the lamatl's lizard, and the inevitable punishment implicit in disobedience or disdain of the sacred precepts.

The sinner will fall, say sacred books, and so will all those who follow too freely the impulse of darkness and evil. And the fallen are dragged into the machinations of an inevitable system, which is capable of transforming grandeur, pomp, and glory into wretchedness and misery. The arrogant, then, can only emulate the lowliness of the basest animals that crawl through the offal on the surface of the Earth, when they would otherwise have been free to fly, to soar across the heavens, to penetrate all mysteries and solve all riddles, for nothing is really denied any of us. The choice is our own.

The mill of transformation, says the arcanum, is driven by the implacable force of the universe, but the same force is ours for the taking, to impel our ascent or bring us to our knees. We will sow, it says, and we will reap. Our bread may be sweet or bitter.

Ixtlacoliuhqui, with his curved cap, trimmed in sharp points like the teeth of a saw, suggests the wheel and its axle. The wheels on his headdress represent an advanced dimension of privileged wisdom. His garments indicate a laborious artisan process. Yet the gods have denied him sustenance. He was hurled naked from paradise to become the god of adulterers, of sinners, of those who failed to keep the sacred light of matrimonial fidelity and so are punished by a hideous and pestilential death, as a warning to anyone tempted to follow their example. The notion of sin, the disruption of the life and structure of the community, are inadmissible. The gods have taken the trouble to express their will and transmit their wisdom. There can be no margin for digression. The price is survival.

The Star of David, in the center of the Wheel of Fortune, becomes synonymous with the advocations of Ixtlacoliuhqui, the vagrant noon star that becomes a constant in the southern sky for one hundred and twenty days, from August until December. Each is determined to persist and to survive beyond judgment and beyond punishment, until it is redeemed, beyond reproach.

ARCANUM XI

MYTHOLOGY OF STRENGTH

The arcanum known in the Egyptian Tarot as The Sorceress, or Persuasion, was in fact associated with the impenetrable mystery of concentration, the power of the mind with all its persuasive force, as undeniable and as effective as the intellect itself is a depository of criterion.

The traditional talisman was used for enhancing strength. It was claimed to be an integral factor in those with a gift for taming wild beasts, according to occultists, by virtue of the invocation of symbolic animals—such as the lion, representing power, or the unicorn, semiotic virginity and the mystique of the unattainable—and was further supported by a bond with the Moon, and therefore with Artemis.

Apollo's twin sister was said to be revered in connection with the word for "bear" or "quail." Her name is even supposed to be related to an adjective, meaning "safe and sound," which would make her "she who heals sickness," thus establishing the parallel with a "sorceress."

The primitive Artemis, however, was an agricultural deity, worshipped especially, like Hermes, in Arcadia. She was the goddess of the chase and of forests, symbolized by the she-bear. From the beginning she was associated with Apollo and was therefore a divinity of glowing light, especially the Moon's.

Her lunar character, however, as befitting the symbolism, began to wane when Selene, the moon goddess, appeared, and Artemis merged with Apollo as a light-goddess. Armed with a bow and quiver, as he was, she bore the epithet *Apollousa*, the destructress, or *Iocheaira*, who liked to "let fly with arrows" or "strike down mortals with her fearful darts" and even "assail their flocks with deadly disease."[1] Like Apollo, she was the deity of sudden death, though usually she confined her reprisals to women. Yet she could be equally benevolent and brought prosperity of a sort to those who honored her. Consider Agamemnon and his sacrifice of Iphigenia in her grove.

---

[1]Felix Guirand, ed., *New Larousse Encyclopedia of Mythology* translated by Richard Aldington and Delano Ames (London: Hamlyn House, 1969), p. 121.

As a moon-goddess she presided over childbirth, and while she had no connection with Tauris, another moon-goddess with whom she was confused on the Aegean islands of Samos and Icarus, the image of Artemis was often interrelated with other lunar deities — such as the Cretan Britomartis; or Hecate, a Thracian divinity, at the same time a moon-goddess and a goddess of the underworld, a concept synthesized in the Hermetic tradition of the tarot.

Artemis's image was glamorized by coins on which she carried a torch, or emblem of the Moon and the stars which surround her head. Sculptors, nonetheless, emphasized her rural association, and showed her to be a young virgin, slim and supple, with narrow hips and charming features. Her beauty however, was severe, heightened by a short tunic called a Dorian chiton, turned up, with the folds held in place by a girdle, and her feet were shod with the *cothurnus* or laced buckskin. She is often pictured in the company of a hind or dog.

Artemis was occasionally presented as the daughter of Zeus and Demeter, or even by Zeus with Demeter's daughter Persephone; or of Dionysus and Isis, thus relating her to the Moon figure in Egyptian mythology. But according to tradition among the Greeks she and Apollo, her twin, were children of Leto, sired by Zeus. They were born after a turbulent odyssey and a laborious pregnancy, on the island of Ortygia, called Delos from the time of their birth, after Hera had banished the twins' mother from the realm and forbade any province or town from offering her refuge. The palm tree, where Leto was said to have hung by her hands from a frond during the ordeal of her labor, is still visible among the ruined temples on the island, where a sanctuary to Apollo was dedicated the moment the birth took place.

When she realized her new position, Artemis went to find Zeus, her father, but instead of pleasures, ornaments, or privileges, she begged him only for a short tunic, hunting boots, a bow, and a quiver of arrows. She spent her youth, say the folk tales, tracking wild beasts and when she tired of her sport she paused to bathe at the clear waters of a fountain in the forest. There was no place for love in her rugged life, while she pursued a lion, roebuck, or boar, and she shunned the "legitimate joys of marriage" because for her "these were repugnant."[2] She finally made a law of chastity and imposed her virginal obstinance on her companions, the nymphs in her forest band, probably in Asia Minor. Once, however, Actaeon caught her bathing, but this only enraged her, despite his enraptured response. She changed him into a stag and the hounds tore him to pieces. Callisto, tricked by Zeus into seducing her, fell under her arrows. She

---

[2]Felix Guirand, ed., *New Larousse Encyclopedia of Mythology*, p. 121.

loved Orion but Apollo, a possessive brother, according to the myth, arranged by a ruse for one of her arrows to pierce his temple.

After this incident she became surly, vindictive, even artful in her cruelty. Yet while she grew bloodthirsty—demanding victims in human sacrifice, flagellation, plagues, outbreaks of madness, murder, and epidemics—she could also be gentle, less barbarous and more forgiving. She loved music, song, and dancing. "When the chase has rejoiced her heart she unbends her bow and enters the vast dwelling-place of her brother in the rich land of Delphi and joins in the choir of the Muses and Graces. There she hangs up her bow and arrows and, dressed in gracious style, leads and directs the choir."[3]

CARD DESCRIPTION

The eleventh arcanum shows a woman closing the muzzle of a furious lion with no effort at all, a smile betraying her self-confidence. The whole of her figure conveys the impression of irresistible power.

Over her head floats the sign of astral light, a figure eight on its side. The hieroglyph indicates a firm hand, signifying strength, in the theosophical ternary of the *Vis Divina* (mental plane), *Vis Humana* (astral plane), and the *Vis Naturalis* (physical plane), revealed in another of the card's names, *Leo Domitatus*, or "Conquered Lion."

In the Egyptian Tarot, an image which extended to the European tarots of the Middle Ages, a young woman is shown with noble attributes, wearing a crown, adorned with a serpent and a condor's wings (plumed serpent), while she tames a lion with the utmost ease.

In the Miquianti cards, the figure is replaced by an Amazon of almost grotesque strength and proportions, seen breaking the column of a Greek temple into two halves. Certain very early tarots indicated "strength" in the Biblical figure of Samson, overcoming a powerful god with the sheer physical magnitude of his force.

---

[3]Felix Guirand, ed., *New Larousse Encyclopedia of Mythology*, p. 122.

In more recent decks, the young woman, apart from the crown of wisdom which indicates her contact with the higher planes of knowledge, wears a hat as a symbol of the Infinite. Her clothes are ample and luxurious, to denote her rank. In certain cards a landscape offers a background for the figure, indicating the perspective in a vanishing point, by means of the mountains and the rich vegetation associated with the paradise of the supreme gods, just as was done in 14th and 15th century Flemish painting.

On other cards the figure is shown with a wreath or garland around her breast, confected of full and perfect roses, instead of a hat and crown, in order to indicate her invincible strength, product of the commitment among the gods and their support of her in the struggle of the spirit.

CARD SYMBOLISM

The card is intended to symbolize the application of those evolutionary forces, which bring about the triumphant knowledge of the astral, as defined in the sign over the woman's head. This is combined with a purity of intention, as implied in her virginity.

The composite is projected onto a faith in oneself, revealed in the figure's unconstrained attitude, her pride, and her self-assurance.

The elixir of incalculable power is ultimately expressed as oneself alone, the integrated force of the microcosm, which motivates all action and which determines a course in a chain of actions—in themselves, events—leading toward the accomplishment of the proposed goal. The process might conceivably imply a temporary downfall—a defeat or digression—but it also implicitly signifies synthesis or reintegration, the potential inherent in cognition. In short, if a harmonious being attempts "illumination" as his goal, then the light, according to Hermetic tradition, reveals the integration of what had formerly seemed to crumble. This implies the unification of what had previously been divided, so that when Light had ceased, this was seen as the downfall of the Angels, which unveiled to the universe the mystery of Death.

Light is life itself, freedom conquered and redeemed, a proposal, a house set to rights. The binary of the soul refers to the Sephira Hochmah, an essential concept curiously similar to that of the Mesoamerican *Chac-Mool*—that is, total restitution, encompassed in the discipline required for the control of any violent or irreflexive act. Jealousy, desperation, compulsion, or a sense of loss and betrayal result from the incapacity of the intellect to achieve this fundamental harmony of being; in effect, "mind over matter."

The lion in the arcanum represents instinct, while the woman, associated with the cult of dynamic Artemis, in this case symbolizes reason. The so-called "animal" aggressions can presumably be tamed, according to this principle, by the gentle application of conviction-in-reason, firmness requiring no more effort than the fact of the thought itself. Love will therefore conquer hate, good will overcome evil. The positive constitutes an invincible barrier, like a wall, as Gandhi said, that can neither be breached nor tumbled.

LAMATL XI

MYTHOLOGY OF CE-ITZCUINTLI (THE DOG)

This thirteen-day period is called Ce-Itzcuintli, "The Dog," and is considered a sign of feasting in gratitude for a fortunate planting and a successful hunt, or a celebration conducted by those elected to high office, in order to announce their newly ratified though possibly short-lived position of power and supremacy.

In certain codices, the sign is governed by Xiuhtecutli, God of Fire. In others, in fact more commonly, this period is dominated by Xipe Totec, the Communion of Spring confirmed in the wearing of the skin of those sacrificed to appease the gods. In both cases, the figure of Xiuhcoatl is invariably present, as the Serpent of Fire, primal light of the world.

Quail were considered a specially prized offering during the feasting that accompanied this sign. One of Artemis' names refers to the root equivalent of the same word. Fine feathers were added to the adornments of the occasion, along with paper cutouts, "wrought by skilled craftsmen who were masters of this significant art." Later the paper offerings were thrown to "feed the fire," while live quail wandered near the flames, and decapitated quail, "the blood still streaming down their breasts," were roasted as an "offering to the fire. Wealthy merchants or festive bureaucrats poured food and drink in abundance on their guests, with song and merrymaking, the strumming of stringed instruments, and a happy choir."[4]

---

[4]Interpretations from the Spanish are from Eduard Seler's *Comentarios al Códice Borgia*, Vol. 1 (Mexico: Fondo de Cultura Económica, 1963), pp. 112–114. Originally published in German in 1904.

The poor were obliged to celebrate by offering *copalxalli*, an ersatz incense, or *yauhtli*, a ground herb, to their fires; yet every gathering, humble or prominent, was regulated by prayer and gifts were exchanged, until the "guests departed far more laden than when they arrived and the host proffered more than he received."[5]

Blankets and tunics were considered the accustomed gifts. The scene, with its music and "merry-making," its mantles and pulque, must have approximated, to a surprising degree, Penelope's dining hall, filled with rapacious suitors, when Odysseus reached home, his arms laden with tunics and mantles not unlike the one granted Artemis by Zeus.

The sign was associated with war and its gods, to the same extent that Mars influenced the eleventh arcanum. Those who celebrated their high office during the banquet were now obliged to declare war on their enemies, to impose their strength and power, and to make a great display of their indomitable spirit. Those who had dined at their table and received their tokens were to come forward to claim a position in the legions of their followers, to offer any kind of complementary business or trade, and to prepare to die in battle if necessary.

While this sign had to do with sudden death in war, it was also a time for commuting a death sentence in the case of a crime, for "then the blameless were taken from the jails and slaves were also freed, at which time they would repair to the fountains and springs of Chapultepec Wood, in testimony of their freedom." Those born under this sign were considered to be destined for riches and good fortune. They were decreed powerful and keenly directed, with "many slaves; and they would be treated to banquets, and would be baptized in splendor." Another ceremony associated with Ce-Itzcuintli involved the coloring of the heads of the dogs that gave their name to this sign, with red earth and ochre, applied by "those who devoted themselves to breeding this specie."[6]

Xipe Totec, called in Tlaxcala the *Ixcuina*, "The Wallowing Dog," is an association with the namesakes of this sign. He was further identified with Teteo Innan, goddess Mother of the Earth. The restorative quality of spring, and the capacity for renewal in mankind and nature, suggested a dominion over the natural elements, powerful enough to open the Earth to make it fruitful, and to make the rain fall in order for the corn to grow. The massive sacrifices at the time of the spring equinox in fact or in symbol were designed to "sprinkle the

---

[5]Ibid.
[6]Eduard Seler, *Comentarios al Códice Borgia*, Vol. 1, p. 128.

earth with blood to make it fruitful."[7] Was the "blood" real or implied? We may never know.

Those two masters of penitence, Quetzalcoatl and "Totec, called also by his other name Chipe (*Xipe*)," were said to have taken the survivors of Tula by the hand "to lead them away from sin and calamity, through villages and towns, until they came to a mountain which they intended to bore through, thus passing below it, yet some say they remained entrapped there and were transformed into stones."

Another version, the imaginative though obviously inaccurate 18th-century interpretation by British explorer Lord Kingsborough, has the twin gods turned into serpents who in effect, burrowed through to the opposite end of this "secret passage to America, from which they emerged in Europe, on the other side."[8]

Though Black Tezcatlipoca is supposed to have betrayed a guileless Quetzalcoatl and provoked the fall of Tula, the Vatican Codex illustrates a populace caught between two mountains or trapped in an abyss which closes over their struggling numbers, while it describes the sins of the Toltecs that angered the gods, who then showed their strength by "bringing about the downfall of Tula's foolish ways."

The red ochre, used to paint the heads of Xoloizciuntli dogs during the period corresponding to this lamatl, is considered synonymous with Tlapallan, "The Place of the Red Earth," later interpreted as "The Site of the Red and the Black," meaning "place of learning and writing." After the fall of Tula, it was said that Quetzalcoatl, weeping and stumbling, found his way to the coast and "there he donned his plumed headdress, his green mask and set fire to himself, until he crumbled into ashes, witnessed by all the glorious and precious birds in the sky, who circled the flames, until Quetzalcoatl's heart mounted to heaven and entered there. The elders say he became the morning star that rises in the East, in the red region, from whence the sun emerges, and was turned to Light itself, to learning, to strength and fulfillment."[9]

---

[7]Eduard Seler, *Comentarios al Códice Borgia*, Vol. 1, p. 134.

[8]See Lord Kingsborough's compilation titled *Antigüedades de México*, 4 volumes (Mexico: Secretaría de Hacienda y Crédito Público, 1964).

[9]Eduard Seler, *Comentarios al Códice Borgia*, Vol. 1, pp. 146–158. See also Bernardino de Sahagún's *Historia General de las Cosas de la Nueva España*, Book 1, chapters III & XIV (Mexico: Editorial Porrua, 1979).

LAMATL DESCRIPTION

Most of the codices associate this lamatl with the figure of Xipe Totec, Quetzalcoatl's other advocation, referring to the two gods doing penance on the Hill of the Thorn.

Xipe's colors are red and white, as the Sun's and Quetzalcoatl's. Xipe Totec received offerings of seashells and conchs and was known to the Tarascans, the mountain people from the pine forest of Michoacán, as the god of the sea. During the festival called *Tlacaxipehualitztli*, prisoners—whose skin had been stripped from their bodies—were offered to him in sacrifice. The skin was then utilized by priests and elders as a sheath, symbol of renewal and rebirth, thus his association with springtime and serpents, who shed their skin along with their desperation and violence, in order to assume a new course of moral action, as opposed to naked lizards.

Xipe Totec, another incarnation of Tezcatlipoca the Red, appears with his body painted red and a quail in his hand. He carries a shield and the quiver of arrows associated with the celestial warrior. In the Bourbon Codex, his body paint is yellow. He wears a moon crescent in his nose, made of the gold with which he is identified and whose color he assumes. He is further adorned with gold earrings and a wand of rattles, shown to be moving in his right hand. His sandals are red and are decorated with quail feathers. Three banners are draped across his back. These are mantles fashioned of bark or reed paper—a kind of papyrus—and they are shown by means of symbols to move in the breeze or while the figure walks, as indicated by the drawing in the lamatl, which also describes the paper's unique sound. The figure wears a gold ring, for he is also the god of jewelers. Various layers of gold simulate the skin drawn over the deity's body. His kilt is made of leaves from the native sapota tree and these also rustle, as if in the wind or with the movement of his steps.

He is accompanied in the lamatl by the dog that leads the souls of the dead into the underworld, the itzcuintli that also serves as keeper of the flame in a brazier, used for an offering of a ball of incense in the

Figure 23. Tlatlauhqui Tezcatlipoca, or Tezcatlipoca the Red, Aztec incarnation of the Zapotec deity from Oaxaca, called Xipe Totec, god of the (red) earth. From the Códice Borgia.

shape of a sphere. The offering represents the Sun, but indicates a fading, or dying sun, the sun in the world of the dead, struck through by night's arrow. An effigy of Quetzalcoatl as Ce-Acatl appears in the brazier, complemented with a reed or *acatl*, the calendrical name for the morning star.

A *cihuatéotl*, a warrior-woman, appears in the lamatl tossing a ball—the heavenly eye, that is, a star—into the world of the dead. She is shown to be speaking simultaneously on three levels, to Heaven, to Earth and to the underworld.

LAMATL SYMBOLISM

Xipe Totec is seated on the red throne of the solar gods. The throne is adorned with the attributes of the jaguar, characteristic of the Huastec region, suggesting this god's position in the Olmec and Maya as well as the Nahua pantheons.

In the Borgia Codex, he is accompanied by Xiuhcoatl, the Fire Serpent, with its fearsome claws and crude scales, graphically emphasized to distinguish him from Quetzalcoatl, the Plumed Serpent. A sacrificial victim appears in the dragon-like mouth, indicating human identification with Divine Strength during the festivals honoring the Earth's rebirth.

The Mesoamerican spring, on the high, dry plateau where the Aztecs lived, unlike most others, is characterized by dryness and dust, a russet sun, and a peculiar tree, the *colorín*, which blossoms before its leaves appear. The Nahuas urged the gods to provide the moisture they needed for their planting and to assure the customary six months of rain below the Tropic of Cancer that brought parched vegetation to green luxuriance and full fruit.

The rain and the reed (*acatl*) like the sexual binary, reiterate this process of rebirth and fertility. The sprinkling of drops of precious blood, symbolic or real, designed to inspire the still more precious rain, was performed in a ceremony as emblematic as it was abundant, in the attempt to bring forth a ravishing in the sacrifice, in turn to provide the most opulent possible response from each of the elements.

The gladiatorial sacrifices were followed by dancing and music, while the dancers wore the masks of the sacrificed. The "Old Bear"—again, a parallel to Artemis—called Cuetlachuehue, personified by the honor guard who had bound the sacrificial victims, was called upon to wail in a doleful funereal plaint, hoping the gods might hear and know their appetites had been sated and their desires appeased.

PARALLEL SYMBOLISM

Both the tarot and *Tonalamatl* recount the problem of the persistent human struggle against the blind power of the Cosmos, of nature and the unconscious mind, the juxtaposition of instinct and intellect, suggesting a victory only when savagery and fury—the lion or the serpent—have been tamed and brought under unquestioning domination.

Only an awareness of the astral and an access to cognition can be assumed to light the way to the Infinite and the Crown of Wisdom. The virginal young woman in the eleventh arcanum, like Quetzalcoatl in his immolation, offer purity, revitalization, and nobility of purpose as part of a chain, which ideally leads toward the ultimate goal of enlightenment.

Both mental and physical strength are necessary in order to foster this personal power, which then reflects on the collective unit, or community. Xipe Totec's appeal to the elements, the urgency in his communion with the natural forces that otherwise overwhelm his existence, represent the voice of the leader who speaks in the name of all his people, yet indicates a single course of action for each individual. His rapacious sacrifices only emulate Artemis'. These massacres, intended not only to limit but to illuminate the survivors, are conditioned by the principle of a fertile—that is, a productive—and active community, a vital unit, unified in spirit and harmonious in intent.

Order from chaos can only be imposed by discipline and dominance of the mind. If the serpent, like the lion, symbolizes the material world, then the fertilizing of that world, like the reptile burrowing into the earth to lay its eggs, represents the potential to one day fly free, unburdened and unrestrained. The Thirteenth Heaven of the Supreme Gods is entered by means of the Word. Cognition, or access to this Nirvana, may only be achieved in an applied effort. Yet both tarot and the *Tonalamatl* stress the self-assurance and the quiet accomplishment implicit in the attempt, expressed simultaneously on the three planes of existence.

Dominion is therefore ordained, say the gods, and the mere proposal contains the virtual accomplishment. Awareness is therefore its own guide and its own fulfillment, as well as its plea, the wail of pain, or the appeal to Heaven.

Quetzalcoatl and Xipe Totec, with their little itzcuintli at their side, like Artemis with her dog or hind, are only sent, according to the logic in mythological philosophy, to show the way. Oneself, unless blinded by useless fury or foolish dismay, is equipped to find one's own way.

ARCANUM XII

MYTHOLOGY OF THE HANGED MAN

The twelfth arcanum describes the rites of the Orphic cult of Diony-sus, the sacrifice which assures the fruitfulness of the Earth and the abundance of the harvest, "when the earth has been made fertile by life-giving rains it must, in order that its products may reach maturity, endure the bite of the sun which burns and dries it up. Only then do its fruits develop and the golden grapes appear on the knotty vine."[1]

The allegory originated in the myth of Semele, generally consid-ered to be the mother of Dionysus, when this daughter of Cadmus, King of Thebes, was "seen by Zeus and yielded to him."

Zeus often visited the palace, it was said, but one day, at the suggestion of "the treacherous Hera, who had assumed the guise of her nurse," Semele begged Zeus to "show himself to her in his Olym-pian majesty." She was unable to endure "the dazzling brilliance of her divine lover and was consumed by the flames which emanated from Zeus' person. She would have been destroyed and the child she carried in her womb would have perished had not a thick shoot of ivy suddenly wound around the columns of the palace and made a green screen between the unborn babe and the celestial fire. Zeus gathered up the infant and, as it was not yet ready to be born, enclosed it in his own thigh. When the time was come he drew it forth again, with the aid of Ilithyia, and it is to this double birth that Dionysus owed the title *Dithyrambos*."[2] Zeus then gave the baby into the care of Ino, Semele's sister, who lived at Orchomenus with her husband Atha-mas.

Another version of the story says Cadmus, enraged at his daugh-ter's wanton affair, enclosed her in a chest and threw her into the sea. The chest was carried by the waves as far as the shores of Prasiae in the Peloponnese, but when it was opened, Semele was dead and the child, just barely alive, was cared for by Ino.

Hera's jealous vengeance was still unappeased. She struck Ino and Athamas with madness. Zeus succeeded in saving his child for a

[1]Felix Guirand, ed., *New Larousse Encyclopedia of Mythology* translated by Richard Aldington and Delano Ames (London: Hamlyn House, 1969), p. 157.
[2]Felix Guirand, ed., *New Larousse Encyclopedia of Mythology*, p. 157.

second time by changing him into a kid. He ordered Hermes, his messenger, to deliver this "kid" into the hands of the nymphs of "Nysa" (an ambiguous name for a "mountain" or "heights"), indicating that the cult of Dionysus flourished from Thrace all over the Aegean.

Dionysus passed his childhood on the fabled mountain, cared for or so the story goes by the nymphs, the Muses, the Satyrs, the Sileni, and the Maenads. With his head crowned by ivy and laurel, the young god wandered the mountains and forest with the nymphs, "making the glades echo with his joyful shouts."

When he had grown, Dionysus discovered the fruit of the vine and the vintner's art. Perhaps he drank immoderately in the beginning, "for he was struck by a short-lived madness," and for his cure he sought the oracle at Dodona. He undertook, then, long journeys across the world in order to spread the inestimable gift of wine among mortals.

Coming down from the mountains of Thrace, he crossed Boeotia and entered Attica, where he was welcomed by Icarius, the king, to whom he presented a vine-stock. Icarius, however, "gave his shepherds wine to drink and as they grew intoxicated they thought they were being poisoned and so slew him, and caused his body to disappear." Icarius' daughter, Erigone, set out to look for her father and, with the help of her dog, Maera, discovered his tomb. Upon confirming his tragic death, she was so stricken, she hanged herself from a nearby tree, thus the reference in the earliest forms of this arcanum to a figure hanging upside down from a tree, whose branches arch out in the form of a "T," heavy with a foliage not unlike ivy or grape leaves.

As punishment for Icarius' death, Dionysus struck the women of Attica with "raving madness," while Icarius was carried to the heavens, along with his daughter and her faithful dog, to be changed into constellations: the Wagoner, Virgo, and the Lesser Dog.

The many adventures, love affairs, and travels of Dionysus are woven into an intricate tapestry, yet the persistent and recurring threads refer to misunderstandings and complicity, dementia, and the symbolic tendrils of the grape or ivy, to a sea of wine, "fragrant and delicious," to dark green leaves and the god himself, become a lion "of fearful aspect."[3]

Beyond continental Greece and the archipelago, he wandered with his retinue into Ephesus, where he fought off the Amazons, then on to Syria where he punished Damasicus because he destroyed the vines the deity had planted. He skinned him alive. In Lebanon he

---

[3]*New Larousse Encyclopedia of Mythology*, p. 159.

visited Aphrodite and Adonis, then moved on to Caucasian Iberia, later continuing his journey across the Tigris on a tiger sent by Zeus, like Quetzalcoatl's jaguar ordered to his aid by Tonacatecuhtli. He joined the two banks of the Euphrates by a cable woven of vineshoots and ivy tendrils, in order to spread his cult as far as India. He was received in Egypt by King Proteus, and in Libia he helped Ammon to reconquer the throne from which he had been deposed by Cronus and the Titans.

By the time he returned to Greece from these "glorious adventures," however, he was received with mistrust, even hostility. He was no longer the robust and rustic god recently come down from the mountains. Now he was soft, a little cynical and even effeminate, robed in the Lydian fashion of the androgynous adolescent. His cult had been infiltrated by orgiastic rites brought from Phrygia, and the rest of his story is a travesty of despair, persistent lunacy, what he called his "unhappy transformations" and the appalling dramas described by Euripides in the *Bacchae*. Women, driven out of their minds, devoured their own children. Pentheus was torn to pieces by his mother. Lycurgus was conducted to Mount Pangaeum where he was trampled to death under the hooves of wild horses. The land, uncared for, went barren and famine was rampant.

Dionysus, in an effort to reverse what he described as "these horrors," took on the successive guises of a young maiden, then a bull, a lion and finally, a panther. He participated in the struggle against the giants. He descended into the infernal regions, which associated him with Orpheus, then just an initiate, in search of Semele, his mother. He emerged from his expedition, after crossing and recrossing the Mediterranean world, through the soporific Sea of Alcyon.

In his attempts at redemption he preached sacrifice, discipline, and the convictions achieved by the circuitous but ultimately well-founded path of experience. If he was distorted or misunderstood, says this arcanum, it was because he, himself, had deviated from his chosen path. Yet the best and most tenacious of his aims were invested in the service to others, to duty and charity, to the Earth itself, and to the process indicated in the Wheel of the Sphinx, the world's mill.

His teachings, which eventually implied a solar cult, encompassed the joyful processions in which priests and the faithful, both men and women, celebrated the vintage, often accompanied by Pan, the flutist. Additional rural divinities implicit in Dionysus' retinue included his tutor, Silenus: fat and old, bald and snub-nosed, invariably drunk. Yet while he swayed on the back of a donkey, like Don Quixote's Sancho Panza, as he followed his adored Dionysus, he largely determined the deity's character and had genuinely molded his personality. From the beginning he had, according to the myths, "inspired in him a love of glory."

Silenus' knowledge, it was said, had no limit. Whether drunk or sober he knew both past and future and could reveal the destiny of anyone who succeeded in tying him up during the heavy slumber that followed his drinking bouts. Plato compared his teacher, Socrates, to this son of Hermes and the Earth, who was born, some said, of the blood of Uranus after Cronus had mutilated him.

In actual fact, the name Silenus came to be applied generically to the Sileni, an entire category of rural divinities, similar to the Satyrs and often confused with them, described as hooved creatures, either goats or horses, with the head of a man. The image ultimately evolved into the icon of the centaur: torso and head of a man on the hairy hindquarters of a horse, said to be related to the Vedic Gandharvas, or to the primitive herdsmen of Thessaly who rounded up their cattle on horseback. The latter had a reputation for rude behavior and gross or cruel conduct, and were generally given to lechery and drunkenness. Yet one of the most enlightened of all figures in Greek mythology, Chiron, who exchanged his immortality for the mortality of Prometheus and who was placed among the stars as the constellation Sagittarius, was in fact a centaur. Educated by Artemis and Apollo, he, in turn, was the teacher of the most exalted heroes in legendary history.

CARD DESCRIPTION

Most cards representing the twelfth arcanum show a man hanged by his left foot. His right leg is bent at the knee and is positioned behind the left, suggesting the form of a cross. The man's arms are folded behind his back, so that the lower part of his body describes a figure, like a descending triangle. In other cards the image is reversed.

The construction on which the man hangs was originally composed of two beams, or the crossed branches of a tree, forming the letter "T," but they can also be shown as two vertical poles. Twelve branches, or knots, six on each side of the pole, when they appear symbolize the twelve signs of the zodiac, that is, the material world. The man is depicted as crucified on the emblem of matter.

Medieval occultists represented the hanging man as Judas Iscariot, hanging by his heel, a punishment assigned to criminals and debtors. He is shown with thirty pieces of silver pouring from his pockets. In the 18th century, he appeared as a fashionable and effeminate young dandy. The Rosicrucians considered the card to indicate an initiate bound by the cord or cables of his own actions, like the vines or tendrils woven by Dionysus.

Yet the hanged figure appears placid and serene, almost in a trance. He is occasionally shown with a single shoe, while flowers issue from around his feet. In other decks he appears with a halo of light around his head. In certain Christian interpretations he is assumed to be the death of the Old Year, a Jack o' Lent or the Lord of Misrule. The Saturnalia of the Winter carnival is derived from these images, originated in a traditional homage to the Sun's activity and energy, and a petition for the reappearance of the fruits of the Earth brought forth by the Sun's presence. The idea encompasses every mysterious solar emanation, with its accompanying transformation into the plants and the animals, all of organic life, warmth, water, the atmosphere. This idea then emerges as the chain in the creation referred to in the sacred texts, the character of the sacrifice of the archetype, brought about in order to assure the salvation—that is, the regeneration—of humanity.

CARD SYMBOLISM

This arcanum symbolizes the uncomplaining sacrifice, a suffering intended to bring about a transformation in the natural order, the emergence of a spiritual from a material world.

Yet, while the spiritual decision produces serenity, hope, well-directed initiative, prophetic insight, even occult power and inner peace, any vague idealism or futile sacrifice, false introversion or hypocrisy, arrogance, or the love of the material that brings about a dependence on the physical world, will denote destruction, abandonment, a violent death, the despair that leads to hopelessness, or even lunacy.

The card is also termed the Messiah, in effect the archetype incarnate, yet if this concept of devotion and charity is confused with false resolution or complacency its enormous power can be dissipated in indecision. The vitality of the Sun, which nourishes every planet in the solar system, is then distorted. If the voluntary involvement in the occupations of others is corrupted by selfish personal pleasure or private benefit, then every Hermetic mystery, resolved in the unity of life, is befouled.

The *duodenary* sign of the twelfth arcanum appears as the mystical cross, while the twelve knots suggest the twelve incarnations of the initiate in his or her odyssey, on a journey toward the attainment of liberation, seen as personal mastery.

This mystical cross is no more than a purely kabbalistic pentacle, giving priority to the upper and right ends, over the lower and left, the superiority of the active principle over the passive, of the subtle over the obvious.

Yet there remains an enigma, implied in the twelve convexities of the cross, transformed into the redeemed cliché, or the unavoidable Law of Sacrifice. This suggests that the concept of the Messiah—translated as human charity, the benevolence of the Sun—carries an implicit message of fearlessness. Only the truly charitable, according to Hermetic tradition, are able to comprehend the serenity in the power and the beauty of this renunciation of the material. The "baptism by blood," actually the birth of Silenus, in effect symbolized in all religions, was originally conceived as the product of the most intense suffering and therefore projected in the symbolism of the tarot as the semiotic power of sacrifice, that which is supreme.

This must remain, however, the province of those who have mastered true enlightenment in a synthesis of the concept of martyrdom. Humiliation, torture, betrayal, even death once indicated the greatest sacrifice, and were considered to incite a renunciation of the relative and the temporal until these had been exchanged for the eternal and the absolute.

LAMATL XII

MYTHOLOGY OF CE-OLLIN (MOVEMENT)

 This thirteen-day period is distinguished by a multiplicity of female deities, a cubistic representation of womankind, described particularly in that intricate counterpart of Xochiquetzal called Ixcuina, "she to whom sexual sin was confessed," one of the four manifestations of Tlazolteotl.

The goddesses of carnal love, and, therefore, of the baccanalia, encompassed the quaternary apparition of the Mexican Aphrodite. They were interpreted as sisters with clearly distinguishable form and design. The first was Tlaelcuani, "Devouress of Filth," or Ixcuina. She was probably a regional Tlazolteotl, an early Huastec deity of fertility and the Earth. When seen as an old woman, however, though still a fertility goddess, she was called Toci, "Our Grandmother," Teteo Inan, "Mother of the Gods" or Tlalli Iyolo, "Heart of the Earth," a reference to the inner- or underworld.

Like Xochiquetzal (Xochiquetzalli), this Tlalli Iyolo was a Mother of Corn. She was the patroness of doctors and midwives, who called her Temazcalteci, "Grandmother of the Temazcal (ritual baths)," or Yohualticitl, "Healer of the Night." She was also the patroness of those who sold quicklime. This ingredient was used by women for cooking corn and especially for soaking the kernels in order to loosen the hard outer skin, for producing a smoother meal or flour.

She was additionally a patroness of the Tonalpouhque or "day counters," those masters of the ritual calendar, who received the confession of carnal sin, intended for Tlazolteotl. Thus Toci was identified with Oxomoco, the first woman to use an accounting of days for divinatory purposes, bringing the concept of the female full circle and binding, according to the codices, intuition to the pragmatic, prophecy to production, in love and sin, Heaven and Earth, world and underworld, darkness and daytime, passive and active.

Corn was synonymous with sustenance and therefore the male-female binary. It was inexorably associated with the Sun, and with that private Heaven reserved for warriors killed in battle, women dead in childbirth, or those who had been sacrificed. This eastern quarter of the heavens received the light of morning, after the Sun had navigated through the night, crossing the rivers of Hell. Its rising was greeted with war cries and applause; and a celebration by the warrior souls to accompany the primal body in its journey to the center of the noon sky. After four years devoted to this service, the spirits in this Heaven were changed into hummingbirds and butterflies, in order to permit "a honeyed existence," sucking the nectar from the flowers in Heaven and on Earth.

It was said that merchants who died in the course of an expedition, if they had outfitted warriors for battle, were also permitted to ascend to the Sun's Heaven. Instead of cremation—a ritual reserved for those bound for the nether-regions—their bodies were hung on a frame or armature, exposed in the treetops.

This lamatl was associated with an indifference to good or evil. Those born under this sign were considered natural penitents and, if well versed in laudable conduct, their lives were destined to prosper. On the other hand, if initiated into evil, then their lives were doomed to suffering and misery.

Since repentance and sin played a vital role in the concept, as well as the cult, of Tlazolteotl, or Ixcuina, this sign was additionally associated with drunkenness. For some, wine does no harm. Others, by contrast, are deeply affected; they fall as told in morality plays, into a stupor, heads down, seated or sprawled. Still others, according to the codices, become violent. They provoke havoc or sudden death.

The codices depicted those unfortunate inebriants, as the reprehensible who neither sing nor converse, but only mumble to themselves, or claim to be rich when they are not, say shameful things about their neighbors, become harsh and rebellious and then insist they had too much wine and had no knowledge of what they had done.

Izquitecatl, the principal god of wine, was honored "throughout the land" in "repeated festivals," as described in the codices, and with his retinue, he received offerings, dancing and recitals of music performed on reed flutes, not unlike Pan's, the goat god included in Dionysus' entourage. The participants in the celebration drank wine from a tub which according to folk tales, had no bottom, for each time the level dropped the tavern-keepers added more of the frothy liquid. New wine, called *uitztli*—probably pulque distilled into a maguey wine—was brought to the tavern in clay jugs.

Like Dionysus, the "Zeus of Nysa," the Vedic god Soma, the Cretan Zagreus, the Phrygian Sabazius, and the Lydian Bassareus,

Izquitecatl—associated with Ixcuina—was considered a god of vegetation, warm moisture, and pleasure.

LAMATL DESCRIPTION

The four sisters, goddesses of carnal sin, "devourers of filth and waste," and considered the instigators of depravity and "clumsy love," indicated, according to this lamatl, the lustfulness associated with women in general, thus implying the potential wantonness in any woman, as depicted in the codices.

According to Sahagún, Tlazolteotl (Ixcuina) was called, by turn, Tiacapan, Tlaco, Teicu and, finally, as the youngest sister, Xucotzin. The inference of carrion and excrement was certainly only symbolic, in recognition of her "inspiration" in matters of the flesh and the innovative gift, as illustrated in the Borgia Codex, of the female once aroused.

In the Bourbon Codex, Tlazolteotl is pictured devouring a quail. Therefore, in this context, she is a representation of sin, but seen more as a digression from the established conduct than in the Christian sense.

In several codices the figure appears under or beside a cube, the House of Darkness or House of the Earth, the symbol of fertility and the primal body, inseparable from the Sun. In other codices Tateo Inan (Ixcuina) is pictured with her face painted yellow, the color assigned to the Solar Gods. A touch of black on the nose and around the mouth, applied by ritual caoutchouc or rubber further adorns the image. She wears a white or yellow nose ring in the shape of a crescent moon, an allusion to pulque, whose fumes, in some codices, rise around her in enveloping clouds. A heavy cotton turban, from which two ribbons trail like grapevines or ivy tendrils, is wrapped around her head. She often appears to be pregnant, or at the moment labor begins, while her red and black colors identify her as a sacred figure from the land of the gods, the Citlan Tlapala.

Figure 24. Tlazolteotl, goddess of filth and also known as the Huastec earth mother. From the Códice Borgia.

In the Vatican Codex, she is painted white, with vertical yellow stripes and the attributes normally associated with Xipe Totec (Tezcatlipoca the Red) and Xochipilli, dual image of the male gods of spring. This is to indicate the integration of Divine Symbolism on the occasion of the equinox, during which one of Ixcuina's two celebrations takes place. She is also associated with the symbol of Nahuin Ollin and the Cosmic Suns, with the flower festival, and with the vintage of the last wine.

The spring and fall festivals, both consecrated to this deity, were the most important in the Mesoamerican religious calendar. They divided the year into two essential parts and honored the planting and the harvest, respectively, occasions concerned with Ixcuina-Tlazolteotl and the favorable auspices of the gods.

LAMATL SYMBOLISM

Tateo Inan, Toci, and Tlazolteotl, as a composite, or each as a separate entity, symbolize the counterpart of Xipe Totec's faculty for fertilizing the Earth and bringing about the seasonal rebirth of the land, its vegetation, the rains, and the transformation implicit in the application of these powers.

In the Mesoamerican celebrations, nothing stands alone. Each deity is another, and its opposite, itself, its representation, its essence and presence, the fact and its denial. Each shade has a meaning and each meaning pours into a spectrum of intent and implication.

The symbolism is furthered in the image of the young slave girl, described in the codices as sacrificed by decapitation on the day of the festival *Ochpaniztli*, when the priest, just as Dionysus when he dons the *nebris* or skin of a panther or fawn, slips the girl's skin over his body.[4] He implies that the sacrifice induces the revitalization of the Earth. The girl then becomes, in fact or in emblem, a new "skin" of green vegetation and growth, the rejuvenation of the year that begins in the spring.

The autumn festival on the other hand, is intended to recover the bounty of a tired Earth, as a result of another sacrifice, which inspires the harvest. The celebration encourages the abundance of the gods, yet the harvest in itself is a sacrifice, when the Earth gives up its charitable offering to sustain its human brethren and offspring. Then the Earth is serene, say the legends, gratified by this bounty, purified in an action intended for the fulfillment of its inherent purpose.

The cubic figure in the lamatl, the House of Darkness, corresponds, according to Léonard André-Bonnet, to the quaternary symbols in the Kabbalah, with four pearls in Ixcuina's necklace and four regions indicated on her breastplate, each composed of three additional symbols, a total of twelve universal emblems.

---

[4]Fr. Bernardino de Sahagún in *Historia General de las Cosas de la Nueva España*, Book 2, chapter XXX (Mexico: Editorial Porrua, 1979), p. 131.

PARALLEL SYMBOLISM

The multifaceted nature of woman, as expressed in the lamatl, finds its parallel in the fragmented image of Dionysus, old and bearded, young and delicate, effeminate, virile, robed or crowned with a turban of vine leaves and clusters of grapes.

If the Mesoamerican priests exercised their rites of sacrifice, the nature of the festivals dedicated to Dionysus were even more extravagant, as they applied the concepts fortified in the twelfth arcanum of the tarot: the Bacchantes immolated a young boy. Human sacrifice was practiced on the islands of Chios and Lesbos, ritual mutilation was commonplace, and flagellation was encouraged on Lymnos, as well as the Asia Minor mainland.

Both cults stress the rural character of the celebration, as the last vintage is used up and the new wine is offered to the regent gods of this sign. All of this is accompanied by flowers and processions, along with devotions associated with the earth and its fruits.

The sun, seen as a destructive force that punishes the Earth, its plants and animals, is also seen to revitalize the seasons and bring forth the harvest. A male-female counterpoint, identified with the Infinite and the Eternal, reaffirms the Sun with regard to human fruitfulness and the juxtaposition of pleasure and sacrifice. When a balance is restored, both Man and the Earth can afford to be charitable.

The gift of the Mesoamerican women for prophecy and divination finds an echo in the oracles, generally a woman's province; and the sacrifice in childbirth—that maternal bounty which sees only love in pain—is emphasized in the birth of Dionysus, a tale of female passion. Yet Semele's wantonness is compensated by male action, as Ixcuina is supported by Xipe Totec and Xochipilli.

If Dionysus was nourished by honey and "the silky fluid of the vine," the warrior souls in the Sun's Heaven were also fed with "the flowers of heaven and earth," while those bodies destined for the realm of fulfillment were hung, like the man in the twelfth arcanum, from beams or a tree, or a frame or armature, exposed in the treetops. If Dionysus, with his retinue, was honored in the festival, Izquitecatl, also accompanied by an assortment of symbolic gods, was similarly celebrated. And if Dionysus spent a good part of his life in orgies and depravity, he found his counterpart in the composite Tlazolteotl, the "four sisters of lust."

The temptations and the corruption of the material world might be revitalized at any time, say both the tarot and the *Tonalamatl* but can be redeemed by the charity of sacrifice, the renunciation of the static or purposeless in favor of the dynamic and purposeful.

ARCANUM XIII

MYTHOLOGY OF DEATH

Arcanum XIII is associated with the Hermetic tradition of "release," that evolved from the hamanic (shamanic) practices of Tibet, where in fact many occultists believe the tarot might have originated.

In this sense, death is but a passage. Even so, there were selected souls or beings, Bodhisattvas or Astrosomes, that by their actions had earned exoneration from the repeated cycles of incarnation. They were seen as initiates, devoted to the initiation of others. The notion of change or renewal was said to have been devised in the City of Shambala on an isle of the four Kumaras, those Lords of the Flames thought to have descended from the planet Venus in order to leave the secret rites of the initiation in the hands of the decarnated beings later pictured as skeletons.

The Egyptians challenged the physical manifestations of death, and even the decomposition of the body, perhaps more successfully than anyone in their time, aided by the extreme dryness of their climate. Their combinations of herbs, potions, and balms probably did more harm to the dead body than if they had left it to nature's devices. Nearly intact corpses of grave robbers, merchants, or casual travelers trapped by the desert were often found in the sand, while the mummies—especially of the most exalted persons—were frequently destroyed by the gummy concoctions of the embalmers' art.

Yet the ancients, complacent with their rites, consigned the most highly prized oils and tinctures for application to the remains of their dead nobles and royalty, to facilitate the passage of the soul along the journey toward the final judgment. By then it could be reunited with its body, as determined by Shaï, or Destiny, often the goddess Shaït. He, or she, was born at the same moment as the individual, grew up with him and shadowed him until his death. Shaï's decrees were inescapable. After death, when the soul was weighed in the presence of Osiris, Shaï could be seen in the form of a god without special attributes, attending the trial, in order to render exact account before the infernal jury of the deceased's virtues and crimes, or in order to prepare him for the conditions of a new life.

When, thanks to the talismans placed on the mummy, and especially to the passwords written in the indispensable Book of the Dead with which he or she was furnished, the deceased had safely crossed the terrifying land between the place of the living and the kingdom of the dead, they were immediately ushered into the presence of a sovereign judge, either by Anubis or by Horus. After the deceased had kissed the threshold, he or she passed into the Hall of Double Justice, an immense room at the end of which sat Osiris under a canopy, guarded by a frieze of coiled serpents. Osiris, "The Good One," redeemer and judge, patiently awaited the progeny who came from earth.

In the center a vast scale was erected beside which stood Maat, goddess of Truth and Justice, ready to weigh the heart of the deceased. Meanwhile, Amemaid, "The Devourer," part lion, part hippopotamus, part crocodile crouched nearby, waiting to devour the hearts of the guilty.

All around the hall, to the right and to the left of Osiris, sat forty-two personages. Dressed in their winding-sheets, each held a sharp-edged sword. Some had human heads, others the heads of animals. These forty-two judges, each corresponding to a province of Egypt, were charged with the duty of examining some aspect of the deceased's conscience.

The deceased himself began the proceedings and without hesitation recited what has been called "the negative confession." He addressed each of his judges in turn and called him by name to prove he knew him and had nothing to fear; he affirmed he had committed no sin and was truly pure.

To the Assyrians and Babylonians, the infernal dwelling-place beyond the abyss of the Apsu was the "Land of no Return," defended by seven-fold walls and seven gates, at each of which a man had to abandon a part of his apparel. When the last gate had closed behind him he found himself naked and imprisoned forever, according to legend, in the dwelling-place of the shadows.

The audacious Ishtar, who had imprudently ventured into the infernal regions, was unable to escape, goddess though she was, and remained there as a prisoner, until the magic incantations of Ea released her. Sometimes the gods gave an especially privileged inhabitant of the underworld permission to come up for a moment into the light. Thus Enkidu, companion of the hero Gilgamesh, was authorized to report to his friend on the events that took place in these regions of eternal darkness, where the souls of the dead, clad, like birds, in a garment of wings, were indiscriminately jumbled together.

The sole sovereign of this subterranean world was Ereshkigal, "Princess of the Great Earth," until Nergal, "Lord of the Great Dwelling," who under another form bore the name Meshlamthea, invaded the infernal domain, thus establishing another male-female binary of the nether-regions.

For the Vedas, the world is a work of art, derived from a purely organic structure. According to the *Satapatha Brahmana*, there are only two paths: for the just, the road to *pitri*, the fathers, and the Sun. For the evil, another path leads to Hell, *naraka*.

In the Rig Veda, the kingdom of Yama existed as a paradise for the good but in the *Puranas* it was also a place of expiation for the wicked. The *Upanishads* explain this journey to Brahma. It is conceived as the reward for perfect knowledge, that attains an abiding place from which there is no return.

The journeys to Heaven imply the reward deserved, for the soul must return to be reborn here below. Transmigration, or samsara, thus demands an existence without end, viewed as the normal state of life. Yet the possibility of reaching nirvana implies a liberation for all time from the process, for those who have completely understood the worldly work of art as the structure of all things. Heaven is therefore, say the Vedas, a place where we possess the same goods as on Earth but without risking the troubles of earthly existence and Hell, in any case is discerned as a tentative and temporary condition, because death cannot annihilate individual existence. After enduring retribution the soul requires a new destiny, according to the kind and quality of its actions.

For the Romans, at the moment of death, the soul was seized by two groups of genii. The first was malevolent, led by Charun (Charon), who carried a mallet or torch. The second was a benevolent group, led by Vanth. Their dispute symbolized the struggle between good and evil. The Romans, being superstitious, had no great interest in worshiping a personification of death, yet their beliefs abounded in ogresses who were said to frighten small children, the ghosts of the dead who returned to Earth to torment the living, the goddess of funerals who collected money at her temple and Orcus, or Death, who carried off the living by force and conducted them to the infernal regions.

CARD DESCRIPTION

The hieroglyph in the thirteenth arcanum is a woman, the intermediary, or medium, in the process of the transformation of life. It is Woman who brings her child to an epitome of earthly existence, from the embryonic state into the atmosphere, and, therefore, it is womankind who suggests the idea of birth, the conditioning, and death, the destiny of all incarnate beings.

The card depicts a skeleton with a scythe. The completed card would be transformed into the picture of a new life, but an as yet incomplete one, underlining the event we call death, that conjurer of the Unique Life, which cuts off crowned and uncrowned heads alike. Yet immediately after these strokes, new hands, arms and feet sprout from the soil like plants, repropagating and unconcerned.

In certain decks the figure of Death is accompanied by landscapes: rivers, flowers, even a skeleton mounted on a horse that gallops across a plain drenched in sunlight, while a group of women and children, protected by the body of a Bishop, welcome him. Normally, however, the skeleton on the card appears with a mantle and scythe, while crowned or naked heads, hands, feet, and an assortment of bones spring out of the grass in an unlikely but serene crop. The faces are smiling. The scene is pastoral, indicating regeneration and the manifold variations of energy.

CARD SYMBOLISM

This transmutation of forces implies the multitudinous forms of the Unique Life. Death only *apparently* extinguishes that which is seen on any given plane. Yet death in fact transforms the *values* of that plane.

The arcanum emphasizes the image of the eternal *present*, since the archetype never dies. The dynamic of this concept represents the whole of the thirteenth arcanum. Its attributes are forever present, as in birth or creation, decline and transformation, death and regeneration, a new life in new forms.

The Hermetic initiatory tradition accepts the Brahmin concept of the cyclic rhythm of life: a large tree, as perceived in man's awareness, once existed as a tiny seed. Now it rises above and beyond the artificial conception of time.

Contradictions, in fact, belong outside the realm of the "nature of things," except to a limited mind, incapable of penetrating the mysteries connected with the knowledge contained in the arcanum, of the *means* to grow and evolve beyond the unknown.

The principle of death, then, is inevitably bound to the "permanent creation" in the chain of causality, a logical and unchangeable consequence of a selected precept: we must die because we once wanted to exist.

LAMATL XIII

MYTHOLOGY OF CE-COATL (THE SERPENT)

The serpent, or *Coatl*, identified with this lamatl, is seen in both realistic and symbolic terms, as the tail of the earthly body or its animal fangs. The sign, say the ancient ones, indicated prosperity, energy, honor, and wealth. Yet, if those born under this sign were negligent in their penitence and loathe to counsel, especially from their elders, it was said they would lose their good auspices, and become slovenly, slothful and poorly augured.

Those born under this sign, according to tradition, would be dearly mourned in their demise, and would be washed and wrapped, and the tears of the mourners, and their parents and children, would wash over them, promise the augurs, like the fountains of the heavens and the nether-regions do cleanse the entrails of the Earth and give ripeness to the green corn.

The regent of this thirteen-day period, Chalchiuhtlicue, was called "She of the Skirts of Jade" or "Our Lady of the Living Water," for water in constant movement was likened to the serpent, "the amphibious beast who cleaves asunder the sinner's soul, like a mass of fire parting before the fountains of heaven."[1]

Chalchiuhtlicue "dwells in the waters and in the sky," as the wife of Tlaloc, the Rain God, and wrenches open the cloud whose beneficent waters will fertilize the earth. She rewards the immortal being "which subsists in the dead man" and leads him "to the world of the Just." She is invoked for the forgiveness of sins committed "under the sway of passing folly." As a goddess of running water, springs, and streams, and as wife-sister of Tlaloc, she was further invoked for the protection of newborn children, marriages, and chaste loves, to counterbalance a cult normally associated with Tlaloc, considered in cer-

---

[1]Eduard Seler, *Comentarios al Códice Borgia*, Vol. 1 (Mexico: Fondo. de Cultura Económica, 1963), p. 160.

tain interpretations as a festival in his honor for which the priests "looked for a large number of babies, which they bought from their mothers. After killing them, they cooked and ate them. If the children cried and shed abundant tears the spectators rejoiced, saying the rain was coming."[2]

This festival, described by 16th-century priest historian Sahagún as the Atlcahualo, "served to sacrifice children by taking them to the heights of mountains, there to remove their hearts."[3] Yet the chronicle historian clarifies that this ceremony, if it existed at all, was "the devotion of isolated fanatics, for if certain of these ministers of the temple, and others called the *quaquacuiltzin* (sacrifiers), and old men, returned afterward to their homes were named *mocauhque* (the isolated), and they were called infamous and unfit for any public office."[4]

According to the codices no sacrifice of children was ever practiced, except in the symbolic sense, as represented by Quetzalcoatl, "who took hold of a child by its hair, in order to cleanse it of sin, by means of penitence and sacrifice. For this purpose the deity carried human excrement in his right hand, as a symbol of foul conduct."[5]

True human sacrifice, in which the chest was opened in order to extract the heart, supposedly occurred only among vanquished warriors, taken prisoner on the field of battle. If we are to believe those who speak of the physical and mortal sacrifice of women and children, however, we would have to assume a total degeneration of religion and the misinterpretation of the Mesoamerican ethic, either as a result of a linguistic or ideological confusion or the ambiguity of Quetzalcoatl's example as described in the earliest colonial chronicles.

As the story is related in the codices:

> This *Quetzalcoatlatopiltzin,* "Our Beloved Son," seeing no end to the sins and labors of the world, and intending to be the first to invoke the gods and do penance, as a sacrifice to arouse the forgiveness of his people, claimed "to sacrifice" himself by extracting his own blood with thorns and other penances. He threw gold, precious stones and incense into the fire, likening his peoples' suffering to their small reverence for their gods, for they not only failed to serve their deities nor offer them the things esteemed in this world, but

---

[2]Fr. Bernardino de Sahagún in *Historia General de las Cosas de la Nueva España,* Book 1, chapter XI (Mexico: Editorial Porrua, 1979), p. 35.

[3]Eduard Seler, *Comentarios al Códice Borgia,* Vol. 1, pp. 172–173.

[4]Eduard Seler, *Comentarios al Códice Borgia,* Vol. 1, pp. 80–81.

[5]Eduard Seler, *Comentarios al Códice Borgia,* Vol. 1, pp. 69–70.

rather they devoted themselves to the pleasures and recreations of this life, thus committing many other sins, in place of homage and a form of appeasement by means of their own blood. So a time passed with Quetzalcoatl at these and other penances to placate the gods, until finally a lizard appeared, that began to dig, giving to understand that heaven's punishment was ended, that the earth would give joyfully of its fruits; and for this four superstitious signs were drawn, to be used until the present: the first is man painted to appear like the ungrateful deer, hoping the gods will commit no error greater than this one, to compare mankind to this vile and foolish beast; the second is a painting on a stone of a stalk of dry corn, to indicate sterility; the third is a lizard which suggests an abundance of water, and the fourth is a green cornstalk which promises fruitfulness. So seeing how Quetzalcoatl had brought them such benefits, the people began to follow his example, doing penance and sacrificing to the gods not only their worldly goods but also the corporal, and their own blood. And, in order to better promote this practice, Quetzalcoatl invented temples, or chapels, where people could commonly pray, four houses: in the first, the lords and others of the nobles could fast; in the second the ordinary people could do the same. In the third, the House of Fear or The House of the Serpent, no eyes of those who entered should be raised from the ground. The fourth was the temple of shame, to which sinners and those who lived badly were sent, those who had intended injury to others, or calumny.[6]

These chapels, said Sahagún, were often misunderstood by historians or misinterpreted by those denied admittance to them, who claimed dreadful customs to be the province of each house but their own. The thorn, however, used in Quetzalcoatl's self-inflicted penance, called the *chalchihuiztli*, or "precious thorn," was normally venerated. Furthermore, an astonishing number of small vessels were found, with Tlaloc's effigy, around Lake Chapala. The blood of the "self-sacrifice" was placed in them, and then they were thrown into the lake as an offering to the water god.

Tlaloc, in fact, was said to live on the tops of mountains, along with the goddesses of cereals, especially maize, and his dwelling, Tlalocan, was amply provided with food. According to the legend, nothing was wanting. Tlaloc, in addition, owned four pitchers of

---

[6]Fr. Bernardino de Sahagún in *Historia General de las Cosas de la Nueva España*, Book 3, chapter III (Mexico: Editorial Porrua, 1979), p. 195.

water which he used for irrigating the Earth. The water of the first was "good" and helped the growth of the corn and fruits. The water of the second pitcher produced spiders' webs and caused blight. That of the third turned to frost and that of the fourth scorched the Earth and destroyed all plants and fruits.

Certain of the dead were sent to Tlaloc's and Chalchiuhtlicue's heaven, especially the hanged, those struck by lightning and the victims of illnesses such as leprosy or dropsy, believed to be caused by the gods of rain and water. Those sacrificed in Tlaloc's name were also assigned a place under his supervision. The souls destined for Tlalocan were not subjected to cremation. Instead, they were buried with *huauhtli*, or wild amaranth, on their faces, a stick or staff in their hands and paper mantles associated with the rain ceremony wrapped around their bodies.

Tlalocan was situated in the first of the heavens above the Earth's surface, where the Moon also lived, and was identified with the east. Thus it was believed the rain gods skulked close to the tops of the mountains, where the clouds gathered, or inside the clouds, which were thought to be gloomy pouches, filled with water.

Certain mountains were considered the personification of these water deities, among them Popocatepetl, Ixtaccihuatl, and Matlalcueye. It was told that a king from the region of Chalco sent one of his hunchbacks to be shut up in a cave on the slopes of Popocatepetl. Since caves and apertures in the Earth's surface were thought to lead to the nether-regions or into Tlaloc's domain, the hunchback only corroborated the king's assumption when he was released from his somber imprisonment, and told of having penetrated to the depths of Tlaloc's palace, a group of four buildings set around a central courtyard. In each, he said, were tubs containing different sorts of water, probably the four pitchers that Tlaloc used for irrigation.

Though the hunchback failed to mention the association, the four buildings surely indicated the four cardinal points. As he described the experience, the gods appeared with their retinue of minor ministers and lesser rain gods, who used the water in these tubs to sprinkle the earth, with flood, with dew, with fine water or foul. The gods carried the water in jugs and used a stick, which when struck upon the jug caused the sound of thunder. And if the jug broke, then lightning struck where the broken fragment fell.

Chalchiuhtlicue, like Hera, wife and sister of Zeus, had to contend with a number of other goddesses in her home, including her rival Huixtocihuatl, the goddess of salt water and salt. Additional inhabitants of Tlalocan were Nappatecutli, the god of mat-weavers and the left-handed Opochtli, the god of fishermen, as well as the gods for each of the hills and mountains associated with this rainy Mesoamerican Olympus.

The Moon, still another resident, was said to be the son of Tlaloc and Chalchiuhtlicue, at times a dissolute sort who was followed by the Centzon Totochtin (The Four Hundred Rabbits), which are the gods of pulque, used to designate the varying degrees of drunkenness. He also frequented Mayáhuel, the goddess of maguey, a woman with four hundred breasts changed by the gods into the plant that proffered its "honey water," a viscous, ever-present intoxicant. She could also have been the deified image of the first woman to perforate the maguey plant in order to extract and ferment its honeyed elixir.

She was normally pictured with a spike or machete, a scythe-like instrument used in the harvesting of the maguey. The rabbit gods were associated with the south. As gods of the hills, they were also water gods, and gods of the woods and forestry, depicted with hatchets in their hands.

Chalchiuhtlicue herself, in a reference to her Zapotec origin from the southern state of Oaxaca, was called the Mother of Zapotlan (Place of the Sapota Trees), and was identified with Xiuhtecuhtli as the more fearsome manifestation of the fire god called Ixcozauhqui, seen as a flaming reptile and associated with terrifying flood waters destroying everything in their path, symbolized by a weapon known as the *atli-tlachimolli*. It was described by Sahagún as the "dart-thrower" or "flame-thrower," a metaphysical designation of war and destruction.

Tlaloc, like the Assyrian Marduk, personified the fertilizing faculty of the waters, so it was he who made the plants grow and the corn ripen. But he was also called upon to prove his courage in other matters, as when the evil genii were provoked and the nocturnal malefactors plotted their rebellion. He was obliged then, factually or metaphorically, to take them to battle and put them to flight.

LAMATL DESCRIPTION

Chalchiuhtlicue, "Skirts of Jade" or "Highly-prized Skirts," the goddess of water and sister of the lesser rain gods, along with Tlaloc, her husband-brother and Lord of Tlalocan, was "honored because it was she who filled with water the sea and the rivers, and who drowned those who went to those places, and she who made storms and whirling water, who stranded ships and sank the vessels that traversed the water."[7]

Her following included freshwater peddlers in their canoes, and those who sold refreshments or drinking water from tubs in the market. She was depicted with a yellow face, crowned with a paper diadem, painted light blue. Her headdress was made of quetzal feathers. She wore a collar of precious green stones and a breastplate of gold, with earpieces of turquoise mosaic.

Her skirts and tunic were light blue, with a trim of seashells. In her left hand she carried a round shield adorned with the broad, round leaf of a lotus-like aquatic plant, called *atlacuezona*, "mother of the waves." In her right hand she carried a kind of scepter with a cross, while she clutched a spindle and the *tzotzopachtli*, the comb used to tighten the woof in weaving, and further artifacts associated with the goddess Tlazolteotl, the fickle goddess of the desires she herself inspired. For she was a "sovereign of the world by virtue of love's omnipotence."[8] Like the Babylonian Ishtar, the Phoenician Astarte, and the Greek Aphrodite, Tlazolteotl was associated with symbolic water, with human fluids and fertility, water's product.

---

[7]Eduard Seler, *Comentarios al Códice Borgia*, Vol. 1 (Mexico: Fondo de Cultura Económica, 1963), p. 80.
[8]Eduard Seler, *Comentarios al Códice Borgia*, Vol. 1, p. 173.

Figure 25. Chalchiuhtlicue, goddess of water, rivers and springs. From the Códice Borgia.

LAMATL SYMBOLISM

The tears and mourning of this sign, the rebirth in death and the continuity of the universe are emphasized in the cycles of the Moon — the cycles, in fact, of all of life.

Fruitfulness, abundance, plenty, and felicity are associated with water. The vital fluids of the planet, the rich liquid translated into ripeness and fecundity, are also interpreted as the response of the gods to human well-being. When all is well with the world the water flows, it falls from Heaven; it scurries in rivers and streams and overflows into the fields; it appears in the morning dew, renewing its contract with the new day.

PARALLEL SYMBOLISM

The fate of the dead, along with other supernatural concerns, are fundamental to the comprehension of the ceremonial polytheism of ancient Mexico. Humankind originated in the Omeyocan, where the Supreme Gods sent them to be born, along with the Earth itself. At the moment of birth, each individual acquired a *tonalli*, a day, and a destiny.

The tonalli was designated according to the day of birth, or the day the birth was celebrated. The sign determined the individual's personality, future, character, even death and the existence beyond. It was the spiritual attribute, inseparable from the person, to whom he or she would pray, yet which could be lost, especially in the case of children, thus producing diseases which could only be treated by means of certain rites, in the hopes of recovering the child's destiny.

Vitality, the senses, intelligence, and what is commonly termed "the soul" were considered to reside in the heart. The word *yolotl* and the concept inexorably linked to it, which was projected onto the Spanish *corazón*, meant the "soul" or "spirit." It appeared in the names of certain gods such as Tepeyolotl, "Heart of the Hill," or Tlalli Iyollo, "Heart of the Earth."

The dead were assigned different resting-places according to the circumstances of their death, yet each site was associated with its own gods and conditions. Thus the souls admitted there were destined to be incorporated into the god's retinue.

Those individuals who suffered a normal death, as a result of old age or common illnesses, went to Mictlan, or Hell, literally "The Place of the Dead," governed by Mictlantecuhtli and his wife, Mictecacihuatl. Hell was associated with the north and was considered the lowest of a series of nine levels. The bodies of such as these were cremated and their remains were packed into a bundle which was buried in the house of the deceased. Various offerings and the objects necessary for the deceased's arrival at his destination in Hell were buried with him, in the manner of the Egyptians.

The dead had to cross a river, the Chicunahuapan, "Nine Waters," which flowed beneath the Earth from west to east, thus joining the waters of the sea with those above ground, but in a course opposite than that of Ra as he sailed under the Egyptian sands.

In order to cross the river a dog was needed, so dogs were sacrificed and buried along with the dead. When the deceased reached the river, there would be a dog waiting to take him on its back to the opposite bank.

The deceased would furthermore have to cross the Obsidian Winds, Itzehuecayan, where the icy winds blew, and cut like obsidian (volcanic glass) knives. For this reason, the dead were buried with paper robes and mantles, to provide protection from such an ordeal.

The dead lived in Hell as they had lived on Earth, in the same fashion as the Egyptians or Assyrians, so their tools of trade, their utensils and relics, personal artifacts, and other necessities, were buried with them. If the deceased had belonged to the nobility or the privileged classes then his or her slaves were also sacrificed for companionship and continued service.

The journey to the underworld lasted four years. During this time the relatives of the deceased buried new offerings eighty days after death and thereafter on each anniversary. Upon arriving in Hell, the dead were allowed to return to Earth once a year, during the month dedicated to the celebration of *Huey Miccailhuitl*, corresponding to November 2 in the Christian calendar and following Hallowe'en ("All Hallows Eve"). For the occasion, the relatives of the deceased climbed to the rooftops of their houses and directed their prayers toward the north. Even today the fasting and prayers continue through November 1, All Saints' Day, then are broken the following day with music, fireworks, feasting and dancing, usually in the cemetery, which has been decorated with flowers and streamers for the occasion, or among the graves in a churchyard. During these days family members honor their departed with a house altar, not unlike the spread laid out for Buddha in pagodas and stupas in Southeast Asia. Flowers, especially brightly-colored marigolds, fruits and nuts, tidbits of prepared food, as well as water, are placed among candles, photographs of the departed, paper streamers and cutouts and, in Mexico, sugar skulls are added, with the names of the living, indicating that they will follow into the realm of the departed soon enough. Incense is frequently burned and earthenware platters and vessels, and even comic figures of musicians or animals accompany papier-maché skeletons garbed in colored tissue paper. This is one of contemporary Mexico's most ingratiating holidays, in a rollicking calendar still joyous with remnants of a culture long past, yet ever-present.

A number of gods in the pre-Columbian celebration were considered "infernal," among them Cihuacoatl, "Serpent Woman," or Yacatecuhtli, "Lord Guide," patron of merchants. Each of the four cardinal points was assigned its own Hell and was governed by its own regents, always in pairs: a god and a goddess. The Mexicans at no time left a deity to loneliness or celibacy.

The lamatl describes the Tlalocan of the east, which finds a parallel in the thirteenth arcanum in its concept of homages and proper conduct. Death is seen fundamentally as a continuation of life, while the glories of the material world are described as transitory and cyclical. Both almanacs, the tarot and the *Tonalamatl*, in fact emphasize the spirituality of humans, or the process of spiritualization, along the path to independent existence, exemplified in the sacrifice (penance) of Quetzalcoatl. An attachment to worldly goods, therefore, and worldly pleasures and sensations, represents bondage and deprivation, for death, in the end, which strips us of all we thought we owned, reigns supreme.

ARCANUM XIIII

MYTHOLOGY OF TEMPERANCE

The chaos of Hesiod, the name of which comes from a Greek root meaning "to gape," simply designates open space. Only later, because of an arbitrary derivation from a word meaning "to pour," was chaos considered applicable to the confused and unorganized mass of the elements scattered through space. Chaos is simply a pure cosmic principle devoid of god-like characteristics, associated with the fruits of the imagination, a harmonizing of the reversibility of all processes.

Yet after the union of Gaea, the Earth, with Uranus, the vault of the heavens, and Uranus' mutilation by Cronus, their son; and after Zeus' overthrow of Cronus, the Titans revolted with a cataclysmic barrage; and the Giants conducted a fearful war. Even Gaea was loathe to resigning herself to the defeat of her children. "She raised up," said Hesiod, "a ghastly monster against Zeus, Typhoeus, whom she had borne to Tartarus."[1]

Typhoeus was a terrifying creature whose hands worked ceaselessly and whose feet were never still. From his shoulders sprayed a hundred horrible dragons' heads, each with a darting black tongue and eyes which spurted searing flame, an image startlingly, even graphically, similar to the Mesoamerican representations in the codices, especially the mythical weapon *Atli-Tlachimolli*.

From the thighs of Typhoeus emerged innumerable vipers. His body was covered with feathers. He was a plumed serpent, the Quetzalcoatl of the Greeks in his most punishing manifestation, taller than the tallest mountain, a black and vindictive Tezcatlipoca.

At the sight of Typhoeus the gods were seized with terror and fled as far as Egypt. But, Zeus, the valiant, stood firm before the monster. Yet despite his bravado, the myriad coils of the serpents quickly enveloped and overpowered even the future King of the Gods. Typhoeus cut the tendons of his hands and feet and imprisoned him in his den in Cilicia. Rescued by faithful Hermes, however, who repaired the nerves and muscles, Zeus renewed the struggle.

---

[1]Felix Guirand, ed., *New Larousse Encyclopedia of Mythology*, translated by Richard Aldington and Delano Ames (London: Hamlyn House, 1969), p. 93.

With his thunderbolts he overwhelmed Typhoeus, who then fled to Sicily. Under the volcano Etna the god crushed him.

The Olympians had by then consolidated their might. Prometheus, the Titan, nonetheless admitted into Olympus and the circle of the Immortals, resented the destroyers of his race and so avenged himself by favoring mortals, to the detriment of the gods. It was said he even created a new species, fashioning the body of the first human into which Athena breathed soul and life. Pausinias said he saw bits of hardened clay which had the odor of human skin and could only have been the residue of the slime employed by Prometheus. It seems, however, that this creation took place after the earlier race of humans had been destroyed in the deluge. It would appear that every mythology, east and west, relates the tale of a great flood, that caused the nearly total disappearance of humankind, verified by British archaeologist George Smith in his labors in Mesopotamia in pursuit of the tablets that describe the epic of Gilgamesh.

The fourteenth arcanum, called Temperance, treats the concept of synthesis, in death and reincarnation, brought about by the Solar Genii, through analysis, then knowledge.

Humans and gods, Pindar suggested, are of the same family and owe the breath of life to the same mother. The first people, contemporaries of Cronus, enjoyed utter and complete happiness, according to Hesiod. This was the Golden Age. Humans lived like their deities, free from worry and fatigue. Old age had no effect on them. They rejoiced in continual festivity. Their lot failed to include immortality but at least they died as though overcome by sweet slumber. The blessings of the material world were theirs while the fruitful earth gave forth its treasures, as he told it, unbidden. At their death, insisted Hesiod, the populace of the Golden Age turned into benevolent genii, protectors and tutelary guardians of the living.

After the Golden came the Silver Age. A race of men Hesiod claimed were inept and feeble obeyed only their mothers. They were sowers of fields with Earth Mother deities. The Bronze Age followed the matriarchy and was marked by conquest. Men had to be robust as the ash trees of Achaea. They delighted in oaths and warlike exploits, to the disgust of their women. They invented metals and made an attempt at civilization, but they also ended by cutting each other's throats and putting the survival of their world in jeopardy.

Next came the Heroic Age, peopled by the valiant warriors who fought before Thebes and under the walls of Troy. Unhappily this was only a prelude, however, or in fact the initiation, of the Iron Age, the contemporary period of humankind, of misery and crime, when according to the myths men respect neither their vows nor justice nor virtue, and all of civilization must necessarily degenerate.

If temperance and moderation became distorted in the Mediterranean world since the outset of the human race, they were still extant in Eastern occultism, in the Karma Yoga which corresponds to the fourteenth arcanum. The principle describes the reversibility of actions and their outcome. It claims no drop falls falsely, from the mysterious gold and silver vessels, held in the hands of Logos, or Solar Genii. Accordingly, nothing in karma can be lost or forgotten. The cycle must necessarily be honored—never aborted.

For the Egyptians, temperance was related to the flow of the Nile, the flooding of its banks which brought a wealth of fertile silt to enrich its soil and renew its faith in its gods. For the Hindus, it was Indra, god of rain and fertility, who encompassed spiritual vitality and the karmic cycle. The Chaldeans saw in Ea the mastery of the oceans under the heavens, from which all wisdom emanated.

This card is related in Greek mythology to Ganymede, the beautiful young Trojan boy, considered the fairest among mortals. In primitive times he seems to have been interpreted as the deity responsible for sprinkling the Earth with Heaven's rain and is compared with the Vedic Soma, who was ravished by Indra and changed into a sparrowhawk. Ancient astronomers identified him with Aquarius, the Water-Bearer. Ganymede was venerated at Sicyon and Philius. He was depicted as an adolescent in a Phrygian cap, a mantle thrown back over his shoulders, either seated beside Zeus or carried through the air by an eagle, the latter presumably Zeus' spirit.

In spite of the honorary position he occupied on Olympus, he was the son of Tros, not of divine birth at all. Some said his father was Laomedon, possibly Ilus, Assaracus, or even Erichthonius. He was distinguished among mortals for his extraordinary beauty, which so charmed Zeus he had him swept up off the plain of Troad, using an eagle in order to effect the abduction. In any case, as recompense to Tros for the loss of his son, Zeus presented him with magical and magnificent steeds said to be "swift as the storm." On Olympus Ganymede became the cup-bearer of the gods and "rejoiced the eye of all by his beauty,"[2] while he dispensed nectar from a golden bowl. By the Middle Ages this tradition had evolved into the eucharistic mixing of the sacramental wine.

---

[2]Felix Guirand, ed., *New Larousse Encyclopedia of Mythology*, p. 138.

CARD DESCRIPTION

The card of the fourteenth arcanum usually presents a Solar Genii, often taking the form of an angel in a gleaming robe, in certain decks crowned with a golden halo, girdled with a golden belt, and wearing a white kerchief. The kerchief in many cases takes the form of an apron on the bodice of the robe on which the pentacles of the Tarot appear, a triangle in a square with a point in its center.

In many ancient decks the angel pours a radiant liquid from a golden vessel into a silver one, without the loss of a single drop.[3] Under the figure's feet a stream of crystalline water can be seen. The stream has its source on the horizon, just under the rising disc of the Sun.

The hieroglyph of this sign describes a fetus, seen as the fruit of the imagination, product of the woman in the thirteenth arcanum. She is the harmony in death and resurrection—that is, the synthesis of life (perfect equilibrium) revealed in reincarnation. The pursuit of harmony is therefore conceived as the astral essence of individuality, which in its separate stages, between incarnations, and still burdened by flesh and blood, appetites and passions, may be satisfied by the balance of planetary influences.

CARD SYMBOLISM

Hermes Trismegistus, the Lord of Immortality, suggests the image of powerful, all-encompassing deduction, or logic in this arcanum, associated with Scorpio, the sign it represents. Polarity combined with the Laws of Charity, must necessarily, says the principle, lead to the synthesis in the leveling of the liquid in the uninterrupted stream between the golden and silver vessels.

This, in effect, constituted the serenity and equilibrium experienced as a pervading peace by the more evolved. It was the most precious possible possession, yet at some time early in evolution the

---

[3]In other decks the vessels are but one color.

universal balance was somehow upset. It was destined to be recovered only through the chain of karmic experience.

Arcanum XIIII refers more precisely to the triumph of intuition than to the victory of action. Every solution is related to a choice, according to this premise. Nothing in the universe, therefore, nor in the life of any man or woman, occurs by "accident." It is selected, provoked, induced, fomented, even constrained and rejected, but the positive and the negative alternatives are manifest in the outcome. They are as much the product of premeditation, albeit unconscious, as of predetermination.

LAMATL XIV

MYTHOLOGY OF CE-OZOMATLI (THE MONKEY)

This thirteen-day period is represented by a monkey, who, like Ganymede, personified a plaything, a diversion that danced and sang, poured wine—or pulque—from a specified container and amused the onlookers with its dexterity and charm.

The *PopolVuh*, the Sacred Book of the Quiché Maya from the Guatemala highlands goes even farther, to describe a race of "monkey people" who lived long ago, in a mythological time long past, and said that they played the flute and sang, that they illustrated their codices and carved cleverly crafted images on the surface of "beautiful stones."[4]

The monkey, however, was also associated with concupiscence and voluptuosity, "sinful" desires, the scatological, and the sexual. He was therefore placed in direct contrast to this sign's regent, the god Xochipilli, "Prince of Flowers," the male twin of Xochiquetzal, whose happy nature, love of beauty, joyfulness in youth and pleasure in music, dancing, and gambling further identified this lamatl with Ganymede. Despite his jovial duties, Xochipilli was depicted with the head of a corpse, as an indication of the convergence of life's pattern, in the inevitable continuity of existence, through senility, death, and reincarnation.

Natives of this sign were considered equally joyful, inclined to music and mechanical enterprise. It was said, however, that when this sign had risen, the gods came down to Earth, but they could just

---

[4]*Popol-Vuh, Las Antiguas Historias del Quiché (Maya)*. Adrián Recinos, trans. (Mexico: Fondo de Cultura Económica, 1952).

as well transmit glory as suffering "to those they brushed against in the streets."

The lamatl refers additionally to Patécatl, "He who lays down happy," a god of pulque and husband of Mayáhuel. Sahagún called him Pachtécatl and wrote that he inhabited Pachtlan, where the *pachtle*, or *paxtle*, a parasitic moss, grew in abundance, and that it was this plant, when added to the pulque, that "gave it the quality of inebriation."[5]

Mayáhuel, his wife "of the four hundred breasts," was converted into the maguey plant. In the Telleriano-Remensis Codex, the breasts were presumed to indicate that the thorns of the maguey were used in the self-inflicted penance of the tongue or other parts of the body, "which incited the gods to graciousness in the granting of food and plenty, but this was also taken to mean the breasts with which the four hundred rabbits were suckled, or innumerable rabbits, for these *cenzonhuiznáhuatl* or *cenzontotochtin* were the gods of drunkenness."[6]

Mayáhuel was identified by association with Xochiquetzal, in her advocation as Ixnextli, "Ash in the Eyes" or "Ashes in the Face." This goddess was seen as the lovely flower of paradise, the personification of fertility and joy. Nevertheless, in this interpretation she indicates penance. The ashes on her face were used to induce tears, and therefore rain. She is depicted with a vessel in her hand, containing human excrement, symbol of sin or the corruption of the soul. Her penance is intended, according to the codices, to cleanse humanity, in preparation for another, more refined and purified, phase of existence.

Mayáhuel was further identified with Chicomecóatl, "Seven Serpents," the goddess of corn and sustenance, of food and drink. She was related to pulque as a nourishment. She was also associated with Tzintéotl, the god of the ear of corn, that is, the "dawn of the gods," for the gods were said to have been created from a ground corn meal, which was subsequently used in forming humankind, as Prometheus had used clay.

A monolith in the Aztec Hall of Mexico City's National Museum of Anthropology, representing Chicomecóatl, was presumedly identified with Mayáhuel as a goddess of corn and plenty. Her body is formed of a portion of a rattlesnake, with serpent scales and ears of corn, suggesting not only the divine origin of corn and the subtle satiation in pulque but in the root of the Nahutal verb *mayaui*, "to throw" or "to launch"—the idea of procreation itself. If the four hun-

---

[5]Eduard Seler, *Comentarios al Códice Borgia*, Vol. 1 (Mexico: Fondo de Cultura Económica, 1963), pp. 339, 340.
[6]Eduard Seler, *Comentarios al Códice Borgia*, Vol. 1, pp. 108, 112.

dred, or innumerable, breasts of Mayáhuel were meant to indicate maguey thorns, then the thorns themselves were seen as instruments of sustenance, more than of penitence. Not only were the thorns applied to the tongue, ears, genitals, and other parts of the body as a petition for fertility and abundance on the part of the gods of the Earth, but the maguey plant itself served as a staple. Its honey water was applied ubiquitously as food, beverage and medicine. In addition, the industrialization of maguey fiber, as rope and textile, brought about a transformation in patterns of living and the application of utensils or woven goods. Furthermore, the blossoms of the plant were considered, then as now, a great delicacy, to be utilized in the most refined gastronomy. The fronds were also used, though by so doing the plant was destroyed. When roasted and applied to a wound these fronds or pencas accomplished curative miracles, with properties under analysis even in today's pharmaceutical industry. So also the roots of the maguey and related agaves were useful. When ground to a powder they produced a substance from which to fashion balls applied in a nighttime sport. They were set afire and batted with poles, as in golf.

LAMATL DESCRIPTION

The god of pulque was illustrated in the most sumptuous and elaborate of finery. In the Telleriano-Remensis Codex, his body, arms, and legs are painted black. His face, seen in profile, is twotone, *chitlpanqui*: black, with yellow spots on the rear half and red on the forward half. If the face were viewed from the front it would be seen painted entirely red. This red and black composition indicates that the gods all originated in a single place, with residence at "the site of change."

Patécatl wears a nose-ring shaped like a halfmoon, or *yacametztli*, of a lightish, almost white color. On his head he wears a crown of cutout paper, *amacalli*, a halo, formed of lesser deities of the mountains. He wears a large bow, or *tlaquechpánytl*, around his neck.

Figure 26. Patécatl, the god of pulque. From the Códice Borgia.

The crown here appears in Quetzalcoatl's colors, brown and white. A band surrounds the crown, red down the center and black along the edges, on which a nose-bone has been mounted, as a sign of the Moon and of the gods of pulque. Others of the elements of his adornment are further associated with Quetzalcoatl, such as the curved pendants shaped like thorns (carved of seashell), a shell necklace, and the black feathers in the headdress emerging from the crown.

The breastplate, on the other hand, a *chayahuac cozcatl*, is considered a typical attribute of the gods of pulque, as illustrated in the Maglabechi Codex, XIII, 3. Patécatl's feather ceremonial piece, in the shape of a fan, additionally distinguishes his apparel, with red feathers bordered by white. In his hand he holds the *itztopolli*, a stone hatchet.

In the Borgia Codex a jaguar appears, stalking under a paper banner, a symbolic image of a warrior, made braver by drink. In certain manuscripts an eagle further accompanies the jaguar, a representation of the Sun, like Zeus, the Solar Genii, the personification of freedom and dexterity, a great warrior from the east, who made war on the jaguar, that deity of the night, symbolizing Black Tezcatlipoca, the shadow, seduction, and magic.

LAMATL SYMBOLISM

The halfsun and the halfnight accompany this lamatl, the halfworld of twilight, a time of desire and transformation, corrupted discipline or deliverance. It is the time of banquets and pouring of the wine and also the time of the appearance of the young moon growing in the darkening sky, promise of maturity and evolution.

Yet it is just as much a time to hold back the night or to stay the darkness, where the transition from life to death, like that of day to night, may be reconciled at the side of the gods.

The banners or legbands on the jaguar and the eagle indicate they have been singled out for sacrifice—their greater destiny. If captured they must die on the stone altar, they and their warrior sect, those squadrons called the Knights of the Eagle or the Knights of the Jaguar.

At the same time, and though disconcerting, the exact opposite is indicated: the tempering of passion is considered a redirection of vitality, to the service of the gods and the honor of humankind, thus fulfillment of the spirit may be achieved. This is interpreted as a preparation for the subsequent transformations of existence, a reversal of the ordinary into the dimension of the extraordinary.

Additional symbols emphasize piety or abundance. The thorn is understood to indicate the brevity of life on Earth. The green plant, the paxtli, further describes the ephemeral. The reptile translates humankind's initial crudity, his labor, and his nakedness, the cold and suffering. The rabbit represents the wine, or pulque. The apparently harmless little animal served as well as the advocate of drunkenness.

The rain or water that falls from Heaven reaffirms life's pleasures and temporary enjoyment, yet it falls on the monkey, a slothful and undirected though curious and resourceful being, and so is cast before the unevolved human. Xochipilli's death's-head further serves as a reminder of divination and destiny: as soon as humans appeared on Earth, death also came into existence.

PARALLEL SYMBOLISM

The parallelism between the tarot and *Tonalamatl* is stressed in the mysterious combinations of fluids, the sacred liquids that identify those who drink of them, while they project their image onto that of the gods themselves.

According to the arcanum, the combination of water and wine endorsed by the Greeks and described by Homer served as a basis for the eucharistic rites of the Catholic Church, yet the mystic symbolism is equally transcribed in the lamatl, the miracle of transformation in "divine blood" or "honey water," an intensification of the communion among priest, citizen, warrior, or god.

Patécatl, like Ganymede, was deified as the bearer of the divine elixir. Yet only the temperance endorsed in the counter-symbols reinforces the potential for harmony. The most judicious incursions, necessarily combined with the severest exercise of moderation, constituted the only reliable formula for genuinely satisfying the cravings of the spirit, to prepare the initiate for his subsequent phases of existence, as illustrated by the two containers depicted in the Bourbon Codex. The abuse of any privilege turns it to a blight. The devotion to pleasure, or the abandonment in sin, can only lead to the obstruction of equilibrium and the devastation of the soul.

The cosmic power of the sun, the Solar Genii, indicated by means of the eagle in both the fourteenth arcanum and the lamatl, emphasizes a universal balance, a constancy in cosmic order: clear, transparent water which brings abundance to the Earth, the flowering and plenty in daily life, the joy in existence tempered with discipline and awareness of every act and its consequence. All of these factors merge in the central figure of both cards while they suggest the ever-present potential for reversibility in Sun and Moon, dark and light, night and day: the "harmony in mixed elements" synthesized in the Hermetic principle.

Wisdom and knowledge, however, for all their availability, will always be filtered through the private personality of the individual being, symbolized in the counterposed images of the eagle and the jaguar, Quetzalcoatl and Tezcatlipoca. For Tezcatlipoca, like Quetzalcoatl, can assume a variety of moods or identities, expressed as much in colors as in cardinal points. He can be north or west. He can be green, yellow, white, or blue, as well as the red and the black with which he is normally associated. There is no limit to the mutations of either himself, his alter ego, or his supplementary manifestations. Like Horus and Seth, the one is a channel for sagacity, a conductor for the valor of the Heavens. The other is darkness and the faculty of magic, again, the reversibility, a mirror, for all things are themselves and their opposite.

Like Indra, "who swills ambrosia, not to live but to get drunk," an intemperate god, foolhardy yet courageous, Quetzalcoatl—who determined the fecundity of nature by his actions—had to confront his counterpart, Black Tezcatlipca, to "conquer him by a superior power, before the wealth of water could shower over the dry land."[7]

As in the case of Ra, in his eternal disputes with Asep, the great serpent who lived in the depths of the celestial Nile and who succeeded during total eclipses in swallowing the solar barque, Quetzalcoatl was obliged to vanquish his enemy, not once, or repeatedly, but always, every day, in constant vigilance. Especially during the twelve hours of darkness, his perils were even greater; he was pushed to ever-increasing prodigies of tolerance until he surrendered his anger. Sumer's Enlil was finally so enraged he sent down the deluge to annihilate the human race. Yet Enlil was good and evil in a single figure. Quetzalcoatl represented the juxtaposition, the counterpoint, the enduring conflict with the human "heart" or spirit, to find and name its soul, its destiny, a meaning beyond the assigned definition of eternity, and his own place in it.

---

[7]Fr. Bernardino de Sahagún in *Historia General de las Cosas de la Nueva España*, Book 2 (Mexico: Editorial Porrua, 1979).

ARCANUM XV

MYTHOLOGY OF THE DEVIL

The card describes Saturn, the god expelled from the sky by Zeus. But this time the Greek king of the gods appears in his Latin advocation as the thunder-god Jupiter, who presided over the heavens, the celestial light of the Etruscans, the brilliance of Rome.

Since this Latin Jupiter was the god of light, that is, the Sun and the Moon, and of all cosmic phenomena such as wind, rain, thunder, tempest, and lightning, his role was given great importance by a placid and visibly bucolic community. This converted him, however, into a counterpart or rival of Saturn, also an agricultural deity and a very old one, considered native to the Italian peninsula; but his conflicting pre-eminence in a rival capacity led to his quarrel with Jupiter.

After the exile of Saturn from the heavens, he was welcomed, it was said, by Janus, another native Latin, the two-headed god considered by Ovid to have been formed as Chaos, when the elements became separate entities. Saturn then enjoyed a rank equal to that of Janus himself, or even Jupiter, for he was synonymous with abundance.

His name came from *satur*, "gorged" or "stuffed"; and from *sator*, "a sower." He was a working god, the *vitisator* of the vine. Under the name Stercutius he attended the fertilizing of the fields. He was associated with Ops, the personification of the Earth's riches. He was supposed to have risen to King of Italy during the Golden Age of the land called Latium that first offered him asylum, and in fact, he reigned beneath the Capitol in Rome itself, bringing great prosperity to his people. His reserved and moderate ways were initially considered an integral part of conservatism until elaborate cunning, a native talent for discipline, and political organization led Rome to the opulence identified with Jupiter and to unsuspected heights of excess and domination. The secret was contained of course in the concept of *totality*, that is, modules or units—of thought, buildings, roads, territories, agencies of government, in squadrons, legions, bodies of entities—that functioned as a single, invincible force.

Faunus, god of fertility, became inseparably identified with Saturn, his grandfather. This early king of Latium gave laws to the still wild tribes. He invented the shawm, a rustic pipe, viewed in early representations as a torch. He was endowed with the gift of prophecy and caused voices to be heard in the countryside, yet his oracular wisdom could only be extracted if he were first bound and fettered, like Black Tezcatlipoca. Equally wily, he would evade his commitment if he could. The festivals in his honor involved the sacrifice of goats or dogs, nudity and laughter, characteristics as well of the Saturnalia, Saturn's celebration, which lasted from the seventeenth to the twenty-third of December and found their echo in Oaxaca, after a circuitous cultural migration which transferred the Latin customs of Italy to the Roman occupation of Iberia and the Spanish conquest of Mexico.

The Saturnalia originally consisted of a series of rural festivities — *sementivae feriae, consualia larentalia,* and *paganalia* — yet assumed their greatest importance after 217 B.C., at a time when the defeat at Lake Trasimene (a prelude to the disaster of Cannae) caused a religious revival among the Romans.

The seven-day fest represented a period of unrestrained frolic. The religious ceremony was followed by an enormous feast, for which guests took the precaution of bathing in the morning in order to remain the entire day at table. Togas were abandoned in favor of light tunics. In memory of the Golden Age, masters served their slaves, who during the festival could say and do as they pleased. All public activity — law courts, schools, commercial and military operations — were suspended for the occasion.

The state treasury was housed in the Temple of Saturn near the Capitol. Also guarded there were the standards of the legions which were not out on campaign. The god's effigy in the temple was bound with woolen strips to prevent its leaving Roman territory. The bands were untied only during the Saturnalia.

In a painting from Pompeii, Saturn is depicted with a sickle in his hand. On coins, he carried a sickle or ears of corn, not unlike the Mexican deities in the codices. He was usually represented as a bearded old man, hunched over and sagging, often with two or even three faces, his eyes popping out of his head. He was occasionally associated with Dionysus or Bacchus, with a retinue of satyrs, Pan, and the genii. At times he was pictured as a horse from the waist down, a reference to the wisdom, skill, and cunning of Chiron. Frequently his animality was interpreted as a goat, sometimes with a long tail.

He appeared during the period of the Templars (early 12th century) as Baphomet, a symbol of the primitive fertility rites, in turn associated with the cult of Amon, in his advocation as the ram-headed god of Upper Egypt, an androgynous goat-without-gender who was named Mendes and passed into Greece as Mendecius. He was further associated with the Ba'al of the Phoenicians, proprietor of the soil and supreme ruler of all subjects, also known as Ba'alat, a "Lady," or Ba'alim, "Lord of the Skies," like the Balam of the Mayas, a supreme deity presented in the form of a "tiger" (the Spanish designation of feline or jaguar in the Americas.)

Normally the name of this god was never uttered, for the Phoenicians, like the Judeans, the Vedics, or the Egyptians, feared that the sound of the word would deprive their god of his strength, leaving him flaccid and vulnerable.

This unconquerable god was encompassed in the Sun. His birthday took place close to the winter solstice on December 24, and was incorporated into Christianity as the birth of Jesus, who was in fact born in February or March, nearer the festival of Faunus and the rites of spring later assimilated into the Passion. The highlight of the original festival occurred when the blood of a freshly sacrificed bull was sprinkled on the Earth as an emblem of fruitfulness and vigor for the coming planting.

The devotion of the Templars to Baphomet, as a Hermetic and kabbalistic symbol, provoked Pope Clement V, Bertrand de Got, to reprisal. As a close friend of King Philip I—called The Fair, son of the Hapsburg Emperor Maximilian I, Archduke of Austria, who founded the Hapsburg dynasty in Spain when he married Juana—and at the insistence of King Philip IV of France, whose concerns involved the Holy Roman Empire, the order was severely persecuted, until the last Grand Master, Jacques de Molay, was seized and burned at the stake of the French Inquisition, in Paris in 1314.

In Hermetic tradition, Saturn was called Satan, the principle of the materialization of the spirit. The Gnostics, who reaffirmed the image and the symbolism of the goat, saw this figure as the Great Pan. The Catharists, who believed that matter was evil and Christ was an angel who neither lived nor died on Earth, committed heresy by converting the Greek lawgiver Solon into the Creator of the World; yet, they said he had spoken with the prophets. They were supported by ascetic Jews of the 12th century, who saw a revelation in Solon's cosmic luminosity.

Perhaps no other symbol has been as misunderstood or maligned, nor as difficult to understand. The fifteenth arcanum has been called Typhon, or The Devil. Yet while it refers to logic, to fate and to the circular vortex, or whirlwind, even to the serpent who tempted Eve, the Knights Templar used Baphomet as an inverted acronym which meant The Priest of the Temple of Peace for All Men. If the Devil, in effect, represented the "Father of Lies" and the denial of awareness, then the Hermetists, like the teachings of the Advaita Vedanta, stressed "non-dualism." The principle emphasizes the path of knowledge rather than action or devotion as the key to liberation, and agrees on the nature of evil inherent in the divisive state.

The complexities of the Tree of Knowledge and the Tree of Life, the dilemma of Good and Evil, the Astral Chain, and the Union of All Nations were further complicated by agents of Pope Clement V's Inquisition, who destroyed every picture of Baphomet, leaving only the symbols applicable to the theory of probabilities in the reversibility of values.

CARD DESCRIPTION

The hieroglyph of the fifteenth arcanum refers to an arrow, as a weapon rather than the "direction" described in the seventh arcanum, but a weapon used either to paralyze its victim into inaction or to defend the path to reintegration, like the Knights Templar storming Heaven in order to escape the narrow abyss of the Earth.

The upper portion of the picture is usually occupied by the traditional figure of Baphomet, in which case he would be seated on a cube, that is perched on the surface of a great globe. On one side we see a man, and on the other a woman. Both are naked. Small horns emerge from their temples. They are bound together by a heavy chain, one end fastened around the neck of the man and the other around the waist of the woman, like Faunus or Black Tezcatlipoca restrained. The chain is locked through a ring fixed to Baphomet's cube.

On the cube sits, in most decks, the androgyne himself, the representation of the signs of the four elements and consequently the ruler of the four Hermetic virtues. The globe of the Earth is placed under his feet. Fish scales, symbolizing water, cover his abdomen. Wings, indicating air, can be seen behind his shoulders. Fire rises to Heaven from the flaming pentagram above his head.

He bears a torch, indicating wisdom, but the flame points downward. He wears the clue to Egyptian occultism around his waist.

The right arm and hand of the androgyne are male and bear the inscription "Solve," indicating a decision, an abrupt incision, a dissolution. The hand points to the bright crescent of the new moon, on the right side of the figure—seen normally, *not* as in a mirror. The left arm and hand of Baphomet are female and have written on them "Coagula," demanding solidification, the process of condensation. They point toward the dark crescent of the waning moon, on the left side of the figure, or on the cube itself. If the waning moon appears in the lower portion of the card then the female hand points downward to it. The new moon would be depicted in the upper section of the card with the male hand pointing upward to it.

Baphomet has female breasts, like the sagging image of the aging Saturn. Certain cards illustrate a double caduceus growing from the figure's groin. Serpent-like heads reach to Baphomet's solar plexus. The astral god appears with a goat's head, whose horns, ears and beard fit perfectly into the reversed pentagram. While a suggestion of evil accompanies the figure, the ternary of the torch dominates the binary of the horns. In the Italian Tarot, The Devil wears horns, bat's wings, and the beard of Mendes, the goat. In the Marseille Tarot, he is depicted with wings, eagle's talons, and the helmet of a shaman or magician.

CARD SYMBOLISM

A diabolic interpretation accompanies this figure, yet according to medieval philosophers the androgyne is more naughty than wicked. His goat's legs remain solidly on the cube and his feet on the globe are a balancing point, says the tarot.

The legs are usually crossed so that the right hoof appears on the left side of the globe and the left hoof on the right side. This mirror-like transposition of the astral or cosmic vision into perceptible language and legible symbols is designed to facilitate the interpretation, in an allusion to the clairvoyant or the somnambulist, who in the manner of the dyslectic reverse their images.

The double current implied in this arcanum emphasizes the ascending potential in the power of creation. Humanity's downfall however, is symbolized in the interpretation of the perverted, that is, the goat, the distortion of the pentagram, and therefore of knowledge. Though the card is considered mysterious, its message is quite clear and concise, as indicated in the words on the Emerald Tablets: Baphomet came from the metaphysically created Heaven to the materialized Earth. He made the transition from the recognition of the

Gnostic Law of Creation to the understanding of the Principle of Sacrifice, from Divine Nature to the secrets of the Logos' incarnation.

He is thus evolved, that is, integrated in his awareness. If he unhappily provoked the division of the human race and the downfall of man and woman, and consequently took up the chains of slavery, he shares them with the couple in the arcanum, to lighten their burden. Yet together, as a unit, the man and woman, in effect Adam and Eve, can dominate, even overcome Baphomet, while they raise themselves to a more rarefied level by disposing of the obstacles to the integration of the parallel or twin values of activity and sensibility. For the cube on which Baphomet sits is "adaptation" as well as "authority."

LAMATL XV

MYTHOLOGY OF CE-TECPATL
(THE FLINT BLADE)

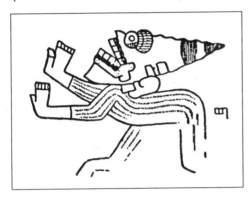

According to the codices, this thirteen-day period is represented by Huitzilopochtli, the joyous god of war, of bravery in battle, of abundance and prosperity. He was feted throughout the season or period of the sign Ce-Tecpatl.

The period had as its secondary patron the flamboyant god Camaxtli, the warrior deity of the fierce Chichimec tribe around Huexotzingo, or Huejotzingo, since the pre-Columbian "x" in certain linguistic variations became the Spanish "j." This region, covering a portion of the present-day states of Puebla and Tlaxcala, was dominated by those Chichimec "Serpents of the Clouds." The primitive Latins of their day, they were known for their skill in the hunt and for their celebration of a *cu* or ritual reverence of Camaxtli's icon. Called the *Tlacetecco*, this included a display of all the deity's ornaments and artifacts, which were placed before him, enveloped in clouds of incense. He was especially honored by the military and by those who fashioned weapons of war, in particular the spears and javelins that struck from a distance.

The most important ornaments, however, were used to honor Huitzilopochtli, and included lavish and highly prized feathers, woven into an irridescent green cape. It was called the *quetzalquémitl* or "cape of quetzal plumes." Another cape, fashioned of layers of glorious blue hummingbird feathers, called the *xiuhtotoquémitl* ("cape of fire feathers") further emphasized the homage to the Hummingbird of the South, the grand and radiant Huitzilopochtli, the Sun in all its splendor, everything that glimmers and illuminates: intelligence, victory, wit, and grandeur.

Still another ornament, a cape of glistening yellow feathers, called the *tozquémitl*, honored Tonatiuh or Solar Fire, the Sun and Lord of the Heavens. It suggested the light of the sun, while the *huitzitzilquémitl*, though it referred to Huitzilopochtli, was described in Sahagún's documentation as a lesser cape, with feathers "only" from a bird called the *cintzon*, not considered significant.

All these capes were laid on rich mantles in the light of the bright sun, which served to heighten the brilliance and the luminosity of their irridescence, a quality in itself divine. And there the image of the god could look upon them and wonder at their marvelous hues. Meantime, he received offerings of rare foods at opulent banquets. On this occasion, the principal guests were the so-called common folk, who made their offerings and then wandered into the temples for their prayers, until later, when the entire population massed together and the "ordinary people" ate alongside the nobles, among those who were Huitzilopochtli's ministers.

The king and lords according to Sahagún's reports, made offerings of flowers to the figure of Huitzilopochtli, those called *yolloxóchitl*, others named *eloxóchitl* and the ones termed *cacaoaxóchitl*. Flowers were woven, arranged, prepared in bundles, isolated for their rarity, or clustered together in order to accentuate their colors. Flowers were distributed among the guests or scattered before the god's image, collected in harmonious or compatible groups in relation to their aroma or placed near the fruits of the plants they came from, like the cacao, to emphasize the utilitarian value in their exotic loveliness.

Offerings were also made of bundles of reeds, in packets of twenty, which smoked and sputtered before the idol like the incense sticks in a Buddhist temple, until the smoke whirled like a dense cloud, leaving the devoted followers hacking and sneezing.

The "Lords of the Maguey," or tavern-keepers, sold pulque for the festival, while they cut the fronds and perforated the hearts of the plant in order to extract the honey-water stored in the natural bowl of its core. The first pulque, called uitzli, was offered to Huitzilopochtli. It was served in the vessels called *ocatecómatl*, to be drunk through the reeds used by the elderly like straws in order to facilitate the maneuver.

Natives of this sign were considered shrewd, reserved, and discreet, yet the very nature of Huitzilopochtli, the left-handed Hummingbird of the South, like Jupiter, propitiated all that was abundance, opulence, extravagance in matters of food. He was clever, honorable, but especially brave; but as in all affairs related to the Mesoamerican divinities, a counterpart existed, in the figure of Chalchiuhtotolin, "The Jade Turkey," a unique advocation of Black Tezcatlipoca, Lord of Lies and Evil, Darkness as opposed to Light, associated with cardinal point north, the precise opposite of Huitzilopochtli.

The sign was further identified with Tonatiuh, Ruler of Fate and the Heroic Journey; and his counterpart, Mictlantecuhtli, God of the Underworld, whose name also indicates the north or right-handedness, and whose private Hell, or Place of the Dead, corresponded to the northern restingplace, the lowest of the nine levels of the underworld.

The *Tecpatl* itself, symbol of this sign, refers to the mysterious flint or obsidian knife, represented by a toothed face inside the knife itself, or a human figure with a face in the form of a knife. The knife, in turn, was associated with human blood—the "vital juices" of the deceased at the moment of death—termed the appeasement for the Devil, and celebrated in the death rites.

Offerings of human bones and skulls were therefore placed before the image of Mictlantecuhtli, or clumps of cotton dampened with the blood of penitents. Certain codices associated Mictlantecuhtli with Ozomatli, a symbol of lust and aberration, related to the excrement which also served as a symbol of spiritual filth, the detritus of the human struggle in a highly moral society, characterized, like the Hindu, by the eternal chain of actions and events, with the planes of existence and reincarnation, in the quest for enlightenment, a oneness with the Sun and all that lies beyond.

LAMATL DESCRIPTION

In the Vatican Codex, the figure appears as the Goddess of the Underworld, wife of Mictlantecuhtli, devouring the mortuary bundle of those who died in filth and sin, or who suffered a disease associated with concupiscence: those condemned to dwell forever in the underworld at the side of the gods of death.

The same codex depicts Tonatiuh, the Winter Sun shining faintly on the Earth beneath his feet. His body is painted pale red, like the deity of the east. He wears green quetzal plumes. His breastplate is adorned with golden bells and turquoise incrustations. He holds Xiuhcoatl, the Serpent of Fire, in his hand.

In the section of the codex devoted to the various combinations of deities in the *Tonalamatl*, Ce-Tecpatl is represented by Mictlantecuhtli as a counterposed image to Tonatiuh, the Solar Lord of Heaven. The god of death is painted black. His head appears as a skull. The chair on which he perches is made of bones and herbs. Before it lie the mortuary bundles and a scattering, like the petals of flowers, of the insignias of the King of the Underworld.

In the Borgia Codex, the Fire God appears on a platform covered with the skin of jaguar, which refers to his Olmec origins. His red color, fiery ornaments, and flaming apparel emphasize his association with the solar god. He is often illustrated with darts in the shape of serpents in one hand and a shield in the other.

This god was designated in Yucatan as the Lord of the Six Underworlds or Six Infernos. In the Telleriano-Remensis and the Bourbon Codices, the regent gods of the sign appear with a sinner between them, suffering his penitence with his head under water, symbolizing the difficulty of abandoning the punishments of Hell.

LAMATL SYMBOLISM

The Bourbon Codex contains an analysis of the complex symbolism associated with the death of the "sinner," he who must dwell in the

Figure 27. Tonatiuh, solar fire and lord of heaven. From the Códice Borgia.

underworld, away from light and the flowers, the birds and their song, to compensate for the brave who died in the battle that he refused to fight and who will receive their reward in the Heaven of the warrior.

The right-living, or those who died of natural causes, are absolved from the wrath of the divinities, the darkness of despair, or the lonely journey to the underworld. The struggle of the will and the capacity for sacrifice may ultimately defeat any temptation. Denial and discipline represent the pathway of the warrior, for death and The Devil are confounded by renunciation, which according to this lamatl will light up even the darkest sky with shining stars, the rain of light in the Pleides.

The Way of Right is revealed as the path of prophecy and divination, a harmony with the Cosmos. Redemption is therefore encompassed in the synthesis of Tonatiuh, the light of day, with the nocturnal Sun of the underworld, until finally, possibly, the "sinner" may contemplate the grandeur and enlightenment of Huitzilopochtli himself.

PARALLEL SYMBOLISM

The fifteenth arcanum is related to man's more negative and materialistic tendencies, the lasciviousness and perdition of the unwary. The sign is characterized, in both the tarot and the *Tonalamatl*, by those who would sacrifice enlightenment for magic, embrace incantation in place of song or the dead plumage of the opulent cape as a substitute for the live wings of the eagle that soars toward the Sun.

Hard work, careful decision, the judicious application of knowledge, the prudent observation of the past, serve as the substance for the fortification of an invincible dynasty, an incorruptible majesty that permits no deviation nor divisiveness. Thus, individuals, entire societies, families, or nations can confirm their vitality only in their definition of purpose. Neither gold nor jewels, an underground sea of oil, the pretense of wealth, the appearance of passion, a show of strength, even the application of might, will ever sway the immutable power of the universe.

The arrow, or weapon, in the arcanum, finds its parallel in the spears of Camaxtli. The feather capes, like Baphomet's wings, are as indicative of Huitzilopochtli's hummingbird as of Black Tezcatlipoca's turkey. The Saturnalia, just as the celebrations of the Ce-Tecpatl, offer abundance and gluttony in juxtaposition with prayers and devotion during the winter solstice. The pulque and the wine of Bacchus incite even the cowardly to valor and the timid to triumph, but the display is false unless supported by a pair of feet—even Baphomet's hoofs—placed firmly on the globe of the Earth.

The leering goat, like the gaping skull, while not in themselves a manifestation of evil or fear, suggest the power of the elements, a retribution for corruption and "sin." The glory of Jupiter, as much as the radiance of Huitzilopochtli, can be countered in the pale light of aberration or the erosion of detrition.

The Devil, or Slanderer, was associated with falling, identified equally with Saturn's or Black Tezcatlipoca's expulsion from Heaven as the parable of the Fallen Angel, lifeless feathers on the dead Earth. He was seen as the supreme personification of the non-righteous, the tempter, a spiritual enemy of both god, and humankind, in fact, God's adversary, as Black Tezcatlipoca was the adversary of Huitzilopochtli and Quetzalcoatl. Yet The Devil is subordinate to God, and is able to act only by His sufferance. Therefore, by symbolic definition, human-kind is potentially a power superior to any conjured by the enemy of the gods. The human is God's ally, the astrosome, a microcosm dependent only on its sovereign fulfillment for the achievement of total, absolute, and unrestricted liberty, on the indulgence of none but the Cosmos.

The Devil is considered the prince of Apostate Angels who, like the all-encompassing Tezcatlipoca, can assume any disguise at will. And, like Mictlantecuhtli, he is the Ruler of Hell. In the Middle Ages, he was generally represented as having horns, a tail—sometimes forked—and cloven hoofs. The Hebrew *Satan* of the Old Testament was translated by the Septuagint as *diabolos*, Greek for "accuser" or "slanderer." In the Vulgate, Satan was cited as the *sairim* or *shedim*, Hebrew for satyrlike demons or the storm demons, respectively. The *daimonion* or *daimon*, the Demon, was also known as Apollyon, Beelzebub, Lucifer, the Archenemy of the Archetype, the Archfiend and, like Black Tezcatlipoca, as the Prince of Darkness.

The powers of the darkness were associated with the "idols of the heathen," which to many were tantamount to malignant spirits. Generally, however, the term, as in the arcanum and the lamatl, came to refer to the symbolic representation of wickedness, imprecation, abandonment, vexation of the spirit, or the negation of discipline. The concept may equally define the excessive or the abundant in both the positive and negative applications, seen as recklessness, the glib as opposed to skill, the pitiable or the pitiless, the extremes of mood or actions, passion, the morbid, the "possessed," the eccentric, falsity, error, the opposite of truth, and corporeality; also the mind, sickness, death, animal magnetism, and hypnotism.

The term further refers, in both the tarot and the *Tonalamatl*, to those instruments or implements that confound the natural course of events or circumstances: weapons; chains; drags; a fire basket; artifacts for grinding or tearing; devices for pushing, lifting, or carrying; those articles which serve to somehow unburden man of his natural limitations, to expand his area of action and his potential.

Baphomet and The Devil are therefore no more negative than Huitzilopochtli-Jupiter in their opulence. The fanatic or the extreme, like the fruitless or the fruitful, are the consequence of a choice. If there is a godliness at all, it can be defined in the alternative, the selection from among the range of all things, the very existence of the polarity. If the gods gave us this, says the lamatl, then they are wise indeed, for the wisdom itself, affirms the tarot, is ours to apply.

ARCANUM XVI

MYTHOLOGY OF THE TOWER

The great life-giving force of the Solar Divinity was encompassed in the stories of Dionysus. His personality, popularity, and the exuberance of the legends surrounding his name led to his assimilating a number of exotic gods into his cult, such as Sabazius, venerated as the supreme deity in the Thracian Hellespont, a solar divinity of Phrygian origin; or Bassareus, a conquering god later absorbed into the composite version of Dionysus.

An element of Orphic mysticism was nevertheless introduced into the legend through Dionysus's identification with the Cretan god Zagreus. The Aegeans considered Dionysus to be the son of Zeus, with either Demeter or Kore. The gods of Olympus were consumed with jealousy, however, and according to the tale, resolved to slay him. They contracted the Titans to tear him to pieces, then threw the remains of his body into a cauldron. Pallas Athene was nonetheless able to rescue the deity's heart and, in the manner of a Mesoamerican priest, bore the still palpitating trophy to Zeus. In retaliation, the Olympian monarch struck the Titans with thunderbolts. From the throbbing heart, that symbol of the spirit of the Mexicas, he recreated Dionysus as the Cretan Zagreus, whose remains were finally buried at the foot of Mount Parnassus, near the sanctuary of Delphi in mainland Greece. The deity was transformed into an underworld divinity who in Hades welcomed the souls of the dead and assisted in their purification.

After this the character of Dionysus underwent a profound modification. He ceased to function as the bucolic god of wine and frivolity, come down from the mountains of Thrace, or the Lydian god of "orgiastic delirium." Plutarch in fact described a god who was destroyed, who disappeared, who relinquished mortal existence and then was born again, to become the symbol of everlasting life.

The mystic notion of a mountain as the key to a cult, indicated in the references to Olympus, Tmolus, and Parnassus, was further emphasized in relation to the various manifestations of Indra, as the Vedic Svargapati, Lord of Heaven, as Meghavahana, Rider of the Clouds and as Vajri, the Thunderer, a metaphysical trinity that inhabited Mount Meru, the supposed center of the Earth, to the north of the Himalayas, and therefore between Earth and Heaven.

"The Lord of pure incantation, making the dead to live," encompassed in the Babylonian Marduk, son of Ea, again stressed heights, while representing the purist definition of humankind's vanity and arrogance, until the god from Apsu passed into the annals of the world's historical legends as the epitome of pride. "Terrible master, without rival among the great gods! In his flames steep mountains are overthrown."[1]

Marduk originally personified the fertilizing action of the waters. He made plants grow and grain ripen. As an agricultural deity he was likened to Dionysus, especially in the Greek god's mysterious appearance as the deity Iacchus in an early cult devoted to Demeter, later associated with another agricultural cult in Italy called *Liber Pater*.

Marduk's fortunes grew with the greatness of Babylon, according to the legend. It was for him, as for others before and after, the city of his choice, for which he abandoned his attribute, the *marru* or spade. He conquered the monster Tiamat, yet before he joined battle he insisted that the assembly of the gods invest him with supreme authority, the privilege of divination, and the determination of the fate of humankind. All this was accorded him. After his victory in this monumental civil war, the gods expressed their gratitude by awarding him fifty titles, each corresponding to a divine attribute. He became (because he earned it, because he was beloved by his peers, or because he demanded it as part of his tribute) "the light of the father who begot him . . . He who knows the heart of the gods, Guardian of justice and law, The creator of all things . . ."[2]

After Marduk had absorbed the identity, functions, and prerogatives of the other gods, he organized the universe at will and fixed the course of the heavenly bodies. He created humans, he said, from the blood of the vanquished Kingu, a captive god of the underworld who had sided with Tiamat and therefore against him during the Civil War.

Marduk was also "Lord of Life," the great healer who took the place of Ea, his father, in magic incantations. He obtained the governorship of the four quarters of the Earth, became the supreme commander of the Anunnaki and determined men's and women's fate in the Duku, the "pure abode," during the feast of *zagmuk*. He was generally represented with a scimitar felling a winged dragon, indi-

---

[1]Felix Guirand, ed., *New Larousse Encyclopedia of Mythology*, translated by Richard Aldington and Delano Ames (London, England: Hamlyn House, 1959), p. 55.
[2]Ibid.

cating his victory over Tiamat, and so he appeared in the Esagil, his famous temple in Babylon.

"I caused a mighty wall to circumscribe Babylon in the east," wrote Nebuchadnezzar. "I dug its moats; and its escarpments I built of bitumen and kiln brick. At the edge of the moat I built a powerful wall as high as a hill. I gave it wide gates and set in doors to be called 'The Gates of the Lord'; of cedarwood sheathed with copper. So that the enemy, intending evil, would not threaten the sides of Babylon, I surrounded them with mighty waters as the billows of the sea flood the land."[3] The Citadel of Babylon was impregnable to assault, yet its destiny was written. The enemy conquered from within.

The literature of Josephus, Diodorus, Ctesias and Strabo, in the cuneiform inscriptions describing the internal power struggles within "the wicked city," also relate the abundant use of stone, water, and gold. The Hanging Gardens of Semiriamis, devoted to that "androgynous queen who flew out of the palace in the form of a dove, in which shape she entered directly into immortality," constituted a technical marvel of their day.[4] The vaulted architecture, the shafts that served as wells using chain pumps to furnish a continuous supply of water, and the stone brought from a respectable distance ironically combined to qualify the children of the demanding and insatiable Marduk as "unworthy of the royal dignity."[5] The god therefore endlessly compelled them to amplify their complex of palaces, their lavish decoration, shining brick reliefs, their miracle of splendor.

Genesis 6:3–4 according to Ceram, describes the Tower of Babel: "And they said one to another, Go to, let us make brick, and burn them thoroughly. And they had brick for stone, and slime had they for mortar. And they said, Go to, let us build us a city and a tower, whose top may reach unto heaven; and let us make us a name, lest we be scattered abroad upon the face of the whole Earth."[6]

Every large Babylonian city had its ziggurat, but none compared to the Tower of Babel. According to an examination of the excavations, 58 million bricks were used in its construction. The whole landscape was dominated by its terraced mass, composed of the "haughty palaces of the priests, capacious storehouses, innumerable exotic spaces, bronze gates, circumambient fortifications with tall portals and a forest of a thousand towers, a staggering impression of greatness and abundance seldom seen elsewhere in the mighty Babylon

---

[3]C. W. Ceram, *Gods, Graves & Scholars: The Story of Archeology*, chapter 20, "Koldeway: The Tower of Babel." Translated from German by E. G. Garside (New York: Alfred A. Knopf, 1952; revised edition published 1967), pp. 284–286.
[4]*Gods, Graves & Scholars: The Story of Archeology*, p. 287.
[5]*Gods, Graves & Scholars: The Story of Archeology*, p. 286.
[6]*Gods, Graves & Scholars: The Story of Archeology*, p. 288.

kingdom." The Jew of the Old Testament considered the sight "a monument to arrogance."[7]

Nabopolassar wrote that at the time Marduk commanded him to rebuild the Tower, which had become weakened since it was razed during the reign of Hammurabi, his instructions specified the grounding of the base securely upon the breast of the underworld, whereas its pinnacles should strain upwards to the skies. Nebuchadnezzar, Nabopolassar's son, continued, "To rise up the top of E-temen-an-ki that it might rival heaven, I laid to my hand."[8]

The Tower, erected by slaves, was built in the hollow known as *sachn*, "a simulacrum of the ancient sacred precinct where was built the ziggurat of *Etemenanki*, the 'House of the Foundation of Heaven and Earth,'" wrote Robert Koldewey, the German archeologist and art historian who began the excavation of Babylon in 1898.[9]

Herodotus described the series of eight superimposed stages. The uppermost terrace, he said, "formed the base of a temple that looked out far over the land. The lower temple housed the image of Marduk, half animal, half human, made of pure gold, seated on a throne beside a large table, again of pure gold, with a gold footstool."[10] According to Herodotus' calculation, the total weight of the statue and accoutrements amounted to eight hundred talents. In one of the priestly houses the "ur-talent" was found, a stone duck, with an inscription that explained a true talent to amount to 29.68 kilograms, or 66 pounds.

Marduk himself was said to hover within the precincts of the Tower. "They say," said Herodotus, during a visit in 458 B.C., "that the god himself lies down upon the temple couch."[11]

Each year the god's statue was carried along the Avenue of Procession, a street in the form of a trench integrated into the city's defense system. This Sacred Way, 73.6 feet wide, was lined with a parade of one hundred and twenty lions, each nearly seven feet long, adorning the walls in colored glazed reliefs, their maws gaping in prideful splendor to bare their teeth, with white or yellow pelts and yellow or red manes, against a background of light or dark blue glazes which repeated the glazed brickwork of the topmost Tower temple. The breccia slabs, veined with red and white, each bore an inscription: "Nebuchadnezzar, King of Babylon, Son of Nabopolassar, King of Babylon, am I. The road of Babel I have paved with Shadu slabs for

---

[7]*Gods, Graves & Scholars: The Story of Archeology*, p. 290.
[8]*Gods, Graves & Scholars: The Story of Archeology*, pp. 279–296.
[9]Ibid.
[10]Ibid.
[11]Ibid.

the procession of the great lord Marduk. Marduk, Lord, grant eternal life."[12]

Tkulti-Ninurta, Sargon, Sennacherib and Assurbanipal stormed Babylon and destroyed the shrine of Marduk, the great and invincible *Etemenanki*, the Tower of Babel. When the god died he was resurrected, like Dionysus, the might of Babylon faded before the rise of Ninevah.

CARD DESCRIPTION

The card of the sixteenth arcanum illustrates The Tower, shattered by a thunderbolt from the dark night sky. Struck by lightning, as the Tower of Babel was destroyed in the Bible, the structure is consumed in flame, "a rain of celestial fire" like that caused by Tletonatiuh, to shower down on the Mexicans.

Two men fall from the top of The Tower. One wears a crown. The other's hair is disheveled, indicating fear. The limbs of the one form a figure similar to the Hebrew letter "Ayin," meaning "a material tie" or bond, "a connection in a state of tension," like the taut coil of a spring.

Physical destruction is clearly visible in the figure of the shattered Tower, like the demolishing of the Babylonian ziggurat that had been intended as a stairway to Heaven. High places were associated with power, authority, or supremacy, as well as the spirit of wisdom in divine communion. The Persian mystic Zoroaster was said to have spent seven years in silence in a cavern on a mountain at Yezd now in Iran, resisting the demons and the temptations of Angra Mainyu, (agonized or negative thought), who offered him an earthly kingdom, which Zoroaster repulsed with his mortal aim described as the striving for perfection in thought, word, and deed. "With the sacred mortar, the sacred cup, the word of Mazda [god of Persian royalty] my own weapon, as with a sword I shall vanquish thee."[13]

---

[12]*Gods, Graves & Scholars: The Story of Archeology*, p. 294.
[13]Felix Guirand, ed., *New Larousse Encyclopedia of Mythology*, translated by Richard Aldington and Delano Ames (London: Hamlyn House, 1969), p. 312.

In certain decks the figure of a woman appears, moaning below The Tower, the "fallen woman" from "the wicked city." In other cards the destruction takes place as a result of the loosening of the bricks and stones used in The Tower's construction. Occasionally one or another tarot illustrates the figure of the tower with drops of rain in the shape of the Hebrew letter "Yod," indicating the collapsing of the Life Force, thus reducing it to the level of material existence.

CARD SYMBOLISM

Lightning and a "rain of fire" provoked the destruction of Babel, and of other real and mythological towers, which dared to brush too close to Heaven. The Supreme Gods as well as the conquering storm gods, not only demanded restitution but unleashed what they termed the weapons of the tempest, the supreme temptation.

The crown, symbol of material ambition and possession, falls from the head of one of the men in the card, as he tumbles from the crumbling structure, as power and vanity equally crumble, or great cities or empires, elevated on pride or personal gain.

The power struggle on the heights is equally manifest at the corporate or the empirical level, yet the person of conscience—like Zoroaster, Zeus, Buddha, Dionysus, or Christ—seeks the top of the mountain in quest of strength and communion, in a struggle with his or her highest moral aims. The catastrophe implicit in the card indicates conflict and oppression, the consternation of the moaning woman, obstacles overcome only with great difficulty. Yet by virtue of the method of the "bond," suggested in the "state of tension," this arcanum expounds logic, *eliminatio logica*, the deduction required in the construction of a hypothesis.

When the confirmation of one thesis results in the logical exclusion of all others, the result is a metaphysical *monomania*. Destruction, therefore, is only relative. The power of concentration in universal wisdom only perpetuates, by means of the authority of The Magician in the first arcanum, a fully protected action. There can be no downfall then, without the potential for recovery and regeneration.

The emblems of Zoroaster became the instruments of the personal fortress of the mind: the sceptre for the condensation of the dispersed ambrosia, the chalice as a fulcrum for the imagination, the sword for dispersing the "improperly condensed"—that is, for repelling an attack—and the pentagram, that mystic reminder of perfect freedom.

LAMATL XVI

MYTHOLOGY OF CE-QUIAHUITL (THE RAIN)

This thirteen-day period begins with the rain, but in this case a "rain of fire," or lightning, thunder, meteorites—every celestial rampage of angry fire from a vindictive sky, born in the province of the fire serpents, the property of a private Heaven.

It was told in the codices that on Day 4 Rain, the Sun of Tlaloc—the Rain God—would fade forever. During this time humankind lived on the seed of an aquatic plant called *acicintli*, "water corn." It all ended, according to the Borgia Codex, when Quetzalcoatl, as Tletonatiuh or Tlequiahuitl, made "fire to rain from heaven" and the thunder and lightning crashed over the face of the earth until humankind took the form of birds.

Quetzalcoatl appointed Tlaloc's wife, Chalchiuhtlicue, to be the new Sun. During this period people lived on teocentli, the wild maize called "divine corn." Yet all existing humans had to be changed into fish as a result of a deluge; the rain was so heavy and so abundant that the skies fell in. After the end of the era, on Day 4 Water, a new Sun had to be created, according to the legend, along with a new race of people. The four Creator Gods decided to build four highways through the center of the Earth, in order to raise the sky again. Tezcatlipoca, here a benevolent deity, with Quetzalcoatl, his brother, made trees in order to lift and hold the new sky in place.

To drain off the waters of the deluge, Tepeyolotl, "Heart of the Hill," built the mountains, and in them stored, as if in a great bowl, the waters of the Great Flood. Tepeyolotl entered the hills in the form of lightning that fell from the sky and symbolized the thunder and fire in the night.

A few men were saved after the deluge, because Tezcatlipoca advised them to row away in a canoe, to a mountaintop, the only dry land that had been spared by the flood. They returned to low ground after the floods subsided. Yet they were very hungry. At the sight of so many fish they decided to prepare a modest feast. One of the men made a fire by rubbing two sticks together. But Tezcatlipoca, enraged at the use of fire without his specific authorization, changed the inventive survivor into a dog called Chántico, "In the Abode," and made it the god of the hearth.

The lamatl is represented by this deity and by Tonatiuh, solar fire, the Sun. Yet the sign's patron is Tlaloc, the Rain God associated with mountains, high hills, and their rings of thunderheads. Among the Mayas the god took the shape of a turtle and was called Ayatl, a likeness of the same turtle believed by the Hurons and the Iroquois to have rescued Ataentsic when she fell from the sky into the abyss left when the Tree of Life was uprooted and nothing remained below but a huge blue lake. The shell of the turtle, then, expanded and became the surface of the Earth.

The Maya glyph, *canac*, means "tempest" and further refers to the torrential rains, the electrical storms and hurricane winds described in relation to the period of Tlaloc's Sun. Tlaloc, in fact, lived in an elaborate palace complex, behind Popocatepetl—the princely sentinel volcano of the Valley of Mexico—and from his terraces and courtyards dispensed the water or droughts, fruitfulness or barrenness, thunder and lightning, drizzle and flood that dominated Mesoamerican life. He was Zeus and Dionysus in Nebuchadnezzar's citadel, an Aztec Marduk who inspired some of the most lavish and monumental cities in Mexico. The Pyramid at Cholula and the ceremonial center at Teotihuacan rivaled the height, the scope, and the grandeur of the mountains around them, so human daring and sheer force of will, a limitless access to building stone, and a reliable supply of slaves finally approximated the magnitude of the work of the Creator Gods themselves.

The slaves, like those of Babylon, came from many nations and spoke in many tongues. Their difficulty in communicating with each other was offset by the overlords, who in fact benefited from their incommunication.

Chicomecoatl, goddess-regent of the lamatl, a sister of the *tlaloques* (the souls of the dead in Tlaloc's heaven who served him as lesser rain gods), was called "Seven Rattlesnakes." She, like Demeter, was a goddess of maize, beans, herbs, and seeds, including the *chía*, which was brewed into a Mesoamerican ambrosia, nectar of the gods.

Tlaloc's heaven, the Tlalocan, served as the abode of young corn, and for the germination of the tender shoots, the eastern counterpart of Tamoanchan in the west, where the flowers grew, where full, ripe corn was harvested and where Cinteotl, the "Goddess of Corn," and Xilonen, "Mother Corn Tassel," the gleaner, had always lived.

Mesoamerica's complex ceremonial organization was closely tied to Aztec political structure and to the strictly observed social stratification. Yet, the great religious ceremonies required the participation of all levels of society. Often the king himself officiated at the sacrifice, extracting the real or symbolic heart of the victim to offer it, as did Pallas Athene, still throbbing, into the hands of the gods. The cult of Tlaloc, the rain god, involved a number of young priests who were equally permitted to participate in the wars and to attain high military rank, awarded in relation to the number of prisoners taken. Other priests remained exclusively devoted to ecclesiastical pursuits and were called *cuicanime*, "cantors." One of the highest religious offices served Tlaloc, the Quetzalcoatl Tlaloc Tlamacazqui, "Priest of the Pluvial Plumed Serpent." Though the lesser rain gods were feted through half the year, during the summer solstice Tlaloc's priests devoted themselves to fasting and ritual baths, sacrifices in the name of the Rain God, and communion with the lesser rain gods from the highest available vantage point, either on or facing the mountains, especially the *Huey Tozoztli*, the hill identified with Tlaloc himself, said to be nearer to heaven than to earth.[14]

---

[14]The "hill" might possibly refer to the graceful Ajusco, a mountain on the southwestern rim of the Valley of Mexico.

LAMATL DESCRIPTION

The lamatl is represented by Tlaloc, the god of rain, accompanied by the deity Nahui-Ehecatl, "Four Winds," called by the Mayas "Hurricane." The god is surrounded by innumerable offerings, exactly like the tribute of the gods of the mountains and caves: a bouquet of herbs, a pouch of copal, reeds, a bundle of bone, and the maguey thorns used in the so-called self-sacrifice. Jaguar paws were also used as offerings, as they symbolized Tepeyolotl, the "heart," that is, the "spirit" or "soul" of the mountain.

Certain codices illustrate a torrent of water sweeping objects and people before it, as an illustration of the destructiveness of the elements. Tlaloc, as Tlequiahuitl, the Sun God, as the incarnation of the "rain of fire," appears with the symbol of tempest and lightning in his hand. Nahui-Ehecatl carries a serpent falling downward, indicating the celestial serpent that carries water which it funnels through its body.

In the Telleriano-Remenesis and the Vatican Codices, Tlaloc appears with a blue pouch of copal in one hand and the emblem of lightning in the other. His figure looms atop a mountain, a volcano from which smoke belches into the sky.[15] Other codices further depict a man carrying lightning in the form of Xiuhcoatl, the Fire Serpent, on his back, describing the suffering and devastation, the death of everything in their path, when the forces of nature are unleashed in all their fury.

---

[15]The entire central plateau of Mexico is dotted with volcano cones, which extend especially into the state of Michoacán to the west. None were more vitriolic and vengeful, however, than Xitle, perched on the lip of the Valley of Mexico above the lava flow called the Pedregal, which it formed when it emptied its entrails of lava over the pre-Classic site of Cuicuilco (600–150 B.C.).

Figure 28. Tlaloc, the rain god. From the Códice Borgia.

LAMATL SYMBOLISM

The divinatory significance of the card is related to destruction and death, the circumstances varying according to the hierarchical position or the power of those affected by the lamatl. The sign indicates personal affliction as much as the wiping out of entire cultures.

The explanation of the cosmic holocaust is inextricably bound to the legend of the Five Suns, describing the cataclysmic devastation during the four eras that preceded our own. Water inundated people and turned them into fish. Jaguars and other wild beasts roamed the Earth and devoured the giants. Fire that rained from Heaven burned men and women alive and the wind blew across the land, uprooting everything in its path. Humans turned into monkeys. According to the legend, Mesoamerica now lives its fifth era, in which humankind is destined to perish by earthquake. On this day, Day 4 Movement, the end is seen to be apocryphal. Stones will tumble from the towering temples. Flames will engulf the crops. Pestilence and famine will accompany the shaking of the Earth's layers, until nothing is left but a blinding light.

PARALLEL SYMBOLISM

The titanic power of the gods and the natural forces of the cosmic elements are counterposed in both the tarot and the *Tonalamatl* with the ambitions, vanity, and pride of humankind. The highest places, reserved for a communion with serenity and wisdom, are invaded by the pompous. The natural cycles of the Earth—consecrated in sowing and planting, reaping and grinding—are interrupted by the construction of great citadels, the waging of wars, passions, abuses, and wickedness, until the gods call humankind to accounts for the violation of all the divine precepts.

The terror of the cataclysm and the loneliness of the aftermath are emphasized in the juxtaposed symbolism of the Tower of Babel and the Pyramid of Cholula, where the men who laid the stones and brick mourned their incommunication while they berated the arrogance of the kings and overlords.

The great structure at Cholula was said to be the tallest of the pyramids of antiquity, erected to rival the mountains themselves, in the hope of providing humankind with a shelter from floods and storms.

Tlaloc represented the benevolent god of the fertilizing waters but he could equally become the malicious Quiahuitl, whose warming rains and fruitful nectar could turn to fire, lightning, thunder, havoc, the devastation of empires, the frustrating of conquest, the disruption of all orderly existence.

If the birth of every child and the demise of every man and woman obliges, in microcosm, a repetition of the patterns of the Earth and the Cosmos, then these processes, far from punishments, must be seen as indispensable stages, visible at any distance. They are as clearly etched as the terraces of Babel, as well fortified, equally vulnerable, equally ephemeral, but in the end, a fragment in a totality far greater than the sum of its parts. The totality is life, the continuity of existence, the vortex that whirls away into space and returns, to begin its cycle all over again.

ARCANUM XVII

MYTHOLOGY OF THE STAR

The seventeenth arcanum is related to the planet Venus, whose rites in antiquity were associated with the warrior Ishtar, of the Assyrians and Babylonians, treated so roughly by Gilgamesh. She was a daughter of Sin, the Moon, and sister of Shamash, the Sun. She personified "lovely" Venus as goddess of the morning and the evening star. She became Athtar to the northern Arabs, Allat to the southern Arabs between the Persian Gulf, the Indian Ocean, and the Red Sea. As Anahita she was particularly venerated by the Chaldeans. The later Moslem Arabs incorporated her into the prestige in which astrology was held, as cold, dry, but a favorable influence. To the Phoenicians, she was Ashtart, the most beautiful of the heavenly bodies in the sky of Ba'al. To the Syrians, she was Astarte, named for the Phoencian queen who confided her child to the care of Isis. She was Astarte as well for the Greeks.

Hesiod's *Theogony*, a poem written in the eighth century B.C. and which represents the oldest Greek attempt at mythological literature, considered Astarte—an early fertility goddess whose domain embraced all of nature—to constitute an important factor in the formation of the cult of Aphrodite, the deity associated with both the most exalted and the most degraded love. An example of the latter occurred when she insisted in carrying off Phaeton. This impetuous boy was especially identified with the planet Venus. He was to have been the guardian of Aphrodite's temple. Unfortunately, the presumptuous son of Eos with Aurora (who was called by Homer the "rosy-fingered dawn with snowy eyelids" suffered a disastrous fate when the unruly steeds of Helios' chariot, at the inexpert hands of the rash youth, brushed too close to Earth. The rivers dried up and the soil began to smolder, until Zeus struck down the boy with one of his thunderbolts.

When the reckless and impassioned Aphrodite, as Venus of the Heavens, appeared in the sunset, the Greeks called the planet Hesperas Aster; as a herald of the Dawn (her fleeting and frustrated mother-in-law), she was Phosphoras Aster. The Sumerians saw her as the guide, Innana, who "lighted the way for the stars." Because she appeared at dawn and with the twilight, this "daughter of the Moon and sister of the Sun" was considered the intermediary between the divinities of daytime and the night.

As she was related to the Sun, she was called "The Valient." When she appeared in the morning, she was "Our Lady of the Battle," who presided over the maneuvers of war and killing. Her sisters included the goddesses of Hell, where the Sun hid itself during the hours of darkness. Religious literature designated her "The Lioness of the Gods of Heaven."

Her bond with the night made Venus one who propitiated voluptuousness. She was the goddess of love and pleasure, and so she was called by the Romans. Her cult was associated with sacred prostitution. She was at home in the heavens or, like Ishtar, storming the gates of the underworld. The "omnipotence of love" gave her far-reaching powers. In spite of the violence and irritability of her character, she could be tender, maternal, even devoted. She was the "Star of Lamentation," who sowed hostility and disorder. She was forever poised with her arrows, as Ishtar was pictured, in a chariot drawn by seven lions, to "cover with combat, arrayed in terror."[1]

Yet, she could speak to Ashurbanipal: "My face covers thy own face like a mother over the fruit of her womb and I will place thee like a graven jewel between my breasts."[2]

To contemporary interpreters of the tarot, she is associated with Mercury, or Hermes, deity of gamblers, though it was actually Venus who was known as the "Queen of Destiny" and "Lady Luck." Such an interpretation, however, in ancient times, led to the card's designation as *Stella Magorum*, the Star of the Magician, mistakenly described afterward as "The Star of the Magi," referring to the priestly covenant that originated among the Median tribe in Persia. Their ritual eventually expressed the ancient Aryan cults that had managed to persist in Azerbaijan, in the mountains of Central Asia.

These early fire-priests evolved into the zealots of Mazda, a god of Persian royalty who finally eclipsed all other divinities, in his particular sphere of influence. There, he became the god of gods, master of the heavens and creator of all creatures, associated with the Sanskrit *medha*, meaning "wisdom," or with *mada*, indicating "intoxication," or with *mastim*, "illumination," considered a dispenser of "transcendent powers." This Ahura Mazda, a metaphysical more than a mythological figure, was represented by the sculptors of Persepolis in the Assyrian style, as a man with a venerable beard, the protective divinity of Darius.

---

[1]Felix Guirand, ed., *New Larousse Encyclopedia of Mythology*, translated by Richard Aldington and Delano Ames (London: Hamlyn House, 1969), p. 58.
[2]Ibid, p. 60.

His body is plumed, with symmetrical and majestic wings. He wears the tail of a bird that plunges vertically, not unlike the sweeping plumes of the quetzal. The hieratic serenity of this Lord of the Heavens hovers, according to the legend, as the evening star in the atmosphere, and bears witness to his royal qualities.

Like the Quetzalcoatl he resembles, he created all things and surpassed humanity in every way, but in contrast to the modest and ever-humble Plumed Serpent of Mesoamerica, Mazda, as a winged prophet and in his own words, had no human weaknesses.

CARD DESCRIPTION

The card is simple in meaning and design. High in the sky a large, eight-pointed star appears, surrounded by seven similar, but smaller, stars, Venus as the Sumerian Innana. Beneath the stars a nude girl is poised, kneeling in the parched grass, watering the dry soil from one vessel while she pours water into a pond from another. One vessel is gold, the other silver.

Behind her a colored butterfly sits on a rose. The right foot of the girl is half-submerged in the shallow, transparent water of the pond. The ground beside her appears infertile, despite the sparse grass. The sterile landscape rolls away toward the bare mountains in the distance.

Occasionally the stars are designed to conform to the five points of the Pentacle, or Star, of Solomon, indicating an association with magic. Other cards illustrate a bird in a tree instead of the butterfly on the rose. Often a lotus, another sacred symbol, appears. The butterfly is sometimes interpreted as Ibis, who is furthermore illustrated in a number of tarots as the Egyptian representation of the soul.

The seven smaller stars are considered in certain interpretations to symbolize the Pleiades. The principal star is indicated as the cosmic energy of light. Very ancient decks depicted only the seven stars, to emphasize the astrological association of the card. Other tarots illustrate two stars of different colors, and superimposed, shining on the figure of the young woman.

CARD SYMBOLISM

The central figure of the young woman is intended as Eve, or Humanity. The bright star, or stars, above her head are considered Human and Divine Nature, often superimposed, source of light itself, translated in the seven-pointed star as wisdom, or as the divine principle that sets the initiate on his or her course.

The star, depending on the composition, may form a double triangle, seen as the counterposed law of Opposing Forces, yet the number seven indicates universal harmony, a reconciliation of violence and tenderness. An eight-pointed star symbolizes the harmony between humankind and the Cosmos, inherent yet precarious, in the balance at all times.

The hieroglyph corresponding to the seventeenth arcanum depicts a throat with a tongue, that is, speech, or hope, communication, an extension of the private dimension in which all things are confined.

Spes, or Hope, another of the Arcana's titles, suggests a radiant light in the darkest hours. Yet without the support of judgement and intuition this hope is false and misleading, the most deadly, according to the Greeks, of the contents of Pandora's box. The living language of nature, however, affords information and guidance, divination, an assortment of practical truths to motivate hope, and to provide the setting to best benefit from all its indications.

Hope is seen as the Source, regeneration through the new freshness of the polarity, active and passive, translated in the gold and silver vessels. This awareness reveals the ability, like that of the butterfly, to distinguish a rose from a weed, and so come to rest on it.

The beneficence of the water, which restores life and fertility to the parched land, is seen as a release from possession and the acquisitive death in the midst of apparent abundance—an abundance of sterile and lifeless objects, for the young woman pours water *into* the pond, rather than drawing water away from it.

Thus the card is a promise, of rebirth and revitalization, the renewal of all that blooms and is lovely—a thought, a deed, the land, life itself—in the enrichment of giving.

LAMATL XVII

MYTHOLOGY OF CE-MALINALLI (THE TWISTED THING)

Quetzalcoatl, the spirit freed from any association with matter, was pictured as the Plumed Serpent. He was Master of Life, Creator, and Civilizer, patron of every art. He might have stolen corn from the ants, or received it from the gods, according to the legends, but he gave it to Chicomécoatl, the goddess of rural plenty, the Mesoamerican Ceres, and she in turn gave it to Cintéotl, the goddess of corn, for when he aroused the maiden Mayáhuel, the maguey goddess of the pulque, it was he who brought love into the world. According to the codices, it would seem these three goddesses were one, three representations of plenty, three faces of Eve.

Quetzalcoatl was traditionally represented as a white-haired old man with a long beard, like the Persian Mazda, dressed in a full robe, his face and body painted black, wearing a mask with a pointed red-colored snout. When the treacherous plotting of Black Tezcatlipoca led to the breaking of his vows on a night of drunkenness and lust, and when Quetzalcoatl had burned his houses, built of silver and shells, when he had buried his treasure, "no longer of any worth," he became the Star of the East, the Evening Star, and joined the realm of Tlahuiz-calpantecuhtli, Lord of the Red Glow of Dawn, Metzli, the Moon and Tonatiuh, the Sun, to become one of the Brothers of Heaven.

The thirteen-day period called Ce-Malinalli is considered "everything twisted," represented as a sickle or a twisted rope, indicated in certain codices as the lower jaw of a skull from which a sickle emerges. The sign's regent is Pactécatl, (also spelled Patécatl or Pachtécatl) Lord of Pulque, at times termed Ometochtli, the rabbit of drunkenness, feted in the harvest season of the Fall.

In the Vatican Codex, Mayáhuel, Quetzalcoatl's tenderly awakened love, appears as the sign's patroness, as the goddess of prosperity and the Earth's bounty, in her advocation as Chicomécoatl, the "Seven Rattlesnakes" of corn, beans, grass, herbs, all that is sustenance, vitality, and abundance.

She appears as well as Cintéotl, or Tomtéotl, the goddess of the ripe corn at the time of the harvest, when the waters of the rainy season have soaked the Earth and brought the land to green lushness. This is the time when the sugar cane and maguey, swollen with ripe juices, are "cured" with pineapple and other fruits, corn and other grasses, to produce the rich and potent brandies, pulques, and wine, the essences and extracts of hallucination and transfiguration, when hope is heightened and illusion becomes reality. Then fear, violence, frustration or confusion are set aside for a time, while "the wild beast is tamed," according to the codices, the rebellious are made docile, the unhappy are blessed, adulterers repent, the wealthy turn generous, and the newborn are baptized.

These gods originated in Meztitlán in the Huastec region, where the Otomi people once lived. This venerable tribe is not only one of the most ancient in Mesoamerica, but is also responsible for worshiping the gods of "the six regions of the world." Among them, Pactécatl was considered of primary importance, while the great goddess Huetztonatzin, Mother of all the Gods, eventually became Chicomécoatl, Goddess of Sustenance, everything that can be eaten or drunk, all that nourishes by means of the mouth, throat and tongue. She is therefore, by inference, communication, the nourishment of the mind and spirit, translated into flavor and festivities associated with eating and drinking, the communion of the table, the cup or vessel, and all that the gods give and receive by virtue of the Earth's riches.

The celebration of these gods varied from region to region but were consecrated throughout Mesoamerica. Especially in "the hot country" along the coastal plains, young people participated in the rites associated with an initiation into puberty, an introduction into the mysteries and the bounty of sex. Pulque, Mayáhuel's emblem, was an important factor in the ritual, which honored this goddess of the four hundred breasts, "she who nourished the earth" with the blood released really or symbolically, from the tongue, ears and genitals, by means of the carefully stipulated application of maguey thorns.

The "self-sacrifice" served as a petition, a supplication before the gods for their blessing in the form of the fertilizing waters and the Earth's plenty. When the dry winter and the parched land broke into bloom with the spring monsoon rains, it was considered that the gods had heard the prayers of men and that the dusty soil, now damp and black with richness, would bear fruit.

This rite of reincarnation, the resuscitation of everything green and living after the long months of dryness, was inextricably bound to the image of inebriation, the limp "dead" form of the drunk restored to "life" after the effects of the drink had passed. The accompanying symbolism usually evolved in a logical progression, from euphoria to violence, to maudlin tenderness, to passivity and remorse, into lucidity, and finally the capacity for revivified action, when the "arrows" of the maguey thorn had found their mark, had released the demons of evil from the soul, and had restored the inebriant to a "restructured" view of his or her position and obligations.

This awareness of life and its cycles demonstrated the extraordinary harmony between humans and their world, in the recognition of the cyclical processes of the human spirit: the soul requires "fertilizer," "hoeing," and "weeding" as surely as the crops, for it is just as subject to the debilitating effects of neglect, blight, insects, thirst, and exhaustion. Humankind, then, was seen as inseparable from its setting. It was its own crop. And while the Earth's bounty rewarded human faith and effort, it was humankind, in its conduct and rectitude, which represented the true and unparalleled harvest of the gods.

LAMATL DESCRIPTION

In the *Tonalamatl* of the Aubin Collection, Chicomécoatl is shown with a pouch for copal, the *copalxiquipilli*, in her hand, while behind her a maguey can be seen and beside it, a tree in bloom.

The Borgia Codex depicts the goddess with a round-bellied jug, the *octecómatl*, ordinarily destined for pulque, with drawings all around it like a Greek amphora. The base on which the vessel rests, in the Vatican Codex, is a coiled rattlesnake dotted with black, symbolizing the starry night. The upper portion of the lamatl illustrates the twilight at evening, composed by means of signs of the Sun and the night, designated as the time of the banquet and the pouring of the ritual pulque. A drinker is seated, facing the goddess.

Figure 29. Mayahuel or Chicomecoatl, goddess of the agave or maguey. From the Códice Borgia.

In the Bourbon Codex and the *Tonalamatl* of the Aubin Collection, the pulque jug is shown along the upper border of this sign's card, against the background of a night sky filled with stars. The drinker is replaced by the figure of a man, carrying a staff across his back. A heart is impaled on the point of the staff. In his hand he carries a banner made of precious feathers.

In the Bourbon Codex, he is further distinguished by the "crown of the starry night," *ihuitzoncalli cicitlallo*, identified with a Black Tezcatlipoca from whom emanate various spirits: the green, blue, yellow, and white Tezcatlipoca. In the Telleriano-Remenesis Codex, in place of the figure, a noble appears carrying the banner of plumes. The *aztaxelli* of his crown or circlet indicates he is a warrior, in a representation of Black Tezcatlipoca, the scurrilous god who plotted Quetzalcoatl's downfall, symbolized in the banner. In place of the staff across his back he bears a hatchet fashioned from ears of corn. He is presumed to represent Cintéotl, the ripe corn.

The Maya god of maize, Yum Caax, the counterpart of the Aztec Cintéotl, was associated with life, prosperity and fruitfulness, but never with death or the flaccid image of the intoxicated drinker. His portrait was normally good-natured, reflecting the Maya's impassioned attachment to the soil. He was shown with the elongated, flattened forehead cultivated by Maya aristocracy, obtained by tying boards to the forehead in infancy. The resulting shape symbolized both the ear of corn and the rattlesnake, key to Maya civilization on the Yucatán Peninsula.

LAMATL SYMBOLISM

This lamatl was related above all else to the spirit, hope, intuition, and the innate gift of divination, encompassed in Providence and supported by a general optimism in the contemplation of nature. The fatality of existence was therefore to some extent alleviated by faith, prayer and ritual, which included a tolerance for fallibility.

If the rains, or the crops, occasionally failed, the fact would be assimilated, within the span of a lifetime, or a century, even an aeon, for another was always assumed, and another after that, providing pessimism was exorcised from daily existence. If the world ended, if the Sun faded or if the stars digressed in their journey, another Sun would rise on another world and different stars would continue another course, for human destiny was neither less nor more grand than the destiny of the Cosmos.

PARALLEL SYMBOLISM

Both the tarot and Tonalamatl stress the bond between the fertility of the Earth and the sacred juices which flow freely with the coming of spring, expressed in a communion through the oral passages.

The young girl in the arcanum, like Mayáhuel or Chicomécoatl in the lamatl, controls the liquids sacred to the perpetuation of life, the moisture required by the soil for its fruitfulness.

Yet the quality of giving is characteristic in both interpretations. These fluids are *offered* and are replenished, by forces beyond man or woman's determination, in an act equivalent to the deliverance in love's abandon.

Both cards refer to reincarnation, to the revival of the dead and the resuscitation of the vital forces in the male-female, that is, the active-passive bond. The lamatl, like the arcanum, stresses the vessel and the pouring, in a symbolic reference to the act of fecundation, and both further depict a plant, the product of fertility, as a resting-place for the spirit.

In the Bourbon Codex, the Moon god Teccitecatli, or Metzli, appears, accompanied by a cluster of stars, interpreted by some as the Pleiades, that cosmic center of the Nahuatl universe. It was told that from a star, Cirius or Aldebaran, the Nahua's ancestors came, and that the Moon god lighted their way across the heavens until they came down to earth in this lusty, beguiling land, where according to the codices the high mountains towered over panting jungles and the plains stretched in the distance until they fell into deep gorges; where coursing rivers tore a path through dense forests until they lunged against the sea, and there they heaved and tossed until the brown waters mixed with the salty blue. There the fish leaped and the white birds glided against the hazy green and shimmering lagoons; and the gods were happy with this place, and content to remain.

It was said that for this reason the Moon god wore the crown of seven stars, which symbolized the secrets of the universe, and the wisdom and the wonder of all the cosmos, of the marvelous roads traveled by other people and other civilizations far away, on the other side of the Milky Way, not visible to this generation of humans because of the blinding light of Venus.

That quarrelsome yet loving planet, which lights the morning and the evening and demands her reward before she will allow this culture to see any farther than it does now, is "only waiting," according to the legend, "for man to display his understanding and his acceptance," but when that day comes, "he will sprout wings, like a bird, and be admitted into the most distant domains, for there lies his true province, the spirit, like Quetzalcoatl, freed from the material world."[3]

[3]Eduard Seler, *Comentarios al Códice Borgia*, Vol. 1, "Four Times Five Guardians of the Phases of Venus" (Mexico: Fondo de Cultura Económica, 1963), pp. 204–205.

ARCANUM XVIII

MYTHOLOGY OF THE MOON

The ancient cult of The Moon was observed throughout the world, inseparably associated with the Sun, for the Earth's satellite, having no light of its own, depended on the splendor of solar radiance, reflected so mysteriously by this elusive, intriguing, often incomprehensible silver body, which waxed, waned, vanished, and reappeared with alarming regularity.

The Moon was considered the First Deceased and was intimately bound to funerary rites and to the journey to the underworld. It was identified with the gods of the Nether-Regions: Ament, Nephtys, Osiris, Neheh, Persephone, Hades, and Hermes.

The Moon was related to Juno and Hera. Because of its dual manifestation, it was both the Gate of Heaven and the Portal of Hell. It was associated with Artemis and Hecate. The former served as a favorable indication, the latter, fearful—Hecate, disposed at will and by her caprice, of youth, magic, and witchcraft.

The ancient Jews were considered Children of the Moon and owed, it was said, their errant and nomadic heritage to its whim. The "King's Daughter," as the Moon is described in the Kabbalah, represented the element Water. In certain cultures, however, the Moon is related to Fire. The Assyrians identified the seductive silver body with Ishtar—"Thou hast loved the lion," Gilgamesh told her, "and thou hast dug for him seven and seven pits! Thou hast loved the steed, proud in battle, and destined him for the halter, the goad and whip."[1]

The Egyptians associated the Moon with Isis, the Greeks with Selene, as the cosmic symbol of the feminine spirit, of fecundity, but also of the erratic, the unconscious, of nocturnal existence and death.

The Babylonians saw Sin, their Moon god, as male, the night from which light had emerged. An old man with a long beard the color of lapis-lazuli, he was Nannar at Ur. He normally wore a turban, and "god's own crown." He was an enemy of evil-doers and he mea-

---

[1] Felix Guirand, ed., *New Larousse Encyclopedia of Mythology*, translated by Richard Aldington and Delano Ames (London: Hamlyn House, 1969), p. 58.

sured time. The successive and regular transformations of this "Lord of the Diadem" lent Sin a certain inscrutable quality. He was considered to be a singular being whose deep heart no god could penetrate.

The various cultures of Indonesia and Polynesia looked upon the Moon as the brother of the Sun. Both were children of a deity or of the first men, or were formed from certain parts of the body. According to the Kavan of central Borneo, the Moon is one of the descendants of the armless and legless being who came from the sword handle and spindle which fell from Heaven.

In the Gilbert Islands, the Sun and the Moon, like the Sea, are the children of the first man and the first woman, in disregard for the concerns of the Supreme Deity, who had forbidden this and who made his wishes known by means of his messenger, the eel. In Minahassa, in the Celebes, the Sun, Moon, and stars were formed from the body of a heavenly girl. In the Society Islands, Samoa, and New Zealand, they were usually thought of as children of Heaven who were later placed in the sky as eyes.

In Queensland, the Sun, a woman, was made by the Moon, with two legs, like humans but with a great many arms, which may be seen stretching out like the rays when these bodies rise or set. In the Palau Islands, two supreme deities created the Sun and Moon by cutting two stones with an adze and then throwing them into the sky. In the Admiralty Islands, the first two inhabitants of the Earth, after planting trees and creating edible plants, made two mushrooms and threw them into the sky—one became the Sun and the other the Moon.

In Woodlark Island the only person to originally possess fire was an old woman. In vain her son scolded her for not wanting to share it. So he stole it from her and gave it to the remainder of humankind. In her rage, the old woman took the fire she had left, divided it into two parts and threw these into the sky. The larger became the Sun, the smaller the Moon.

Among the Euahlayi, at one time there was no Sun, but only the Moon and stars. According to the Arunta of central Australia, the Moon in the mythical period was the property of a man in the Opossum totem. Another man stole it. The man was unable to catch the thief and shouted to the Moon to get into the sky, which it did. On its way, however, it fell off a rock and hurt its back. Thus, from time to time it appears bent over with pain.

At Aneityum, in New Hebrides, the Sun and Moon were considered husband and wife. They first lived on the Earth, somewhere in the east, but later the Sun climbed into the sky, telling the Moon to follow him, and she obeyed.

According to the Warramunga of northern Australia, the Moon emerged from the ground in the form of a man. One day he met a woman, called to her and they sat down to talk. A fire caused by the carelessness of the hawks surrounded them and the woman was seriously burned. The Moon then cut one of his veins and poured the blood on the woman, thus restoring her to life. They then both went up into the sky.

The shore-dwellers of Princess Charlotte's Bay tell of the Moon who assisted a man whose arm had caught in a tree while he tried to reach for honey. When the man had freed his arm he avenged himself on all who had refused to help him, by setting fire to a bush. But first he looked after the Moon's safety by moving him to different hiding-places, finally placing him in the sky to escape the fire.

According to a legend from Papua, New Guinea, a man digging a deep hole one day came on a small bright object. He picked it up, but the object began to grow bigger; then slipping out of his hands it rose up in the sky and became the Moon. The light would have been brighter if it had stayed in the ground until it was born naturally, but as it was taken up prematurely, the light it gives is weak.

In the Cook Islands, two deities were debating the paternity of a child. Each claimed to be the father. To pacify them, the child was cut into two pieces. Vatea took the upper half, which was his, and threw it into the sky, where it became the Sun. Tonga-iti at first kept on Earth the lower part which had been allotted to him, but later, in imitation of Vatea he threw it into the sky, where it became the Moon. But as it had lost its blood and had begun to decay, it shone with a paler light.

In the Marquesas, this lesser light was justified by the failure of the deity who created the Moon to restrain his longing to eat porpoise, the skin of which was black. Conversely, the whiteness of the Moon's light is explained by Hanua, its mother, eating the pulp of the white coconut while she was pregnant.

The spots on the Moon gave rise to various versions. One of them describes Rona, who one night in New Zealand went out by moonlight to draw water from a stream. But when she reached her destination the Moon disappeared behind a cloud so that Rona stumbled over the stones and roots. In her annoyance she insulted the Moon. He became so enraged he came to Earth, seized Rona and carried her off with her water gourd, her basket and the tree to which she clung, which can be seen to this day.

The phases of the Moon are explained by the Maori myth of Rona, in this case male, in pursuit of his wife. He appeals to the Moon, also male, who refuses to help him. He and the Moon then spend their lives eating each other, and so the Moon diminishes. Then they both regain their strength and their vigor by bathing in the live water of Tane, after which they begin their struggle again.

CARD DESCRIPTION

Of all the arcana, the eighteenth is considered the most ominous and unfavorable, despite the various associations with the Moon throughout history. It describes the most dangerous conditions in which a human can place him or herself, that is the absence of insight, symbolized in the roof that appears in the hieroglyph. But far from the protective shield against external vagaries, this is a limiting and oppressive roof, an obstruction, freedom compromised, disaster and calamity.

At the top of the picture, the Moon sheds its light, in exact accordance with the laws of the physical world, in effect, fate. The Moon directs its rays toward the Earth but this is an insubstantial and reflected light, without warmth, without radiance or the ability to really illuminate.

In the background of the picture the binary of two towers, or two pyramids as shown in earlier decks—symbolically considered the Pillars of Hercules (Herakles) at the entrance to the Greek underworld, or the kabbalistic columns of Boaz and Jakin—are separated by a twisting path, strewn with clean sand, on which are clearly visible a few drops of blood. Vital energy has been dissipated in ignorance or materialism, says the sermon, indicated in the two mysterious towers, like the vitality or the essential energy of past or future incarnations.

In the foreground of the card a wolf, considered man's obvious and traditional enemy, sits on the left. To the right of the "tragic path" sits a dog, revealed as a "false friend." Presumably, only a moment ago, it was licking its master's hand. Both animals are howling at the Moon. A puddle shines in the moonlight. A lobster crawls through the water of the puddle.

CARD SYMBOLISM

The Law of Hierarchy establishes the priorities of the community over the private interests of a single entity. Self-preservation, as indicated in the mystery of Baphomet, has been resolved in the group, which necessarily dominates the individual. Yet *Crepusculum, Hierarchia Occulta, Hostes Occulti* and *Pericula Occulta*, other names by which the arcanum is known, suggest the ominous materialism becoming treacherous.

The physical dangers implied in the card are no more than the ordinary risks in any enterprise, on any passing day. The only difference is expressed as imminence. Implied dangers have become a reality. Our luck has run out. No protective shield stands between us and the fall.

Enmity and betrayal, implicit in the message, further suggest weakness and disunity, expressed in the binary. Both our conduct and our choices, suggested in the twisting path, have deviated from rectitude and coherence. The pale light will be our only light. Yet it shines equally on evil and faithlessness, expressed in the wolf and the dog. Nevertheless, it attracts, even distracts them. Perhaps we will come to our senses long enough to make use of the diversion. Yet we, ourselves, have propitiated the falsity. We became susceptible to flattery. We grew vain. Our world was transformed by moonlight. Ruse has replaced strategy. Wit has eclipsed intelligence. And the common aide has been recruited in the absence of a friend.

The Arunta myth of the Opossum totem describes a man who died and was buried but some time later came back to Earth in the form of a child. On reaching adulthood he died a second time and went up to Heaven, where he became the Moon. Since then, the Moon dies and is periodically reborn.

"The Moon," said Plutarch, "is the mansion of the good man after his death. There he lives a life neither divine nor blessed, but at least exempt from pain. Man must die twice. Once on the Moon during his process of decarnation and once as a prelude to reincarnation."[2]

---

[2]Plutarch, *The Lives of the Noble Grecians and Romans,* in *Great Books,* Vol. 14, "Theseus," Dryden Translation, (Chicago: Encyclopedia Britannica, 1952), p. 14. Also available from AMS Press, New York, under the title *Plutarch's Lives of the Noble Grecians and Romans,* 6 volumes, translated by Thomas North, 1986.

LAMATL XVIII

MYTHOLOGY OF CE-MIQUIZTLI (DEATH)

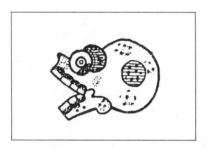

Natives of this sign were counseled not to quarrel or to mistreat their slaves, especially at this season. In fact, according to Sahagún, "At this time it would be prudent to visit every indulgence on one's slaves, to soap their heads, bath them, make them gifts, for they are beloved sons of *Titlacauan*."[3]

Tezcatlipoca, honored during this thirteen-day period, would, in the absence of the prescribed conduct, "procure sickness, poverty, ill-fortune and the lot of the slave. He would take away what one owned and had gathered together." Therefore, and despite all the god's "annoying" admonitions, no one should "despise Tezcatlipoca, nor wish his death, for then that person would die."[4]

The inference however was considered more a chastisement than a threat. The persistent subject of death was neither shunned nor repulsed among the ancient Mesoamericans. On the contrary, it was lauded: in art, legend, and religion, in the calendar, in ceremonial and political organization, in every phase of the life in which it played such an inextricable part. Death was additionally significant in construction and architecture. The gigantic scale of Teotihuacan, the astonishing proportions of its extension and the magnitude of its grandeur, were essentially consecrated to death, and to the Sun and Moon.

The Pyramid of the Moon, the oldest temple in the city, though smaller than the Pyramid of the Sun, was not only harmonious in proportion but dynamic in its role. It was there the Avenue of the Dead ended, at a broad plaza, beyond which a wide stairway, divided by terraces, ascended to the temple on the structure's crown.

---

[3]Fr. Bernardino de Sahagún in *Historia General de las Cosas de la Nueva España*, Book 4, Chapter IX (Mexico: Editorial Porrua, 1979), p. 232.
[4]Translated by the authors from Fr. Bernardino de Sahagún, Franciscan; Angel Maria Garibay K., ed., 1979, Mexico, Editorial Porrua, S. A., Book 4, chapter X, p. 233.

This temple honored Tecciztécatl, "He of the Seashell," the Moon. It was said that the world was first lighted only by the fires of the Creator Gods, until they produced a sadly insufficient halfsun. A grand council concurred that a "Sun should shine on the earth and this Sun would nourish itself on human hearts and quench its thirst with blood." For this reason, according to the codices, "there must be War, to supply the Sun with hearts and blood." *Hearts* originally referred to "the spirit" or "the soul" of men. The blood, symbolic or otherwise, so dearly beloved by all ancient cultures, involved "the ritual blood of human vitality, blood which makes the gods themselves beholden."[5]

The gods then gathered at Teotihuacan, for they needed a candidate, a volunteer for the personage who would become the Sun. Only Tecciztécatl, "He from the Place of the Seashell," came forward. There could be no contest, however, without another candidate, so the gods selected Nanahuatzin, "The Pustule," known also as "the Syphilitic," one of the most derided and despised among the Mexica pantheon. This could also be interpreted as an allegory regarding appearances, that most deceptive of characteristics.

In preparation for the ceremony, a great fire was lit and the two candidates spent four days at fasting and offerings. Tecciztécatl was very wealthy, so he was able to offer thorns—a reference to Quetzalcoatl's penance or sacrifice—fashioned of coral and precious stones, as well as rich bundles of quetzal plumes, pouches of gold and copal.

Nanahuatzin was poor. He offered only bundles of green reeds, emblem of Quetzalcoatl as Ce-Acatl, lumps of the sacred moss called *pachtli*—the herb used to season the ritual pulque—maguey thorns anointed with his own blood and, in place of the pouch of copal, the scabs from his pustules.

The gods then caused "a tower like a mountain" to rise in honor of each candidate. These became the two pyramids at Teotihuacan. Following the penitence the contenders were dressed and led before the fire. "It first fell to Tecciztécatl, whom the gods ordered he throw himself into the fire." He tried four times and each time he hesitated. He was unable to fling his purified body into the flames.

The gods then spoke to Nanahuatzin, who closed his eyes and unhesitatingly leaped. At the sight of his unswerving devotion Tecciztécatl gathered his courage, and finally stumbled into the fire. Nanahuatzin of course was instantly converted into the Sun. His hideous figure was glorified in his devotion to duty; his redemption in the brilliance of the warming light of the Sun was complete. He

[5]Fr. Bernardino de Sahagún in *Historia General de las Cosas de la Nueva España*, Book 7, Chapter I (Mexico: Editorial Porrua, 1979), pp. 431–432.

thus served as an example to the pious never to be deceived by the shallow or the superficial.

Tecciztécatl, on the other hand, became the Moon. Its lesser light, the gods explained later, was due to the fact that they had looked upon the scene with "a rabbit before their faces,"[6] thus obscuring a portion of the light, but in fact, the description refers to the ritual *tochtli*, or rabbit, of the pulque, that is, of inebriation.

Another version, however, clarifies that the dimmer light of the Moon was the result of the diminished fire. By the time Tecciztécatl threw himself into the "sacred conflagration" nothing was left but the coals.

If was said that the Sun was the child of Quetzalcoatl, while the Moon was the son of Tlaloc and Chalchiuhtlicue. Nonetheless, despite the dynamic of these geneological references, the movement implicit in the Rain and the Wind, the slithering or the plumed creatures that were their symbols, these heavenly bodies, upon their appearance in the sky, remained perfectly static. The gods realized they would have to devise some means of setting them in motion, and so "allowed themselves to be slain by Ehecatl," the Wind, an advocation of Quetzalcoatl, who managed to capture each of the resigned but reluctant gods in turn. The rush of their souls leaving their bodies instigated the momentum which set the Sun and Moon on their course through the heavens.

One of the gods, however, the mischievous page called Xolotl, like Hermes, managed to escape. Quetzalcoatl nevertheless captured this God of Duplicity after he had exhausted a number of disguises, including animals and plants such as corn and maguey. Xolotl was finally trapped beneath the water, like the lobster in the eighteenth arcanum.

The Moon began its journey *after* the Sun. It seems it had been anchored to the horizon by the Demons of the Night, the malicious *tzitzimime*, until sunset, in a premeditated confounding of Quetzalcoatl's intentions.

The ancients utilized both the lunar and solar calendars, along with the synodic reckoning based on the course of the planet Venus, but favored the greater precision of the Moon's indications. The Mayas believed eclipses were produced when ants ate away at the Moon, yet their calendar was a marvel of calculation and deduction, surpassing the Egyptians, the Greeks, the Romans, and the Jews in their cyclical divisions.

---

[6]Fr. Bernardino de Sahagún in *Historia General de las Cosas de la Nueva España*, Book 7, Chapter I, p. 433.

LAMATL DESCRIPTION

Tecciztécatl, the Lunar God, appears in most of the codices as the figure of a man with a staff in his hand, depicted with the attributes of a priest. He is often shown with white hair and the features characteristic of old age. He is always associated with the image of a seashell. He usually wears a crown of stars or is accompanied by the symbol of midnight.

In the Bourbon Codex, he appears with attributes related to Mixcoatl, the God of the Hunt, one of the Four Creator Gods, another manifestation of Black Tezcatlipoca. He is shown with a deer caught in a trap and bound by the hunter, a reference parallel to Artemis, or Diana—the Greek and Roman, respectively—goddesses of the hunt, also associated with the Moon.

Androgynous Tecciztécatl is shown in certain codices in a dual manifestation, as the solar god face to face with the lunar deity. The identification with the seashell apparently refers to the mysteries of fecundity, a curious association with Astarte-Aphrodite. She was said to have been born of a seashell in the spume which appears in the sea, a foam that bubbled and boiled from the wine-dark cauldron, when the drops of blood from Uranus' offended members were hurled into the water by Cronus.[7] The ancient Mesoamericans, who practiced ritual self-mutilation, presumably applied a maguey thorn or any other sharp object to the earlobes, tongue, lips and nose, but especially to the male organ. When flayed, pierced, perforated, or sliced, the penis then "gave forth of the beneficent blood which brought fertility to all it touched, nourished the gods and made them beholden to man, who in his renunciation and his sacrifice, his penance and his love, anointed his god with his own vitality."[8]

---

[7]Felix Guirand, ed., *New Larousse Encyclopedia of Mythology*, translated by Richard Aldington and Delano Ames (London: Hamlyn House, 1969), pp. 130–131.

[8]Fr. Bernardino de Sahagún in *Historia General de las Cosas de la Nueva España*, Book 4, Chapter IX (Mexico: Editorial Porrua, 1979), pp. 231.

Figure 30. Tecciztecatl, of the sea conch and god or goddess of the Moon. From the Códice Borgia.

LAMATL SYMBOLISM

In Mexican mythology, the deer is always associated with the Moon. Its soft color, say the myths, identifies it with the Sun that pursues, teases, or plays with the Moon in order to finally surrender before its gentle beauty. The rabbit also represents the Moon. The gods were said to have "struck the moon across the face with a rabbit," or that "a rabbit came between them and the Moon," though the interpretation probably refers cryptically to inebriation.[9]

---

[9]Fr. Bernardino de Sahagún in *Historia General de las Cosas de la Nueva España*, Book 4, Chapter X, pp. 231–232.

The lamatl confirms the Moon as a deity of the night, intimately associated with water. The Moon is depicted as Tecciztécatl with his staff, symbolizing the metaphor of the Moon as a nomadic old man—the "Wandering Jew" or Mazda, even Quetzalcoatl—who occasionally is obliged to confront the Sun, symbol of power and wisdom, with the sagacity of his own experience. Thus the lamatl implies a transitory death. Tecciztécatl-Tezcatlipoca and Tonatiuh appear as the Moon and the Sun of daytime, reborn with each dawning, after which they must again cross the heavens, confront each other, vanish in the firmament and reappear, as the counterposed images, or images in pursuit of each other, of the complement, and of the essence of light—that is, fire and water, night and day, feminine and masculine.

PARALLEL SYMBOLISM

Both the tarot and *Tonalamatl* describe the abundant, intricate, often contradictory and definitely ambivalent symbolism surrounding the Moon, with astonishing coincidences in a lunar disc with a feminine face despite the reference to the "man in the Moon" characteristic in Western Civilization, seen in a vessel containing water, with a rabbit or other animal trapped in the liquid, in a parallel to the image in the tarot, or the male-female juxtaposition of the solar and lunar figures.

The esoteric almanacs visualize the Moon as an errant body, regularly traveling through space, appearing or disappearing with beguiling constancy, like the menstrual or ritual blood whose drops appear in the eighteenth arcanum, associated with penance and fertility.

The dog and the wolf in the tarot, like the deer in the lamatl, involve our (humankind's) complex association with the animals of the Earth, on which we depend, not only for sustenance or companionship, to share our burden, or the vicissitudes of our existence, but which also symbolically reflect our own virtues or defects. In our anthropomorphic folklore usually howling at the Moon, moonstruck, or "lunatic," reveal especially our rejection or our identification with the so-called "lower echelons" of evolution. The ritualized aggression of the wolf pack or of wild hunting dogs or of hyaenas corresponds not only to our own atavistic hunting hierarchies but to our political and ceremonial organizations as well, to such an extent that our human society frequently qualifies this connotation of our own attitudes and structures as the counterpoint of our spiritual aspirations, the negative of the appetites as opposed to the positive of prayer and penitence: instinct as related to reason, the unconscious as the counterpart of the conscious, the id as opposed to the super-ego.

Yet this hierarchy, in both humans and animals, indicates the capacity to consult and decide, advise and consent. Such a parliament of consensus permits the survival of many, in contrast to the convenience of a few. Therefore the Moon is tantamount to death. While the semiotic relationship is expressed in the lunar deities or in the divinities who were somehow involved with the dead in the nether-regions—Ishtar, Isis, Artemis, Mixcoatl, Hermes, Quetzalcoatl, Black Tezcatlipoca—these gods were equally allied with the hunt or with battle, with predators who strike in the night, those circumstances which eclipse the radiance of the Sun and leave only the pale gloom of night everlasting: the dark Cosmos, lighted only occasionally with the glimmer of stars like the torches or lanterns of Hell.

The divinatory arts of the *Tonalamatl*, which, like the tarot, refer to vanity, betrayal, false loyalties, and the illusion in physical appearances, were reinforced in the sign called Ce-Miquiztli, or Death, represented in the codices by a skull, or death's head. Rather than the gaping skull of any other lamatl, however, this figure is silent, leering, and serene. "Truly," describes the Maya *Popol-Vuh*, "there was at one time little light over the Heavens and Earth, which existed, but the face of the Sun and the Moon were completely covered, and gave no expression."[10]

For the Mayas, the Moon was a woman, the Sun's wife, in a vision similar to certain of the cultures of Oceania. This lunar goddess protected and aided women during childbirth and was the goddess of medicine. According to the legend, the Sun and Moon lived together as a couple on the Earth, "and were happy," like the god-twins who "came to this land before man was created, and overcame a giant and his two children, divinities of the earthquake. The divine couple, our Mother and Father, turned one of these into a stone and the other was made to carry a mountain on its back. They poisoned the giant."[11]

The Toltecs, after their occupation of Teotihuacan, also spoke of a giant, or a race of giants, the *quinametzin*, who ostensibly designed the city and conceived it in their own massive proportion. The enormous pyramids of the Sun and Moon, the colossal citadel and the monumental Avenue of the Dead, along with hundreds of lesser structures, were erected stone on stone from the lava that had long before been hurled out of the bowels of the Earth by three ancient volcanoes.

---

[10]*Popol-Vuh, Las Antiguas Historias del Quiché (Maya)*. Adrián Recinos, trans. (Mexico: Fondo de Cultura Económica, 1952), pp. 32–33.

[11]Felix Guirand, ed., *New Larousse Encyclopedia of Mythology*, translated by Richard Aldington and Delano Ames (London: Hamlyn House, 1969), p. 450.

Though no one knows who built Teotihuacan originally, it remained for all time as the city where humans turned into gods for there, it was told, the Sun and Moon were created. According to the legend, its streets were paved with gold. The brightly painted murals on the temple walls, the irrigation systems, aqueducts, homes, and palaces served as the setting for the Moon cult, among others, for more than four hundred years.

While the Moon of the eighteenth arcanum is described as negative, the lamatl claims the disaster or destruction to be relative. The ancient Mesoamericans were adamant on the subject of fatality, yet equally obsessed with self-determination, the mutability of destiny in response to supplication, penance, or the reassembling of emblems, as well as a merely temporary withdrawal until more favorable indications incited the passive to renewed action. Failure could then be conceived in terms of a reduction of losses. Calamity was depicted as recoverable.

On these terms their philosophy resembles Zen, in which nothing is "bad" or "evil" as such, except in the interpretation or in its application to its accompanying elements. Yet even these can be reversed, diverted, reconstructed, or negated. The hand is dealt. It will be played well or badly depending on the will of the player, his or her adaptability to the conditions of the moment, his or her stamina, and perseverance, and his or her sensitivity to the waxing and waning of circumstance.

Destiny, then, may be written by the gods. But for humankind, fate will always be reduced to the conjunction of the imponderable.

ARCANUM XVIIII

MYTHOLOGY OF THE SUN

The Sun has been the king of the heavens since the beginning of civilization on this Earth. He is bright, radiant, and luminous, associated with everything warm, healthy, alive, joyous, the ascendance of the victorious, all that commands respect and glory.

The Cult of the Sun, the Royal Hunt of the Sun, the lust for gold, yellow flowers across green fields in summer, Monet's dappled gardens, are all associated with the astral monarch. For the painter Van Gogh, the rapturous yellow of his palette was love and the sun, forever united. When his colors turned dark, as had happened with other painters, he had entered, according to brother Theo, the darker phases of the night and the attraction of the Moon, which served to confirm his lunacy and decline.

The Sun, along with its inseparable companions, the Moon and the stars, governed the firmament, and was encompassed in the figure of heroes, conquerors, giants, the Creative Force, and the vital source of all that was heat and light. Egypt's Ra and Assyria's Asshur—the winged disc—were not only supreme deities but great gods of fertility. "Kiss the feet of the King of Asshur, and in his name thou shalt surely triumph over thine enemies."[1]

The Babylonian Gilgamesh sought the secret of escaping the inevitable fate of death and so undertook the journey to consult Uta-Hapishtim, that fortunate man who survived the deluge and "so received the gift of immortality from the gods." The road was long and dangerous but the prodigal Gilgamesh "would face all perils. If I meet lions and am afraid I shall raise my head and call upon Sin, the wisdom of the Moon. To Ishtar, courtesan of the gods, my prayers shall rise."[2]

And so he reached Mount Mashu, "and here, every evening, the Sun reposed." The gates of the mountain were guarded by scorpion men, "whose heads touched the terrace of the gods and whose

---

[1]Felix Guirand, ed., *New Larousse Encyclopedia of Mythology*, p. 57.
[2]C. W. Ceram, *Gods, Graves & Scholars: The Story of Archeology*, Chapter 19, "Geo Smith: The Story of the Flood." Translated from German by E. G. Garside (New York: Alfred A. Knopf, 1952; revised edition published 1967), pp. 275–276.

breasts reached the netherworld. Their dazzling brilliance overthrew mountains."[3]

The cylinder seal of the Phoenicians associates Hau-Tau of Nega, hero of another saga, with the Egyptian sun-god Ra. He was later identified with Ba'al, and with the cult of Adonis, in a wooded region where various kinds of conifers grew. This spirit, called the "forest vegetation" eventually metamorphosed into a tree, like those used by Quetzalcoatl and benevolent Tezcatlipoca to raise the sky after the deluge. The Egyptians adopted Hau-Tau and related him to Osiris. The resin of the conifers was, according to Plutarch, Osiris' tears. The pyramid texts mention Hau-Tau of Nega, with whom the pharaoh is identified in his tomb, in a supplication, that the dead king be absolved from the fate of Osiris, that is, the transformation into a tree.

In the first millennium B.C., when every town in Phoenicia honored Ba'al, yet refrained from uttering his name, this solar deity was worshipped at Gublia and Berytus as the female Ba'alat, identified with the Egyptian Hathor, with the Greek Astarte—or Ishtar-Aphrodite—and finally, by virtue of the characteristics of a marine deity, as the divinity of the all-important Phoenician ports. Now male, the figure became Melkart, the hero, "God of the City," equated with Herakles, and with Adonis, that direct successor of Hau-Tau of Nega, who replaced the vegetation gods of the Ugarit poems.

Adonis had been born, according to the legend, of a tree into which his mother had transformed herself. At his birth, Aphrodite placed him in a coffer which she confided to the goddess of the underworld, Persephone. But, when she came to reclaim the coffer, Persephone had already opened it, beheld the great beauty of the figure inside, and refused to relinquish it. During the ensuing dispute, Zeus intervened and decreed that Adonis, like Persephone herself, should remain half the year in the underworld and half on the surface of the Earth, with Aphrodite, who as was her custom, had fallen deeply in love with the young god.

This Adonis was manifest in the seed of corn. His name, a Hellenized version of the Semitic adoni, "my Lord and Master," was likened to the Tammuz of the Assyrians, the Mesopotamian vegetation and corn god. He was Eshmun, the god of health, associated with the Greek Asclepius. He was Aleyin and Mot in the saga by Panyasis. He was described by Damascius. His cult flourished near the source of the Nahr Ibrahim, between Lebanon's Byblos and Baalbek in the grottoes and the splashing rivers that coursed along verdant, wooded

[3]C. W. Ceram, *Gods, Graves & Scholars: The Story of Archeology*, Chapter 19, "Geo Smith: The Story of the Flood," p. 277.

banks, before the river finally plunges into the depths of the gorge, and there the god perished.

Although the Greeks considered Apollo, like Tonatiuh, to be the god of solar light, the Sun itself was personified in Helios, especially on the island of Rhodes, consecrated to his worship. The colossal statue of Helios, the renowned work of the sculptor Chares, ninety feet high, called one of the eight wonders of the ancient world, permitted ships in full sail to pass between the god's legs. When the bronze sculpture had been toppled by an earthquake, it was told that Helios was drowned in the ocean by his uncles, the Titans, and then raised to the sky, where he became the luminous sun.

Every morning Helios emerged in the east from a swamp formed by the river-ocean in the far-off land of the Ethiopians, later defined as the source of the Blue Nile, the power and thrust that drove a Nile finally green onto the sands of the desert, where it could be worshiped by the Egyptians.

To his golden chariot, which Hephaestus had fashioned, the Horae or seasons harnessed the winged horses, dazzling white, their nostrils heaving forth flame.[4] Helios then took the reins and climbed the vault of Heaven. "Drawn in his swift chariot he sheds light on gods and men alike; the formidable flash of his eyes pierces his golden helmet; sparkling rays glint from his breast; his brilliant helmet gives forth a devastating splendour; his body is draped in shining gauze whipped by the wind."[5]

At midday Helios reached the zenith of his course and began his descent toward the west, arriving at the end of the day in the land of the Hesperides, where he seemed to plunge into the Ocean. There he found a barque or a golden cup, also formed by Hephaestus, in which his mother, wife, and children awaited him. They sailed all night and in the morning regained the point of departure. The abode of Helios was said to be the isle of Aeaea, where his children, Aeëtes and Circe lived. His horses rested on the Islands of the Blessed, at the western extremity of the Earth, where they browsed on a magic herb.

As a reward from Zeus, Helios was granted an island just emerging from the waves, which he named after the nymph Rode, whom he loved. He disputed the Isthmus of Corinth with Poseidon. He owned, on the isle of Thrinacia, seven herds of oxen and seven flocks

---

[4]Although this word can be literally translated as "hours," it originally denoted the seasons of the year. (Edward Tripp, *The Meridian Handbook of Classical Mythology* (New York: New American Library, 1974), p. 307.

[5]Felix Guirand, ed., *New Larousse Encyclopedia of Mythology*, p. 139.

of ewes with beautiful fleece, each herd consisting of fifty head. The number always remained constant, like the three hundred and fifty days and nights of the solar year. When Odysseus and his companions "cut up the flesh of the sacred cattle and fixed it to their skewers,"[6] Helios threatened to shut himself up in the kingdom of Hades and shed his light on the Dead, but he was placated by Zeus.

As god of light he saw everything and knew everything. Like the Mesopotamian sun-god Shamash he discovered the crimes of the wicked. He loved, but in Greek tradition was faithless. If one of his loves died of despair, as Ovid said, he tried to bring warmth to the frozen limbs, but in vain. The deploring Clytie, like any other scorned lover, could only quench her thirst with the dew and her own tears. Her body at last took root in the soil, as the fragile heliotrope. The myth says that her head became a flower bright as the violet and in spite of the root which held her fast to the ground she turned her face toward Helios, whom she never ceased to worship.

CARD DESCRIPTION

The hieroglyph of the nineteenth arcanum refers to an axe, the vehicle or implement of liberation, the means of nullifying the oppressive roof in the eighteenth arcanum.

The Sun depicted on the card is illustrated with a human face, surrounded by rays of light and drops of dew, a golden moisture that sprinkles over and around two children playing under this astral protection. Some of the rays are smooth, others are seen to be undulating.

In the most ancient tarots, instead of the children, two young lovers are illustrated, walking hand in hand across a grassy knoll surrounded by flowers. Other cards show a man spinning, or pulling, a thread from a skein he holds in his hand, referring to the spindle from which the world was formed. In another deck a euphoric child appears under the Sun, mounted on

---

[6]Ibid.

a white horse and holding aloft a flag or banner, like St. George. He has vanquished the reptile from which a chaotic world evolved, in order to reign benevolent, in light and good deeds.

Most modern tarots depict the two children, nude or clothed, playing within a circle drawn on the grass in front of a low wall.

CARD SYMBOLISM

Since the card is equated with light, that is, hope and progress, this arcanum is associated with the ultimate truth of being, expressed in its first title, *Veritas Fecunda*, Fruitful Truth. This fertile light is intended as the Law of Hierarchy which indicates the second title, *Virtus Humana*, Human Virtue, and the elixir of life, expressed in the third title, *Aurum Philosophale*, Philosophers' Gold.

The mystery in true understanding, as encompassed in this "transitional" arcanum, refers to philosophic alchemy, in which knowledge is genuine power, a concept expressed by Athene in her temptation of Paris.

The resplendent light of the Sun, transformed into the golden rain over the heads of the two children in the card, is then interpreted as human enlightenment, gone beyond the dimension of the ordinary, into the realm without limit which deplores the conditioned or the predictable, despite the limitations imposed by the wall, which in effect serves as protection. Rather than a restriction, the circle or fence determines the place over which the rays of the Sun are shed, an enlightened demarcation for the eternal child, playing his eternal game in the eternal garden.

And if children are presumably free of the "poverty of spirit" imposed on adults through conditioning, then their ingenuousness also relieves them of preconceived evil or sin. They frolic unhampered, under the blessing of divine light, within the precinct of a moral law they are more than prepared to respect, for it represents their protection, a defense against external danger.

If for some the card indicates the fraternity of the vain and the hypocrisy of the presumptuous, the stones in the wall are then seen as the hieroglyph of truth, of the absurd, and of the infinite in the philosopher's stone; the wall is prodigal, blessed by logic against the vagaries or the imposition of convention.

If the rays of the Sun are often rich and warming—that is, smooth—they can extend beyond their stipulated province. The ancient cultures spoke of many suns. When one grew too hot or powerful it was destroyed by earthquake, a "rain of fire" or flood, until it could be recreated within its assigned jurisdiction, for even the Sun, exalted deity, a motivating force, a commander of all it surveyed, might never presume to absolute omnipotence. A force even larger, brighter, and stronger lies beyond its reach.

LAMATL XIX

MYTHOLOGY OF CE-XOCHITL (THE FLOWER)

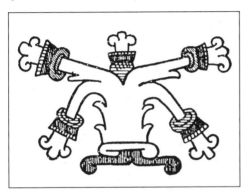

The flower which symbolizes the thirteen-day period called Ce-Xochitl describes the beauty, the pleasure and splendor, in the lush abundance, fertile bounty and unrestrained voluptuosity of nature.

Everything considered lovely and which contributed to life's joy — art, craftsmanship, skill, music, games, dance, poetry, love, and erotic delight — were associated in the Mesoamerican world with this sign. Its goddess-regent, and all the wealth in its symbolism, was incarnate in the figure of Xochiquetzalli, "Quetzal plume" or Quetzal flower," goddess of the flowers, of the water that bubbled forth from mountain springs and the beauty of the birds in the forest, expressed in the tropical quetzal bird, whose vivid green plumes in fact swirled, and were described as a river, or a cascade seeking its final abode.[7]

Xochiquetzal was the goddess of spinning and weaving, the womanly arts and crafts, a parallel to Athene, who counseled the wise application of her knowledge. She was often identified with Tonacacihuatl, "Our Lady of Sustenance," who presumably fashioned the young goddess from her own hair.

In the legends of the various tribes from Tlaxcala, Xochiquetzal was Tlaloc's wife and was therefore, in a variation of Chalchiuhtlicue, the goddess of water. Yet she violated her vows when she ran off with the seductive and malicious Black Tezcatlipoca, so she grew old

---

[7]Though Sahagún writes "Xochiquetzalli," the codices normally refer to "Xochiquetzal." In either case the term refers to the same deity and the spelling, here as elsewhere, can only be an arbitrary interpretation of the original texts, as documented by later priests and scholars.

and wrinkled, according to the myth, and too corrupt to remain in her happy land. Until then however, she had lived in a delectable place, in which fountains, rivers, and flowers abounded. There, jesters entertained her with music and dances while she applied herself to her womanly spinning and weaving.

The patron of these musicians and dancers was Xochipilli, "Prince of Flowers," a beardless young god described as a model of manly grace and fine figure. He was said to have come from *Tamoanchan Xochitlicacan*, where the flowers are thrust from the ground, located to the west, where Cintéotl, the corn-god was born, and where *Chichihualcuautli*, "the suckling tree," distilled the milk which fed the souls of young children who had died, say the codices, before the age of reason. There they all frolicked at the foot of the *Tonacacuauhtitlan*, "The Place of the Tree of Sustenance," in the Heaven inhabited by the Creator Gods, the Lord and Lady of Abundance.[8]

Here were all manner of trees and fruits, and the souls of children, joyfully transformed into hummingbirds, who "suckled the honey from the plants." This reference to Huitzilopochtli, the hummingbird, God of the Sun, and to sweet fluids and dew — the radiance of the Sun turned to drops of wisdom, fulfillment and plenty, suggests the heroic Gilgamesh, who filled a pot of jet with honey and offered it as a gift to Shamash, the Sun.

If Xochiquetzal, "of the flowers," was originally young, uncorrupted, fresh, and tender, the Mexicas claimed it was because she was spun from the hair on the head of their Mother, the first woman on Earth. She was fruitful and joyous, they said. She who saw in love the flower of fulfillment rather than the perversity or aberration, "that which incites a tired spirit to prodigies of further exhaustion."

She had been created, they insisted, as a companion for the diaphanous solar deity, Piltzintecuhtli, son of the Creator Gods, occasionally seen as the infant divinity associated with the young Quetzalcoatl, or with the corn god Cintéotl. The latter was said to have been born to them after the deluge.

This fourth section of the *Tonalamatl*, One Flower, designates as its regent the Old Coyote, Huehuecoyotl, the god of song, dance, music, voluptuous sexuality, and perseverance. He was undaunted, even overwhelming, in his vital generosity. His garments, as illustrated in the codices, describe him as a god of fire and the Sun. His red face, decorated with yellow, reaffirms the characteristics of a solar deity. He caused sound to erupt from musical instruments and lightened the hands of craftsmen. He turned the feet of dancers "into

---

[8]Fr. Bernardino de Sahagún in *Historia General de las Cosas de la Nueva España*, Book 1, Chapter XIV (Mexico: Editorial Porrua, 1979), p. 40.

feathers," that never "touch the ground, so they may proceed through the night, bringing life to the dark earth until the sun emerges at dawn."[9]

Huehuecoyotl is one of the oldest divinities in the Mesoamerican pantheon. The Otomies, the most ancient inhabitants of Mexico, said to descend directly from the Olmecs, worshipped him as Tatacoada, the Old Father, or Progenitor. He is always accompanied by musicians and attendants, whose melodies provide his entertainment.

In the Aubin *Tonalamatl*, Huehuecoyotl is accompanied by Macuilxochitl, elsewhere called Xochipilli, God of Pleasure, or the "Jovial God." He, like Hau-Tau of Nega, son of Ra, was the son of Piltzintecuhtli, "offspring of the Sun." An ingenuous god of youth, of song, dancing and flowers, he expressed the awakening of nature in the springtime. The cantors who praised his glories in their songs said he came from that distant and idyllic place of flowers, and appeared specifically to perform the duties of the priest who accompanied the Sun. He was Tlahuizcal-pentecuhtli, the "Great Red Lord of the Dawn."

Certain versions describing the First Couple depict Huehuecoyotl, the Old Coyote, as "the Cuckold," defined as he who permitted betrayal. His wife is Ixnextli, "Face of Ashes," charged in the codices as "she who sinned by cutting the roses."[10] As a result of Ixnextli's transgression, the couple were expelled from *Tamoanchan*, and were sent to follow a prodigal Piltzintecuhtli, who went to the underworld and returned, though he died eventually, like Gilgamesh, in the quest for immortality.

---

[9]Fr. Bernardino de Sahagún in *Historia General de las Cosas de la Nueva España*, Book 4, Chapter VII, p. 230.
[10]Ibid.

LAMATL DESCRIPTION

In the Bourbon Codex, Huehuecoyotl is represented as a human figure with a coyote's mask. As a breastplate he wears an enormous pectoral of jaguar skin, adorned with seashells, symbol of his alliance with Tecciztécatl, the Moon, who ruled the tides of the seashore whence he first came to Teotihuacan. The figure is highlighted by a conch cut in cross-section, symbolizing Huehuecoyotl's high standing in the priestly hierarchy.

His garments are decorated with eagle feathers, which identify him as a solar god. He is accompanied by characteristic weapons. These personify his standing as a warrior in the "hot country" of the Huastecs. His headdress is fashioned according to the dictates of Tonatiuh, to emulate the Sun God he is also intended to represent, and with whom he is equally associated.

In the Vatican and Telleriano-Remensis Codices, Huehuecoyotl is accompanied by the goddess Ixnextli, an advocation of Xochiquetzal, but specifically after her transgression. In this instance, Huehuecoyotl is not only the husband in the respective phases of the two women, but is the priest as well, who must pass judgment. If he so chooses, he is permitted to offer forgiveness, as Menelaus had the choice of forgiving Helen, by means of certain rites, here involving the required emblems, illustrated in the codex as copal and bundles of fresh flowers, which will cleanse the penitent of sin.

In the *Tonalamatl* of the Aubin Collection the Old Coyote is represented as the red dog, Xolotl, who guides the Sun on its journey through the nether-regions, until he becomes Huehuecoyotl, the Nocturnal Sun, a dual appearance as the rising and setting Sun surviving the mysteries of its wearying and otherwise inexplicable odyssey.

The rites of this god are associated with the fertility of the Earth, represented in the pleated panels or pages of the Bourbon Codex and described in the magic potency of herbs, the redeeming quality of flowers and disposition of the priest to cleanse the wrongdoer of his

Figure 31. Huehuecóyotl, the old coyote known as the god of sexual drive and lord of the dance. From the Códice Borgia.

sin. The ceremony is a joyous one according to Sahagún, in which dancing and profusions of flowers serve to embellish the songs and the sacred hymns. The grand lords and priests, in their daily ritual of the adoration of the Sun, and to honor the spirit of Xochiquetzal, are depicted with the flowers they will offer the king of the heavens, the great Tonatiuh, God of solar Light and Fire.

The heat and the fervor inspired by the Sun are further indicated in the fallen figure of a man, collapsed from the sensual zeal of the ceremony, indicating the semiotic relationship of the Old Coyote to the Fallen Man, that is, the Sun itself as the Transgressor.

LAMATL SYMBOLISM

The lamatl symbolizes the blessedness of life in nature. This joy is manifest in the protective presence of the young solar god, Macuilxochitl, the deity of music and dancing, who watches over the youthful revelry of the ceremony.

At the same time the Old Coyote is present at the ritual, personified as the Old King, the astral god grown weary, the perennial light of the Sun in its persistent journey across the heavens, through the underworld and back again.

The presence of Ixnextili, "weeping ashes," serves as a reminder that even the gods are susceptible to moral transgression, and therefore must be punished. In occasional versions, she has broken her sacred fast. In others she has disobeyed, or betrayed, her husband. The "cutting of the roses," according to most interpretations, indicates adultery. Her arrogance requires a penance and she is forever condemned to weep ashes, which course dolefully down what are described as the abysses grown in her face: decadence and decrepitude.

Natives born under the sign of Xochitl were cautioned against the fleeting blessings of contentment, which "can so easily turn to disgrace, like the sun, which shines brightly during the whole of the day but so quickly becomes the gloom of twilight and the darkness of the night."[11]

PARALLEL SYMBOLISM

The dual parallel of Adonis and Aphrodite, seen in Piltzintecuhtli and Xochiquetzal, or in Huehuecoyotl and Ixnextli, celebrates human felicity, love's longing and the beckoning of destiny, but cautions against the disfavor of the gods, provoked by transgression or excess, for then the reward can only be punishment and darkness.

The Sun is encompassed in abundance and fertility, like the fruits of the Earth, emphasized in Adonis and Cintéotl, yet the loss of clarity in a course of action equally disposes the darkening of the road along the journey. Then the Black, or Nocturnal, Sun—a setting sun, without warmth or heat—serves as a warning of the coming darkness, weariness, the loss of youth and vitality, the onslaught of senility and death.

Life may be lived more than once. Both the arcanum and the lamatl stress the element of multiplicity in existence. If the Sun sets

---

[11]Ibid.

then it rises again, in a renewal of all it promised on the previous journey. Yet the fact must never be assumed, for the celestial body may be obscured, diminished or made to disappear from the heavens, temporarily or for all time, until the Supreme Power decides whether or not to create another Sun and bring Light back to the Earth.

The presence of flowers in both the tarot and the *Tonalamatl* serves as an indication of love's freshness, while the quality of perseverance against all obstacles further emphasizes the fragility of existence, the freshness of youth as only temporary, the futility in the pursuit of sensuality when enlightenment extends beyond any such physical limitations into the rarefied dimensions of eternity.

Apollo personified the light of the Sun. This Xochipilli of the Greeks exiled himself to Thessaly to be purified, or expiated like Quetzalcoatl from the stains of the blood of the dragon-serpent, the *Cipactli* he had destroyed.

When Apollo returned to Delphi his head was crowned with laurel, as Xochipilli wore the crown of the fresh blooms used by the priests of Tonatiuh, and with which Huehuecoyotl cleansed the penitent of sin.

Apollo's charm, like Xochipilli's, was that of youth, vigor and grace, of music, fresh bubbling springs, memory, poetic inspiration, and the arts. Yet his greatest gift was divination, the prophetic powers implied by the Mesoamericans in their sacred almanacs. Apollo changed Cyparissus into a tree. From the blood of Hyacintus' discus wound he created a flower. He protected Miletus from the wolves. If he was the light of the Sun, his twin, Artemis, was the Moon. Together, for they loved each other, they indicated fertility. They represented, like the Aztec twins Xochipilli and Xochiquetzal, power, fruitfulness, benevolence, or its counterpart, sudden destruction.

Apollo was the god of magic who reveled, like Huehuecoyotl— whose name in *Nahuatl* means "Flower and Song"—in music, dancing, punishment, and purity, in the blossoms of springtime laid on the altar of the gods, in the celebration of reason and the dominion of the spirit. He was quick to judge and repelled by arrogance. He was transfigured by beauty. Yet he was irreverent in love, even promiscuous, often indiscriminate, incautious, or demanding. He was a curse or a blessing, not unlike Aphrodite or Xochiquetzal.

Aphrodite's sovereign power indicated her life-bringing, that is, fertile, felicity. At her appearance, said Lucretius, the heavens were assuaged and poured forth torrents of light. Yet these parallel divinities of young romance could equally fill women's hearts with the frenzy of fruitless passion, in which case, he said, they would betray their own families, abandon their homes to follow a stranger, or would be overcome with desires he describes as monstrous and bestial.

Aphrodite could be gentle, loving, and tender. She fed children on milk and honey, like Chichihualcuautli. She brought cold stone to life. She made mortal men who lay down with her to suffer premature old age, yet she salvaged the errant by restoring the illusions of youth and vitality. While she flaunted immodesty she inspired piety. And though she visited whole cities with plague, her vision was boundless.[12] She told Aeneas, her son, to leave Troy, to found a new city in "another place," which became Rome, as Xochiquetzal and Piltzintecuhtli sent Huitzilopochtli to lead the Mexicas to glory everlasting.

These multiple images encountered their parallel in Huehuecoyotl's indulgence with Ixnextli. The voluptuousness recovered in tenderness, at the dawn or dusk of life or the day, offers a renewed vitality to extend the dimensions of fate for man on the Earth. This revelation indicates the generosity of the Creator Gods themselves who quicken the blood with light and according to Sahagún's report, flush clean the aimless heart with a recovered vision of joy.

The idea of mystery associated with the Underworld, the verb "to see" made over in the concept of "The Invisible," reiterates a notion of the mournful, where the trees are burned away and all vegetation is dead, turned to ashes, like those that course from Ixnextli's eyes. The Afterworld, Helios' daughter Circe told Odysseus, lies at the extremity of the Earth, beyond the vast ocean. Yet freshness and abundance for the Mesoamericans were encompassed in the opposite extremity, in *Tamoanchan*, like the bounty of the love and the Sun, source of the Nahr Ibrahim, among springs and fountains, lush trees, and verdant banks. There everything gracious and pleasant was indicated in song, succulence, and joy, until it ended, in betrayal or the precipice.

---

[12]Felix Guirand, ed., *New Larousse Encyclopedia of Mythology,* translated by Richard Aldington and Delano Ames (London: Hamlyn House, 1969), pp. 130–131.

ARCANUM XX

MYTHOLOGY OF JUDGMENT

The twentieth arcanum, called "Judgment," is described as "The Resurrection." Its origin lies in a multiplicity of abstract myths regarding the mysteries in the quest of the initiate for personal integrity through spiritual transformation.

This interweaving of symbols involves a seemingly inexhaustible variety or combination of divinities. Especially in India and Mexico, these assume an almost interchangeable character. In the end the gods can be reduced or synthesized, one to another according to the point of view of the worshipper. Yet under this swarming polytheism is hidden a profound doctrine of unity. God is One, says the Rig-Veda, but the sages, *vipra*, give Him many names. When Brahma spoke to the Rishis, he said:

> In the night of Brahma, when all beings were confounded in the same silent mobility, I observed the great Narayana, the soul of the universe, with a thousand omniscient eyes, at once being and not-being, brooding over the waters without form, supported by the thousand-headed snake of the Infinite. Blinded by the shining I touched the eternal being and asked: "Who are you? Speak."

> Then, lifting toward me his eyes like still sleepy lotus flowers, he stood up, smiled, and said: "Welcome, my child." I was offended and replied: "How can you, a sinless god, treat me as a master treats a pupil, and call me child, I who am the cause of creation and destruction, the creator of a thousand universes, the source of all that exists?"

> Vishnu replied: "Do you not know that I am Narayana, creator, preserver and destroyer of worlds, the eternal male, immortal source and centre of the universe? Even you were born from my imperishable body."

> And we argued together sharply over the sea without form, when to our eyes there appeared a glorious shining lingam, a pillar flaming with the light of a hundred fires able to destroy

the universe, without beginning, without middle, without end, incomparable, indescribable. The great Vishnu was disturbed by these thousands of flames, as I was, and said: "We must seek the source of this fire. I will descend, and you will ascend with all your strength." Then he took the form of a wild boar, like a mountain of blue collyrium, with sharp tusks, a long snout, a deep grunt, short strong feet, vigorous, irresistible. He descended for a thousand years but could not reach the base of the lingam. Meanwhile I had changed into a swan, entirely white, with burning eyes, wide wings, and my flight was as swift as the wind and thought itself. For a thousand years I flew up, trying to reach the top of the pillar, but I could not reach it. When I returned I found the Vishnu had already returned weary. Then Siva appeared before us and tamed by his magic we bowed before him. On all sides rose up his Om, eternal and clear. Vishnu said to him: "Our discussion has been fortunate, O god of gods, since you have appeared to put an end to it." And Siva replied: "In truth you are the creator, the preserver and the destroyer of worlds. My child, maintain both inertia and movement in the world. For I, the supreme indivisible Lord am three—Brahma, Vishnu and Siva; I create, I maintain, I destory."[1]

The most perfect model of humanity, described in Rama's peaceable courage, is permanently disposed to the service of virtue, his passionate devotion to duty, his fine and delicate sensibility, his filial piety, his conjugal tenderness, the communion of his spirit with all Nature, are traits of eternal beauty which, according to the Upanishads time can neither destroy nor weaken.

These represented another of Vishnu's incarnations, a portion of the solar myth which exemplifies the human quest for eternal redemption and immortality. Meditation, radiance, and the consolation of the lonely constituted the substance of existence on the Earth, a Vedic hermitage devoid of grievance, beyond the realm of wind, darkness, hunger and the great terrors, into asceticism, indicated in reserve and modesty, the way, according to esoteric scriptures, toward life everlasting.

The intervals of successive creations were seen as a slumber rather than death, a state in which the soul's virtuality slowly ripens, to unfold again in another dimension or universe. Trust, love and the gift of self offered into divine keeping, afforded each being with a

---

[1]Felix Guirand, ed., *New Larousse Encyclopedia of Mythology,* translated by Richard Aldington and Delano Ames (London: Hamlyn House, 1969), p. 378.

potential godliness. Persistent and unredeemable gloom, an aimless odyssey through the underworld, endless condemnation, remained the providence of a hapless dictate, according to philosphers and mythology.

The principle of light "penetrating" a whole universe occurred in a universal syncretism. Each successive or simultaneous religion therefore incorporated all that was foreign and all it was unable to understand. These webs of divergent ceremonies, beliefs, and superstitions, as they crossed and recrossed the world, evolved from the most ancient agricultural rites, while they associated the ideals of love and beauty with the prestige of the supreme gods.

As a result, a succession of Masters appeared in the various cultures, seen as deities or deified concepts, often encompassed in animal forms, in colors or traditional attributes. The path of salvation was projected onto transcendent entities, in the metaphysical principle of the Great Vehicle, the doctrine of mercy, a remedy for evil in healthy reality and the prestige of omnipotence, a notion intended to fill the sky, like sunlight or stars.

The Great Miracle of Sravasti describes the religious fundament in all cultures. In the "miracle of fire and water," the Bhagavat, or Blessed, "plunged into meditation so profound that as soon as his spirit entered into it, he disappeared from the place where he was seated and shot into the air toward the West, where he appeared in the four postures of decency: he walked, he stood up, he sat down, he lay down. He then rose to the region of light, and no sooner had he reached it than different lights spread from his body: blue, yellow, red and white lights, and others with the loveliest tints of crystal. Then he performed other miracles. Flames spread from the lower part of his body, while from the upper part fell a rain of cold water. He repeated in the South what he had done in the West and again in the four points of space."[2]

Buddha, like Quetzalcoatl, prescribed "the middle path" toward spiritual integration. The two extremes, he said, were to be avoided ". . . a life of pleasure, which is base and ignoble, contrary to the spirit, unworthy, vain. The other is a life of self-maceration. . . . the middle path which leads to rest, to knowledge, to enlightenment and nirvana [implies] the truth about pain. Birth, old age, sickness, death, separation from what we love, are pain. The origin of pain is the thirst for pleasure, the thirst for existence, the thirst for change . . . . the truth about the suppression of pain [lies in the] extinction of that thirst through the annihilation of desire."[3]

---

[2]Felix Guirand, ed., *New Larousse Encyclopedia of Mythology*, p. 354.
[3]Felix Guirand, ed., *New Larousse Encyclopedia of Mythology*, p. 353.

CARD DESCRIPTION

The card normally illustrates an angel in the sky, blowing a horn. The sound symbolizes the "call of the Archetype," interpreted as the horn of the archangel Gabriel, who was generally called upon to awaken the dead from their eternal sleep. He might also be interpreted as Hermes, obeying the dictates of the Lord.

In certain cards a swan, the transformation of Brahma, appears in place of the angel. As it descends from Heaven to announce the forthcoming spring or the phallic lingam it also suggests the renewal in Vishnu's incarnation as it embodies the spirit, of the resurrection, and the quest for redemption in eternity, in effect the *Transformatio Astralis* implied in the arcanum's second title.

Below the angel a banner appears, with a cross in the middle. In the foreground a man is depicted, described in his nakedness as he stands before God, accompanied by a woman and child, arising from coffins or graves. Numerous figures in the background repeat the action.

The scene indicates the Day of Judgment and a general resurrection, in both poles of humanity—male and female—with the neutralizing element in the Hebrew letter *Vau* present in the child beside its parents. They return to life from the realm of death.

This effort at change, at a liberation from the ominous roof, in the beginning only leads to a change of setting, as the unenlightened spirit would find itself in another body or form, just as limiting as the former. Yet the *Attractio Divina*, Divine Attraction, implied in the clouds, provides the incentive to the "collaboration with Nature," assigned by Thot, the Hermes Trismegistus who weighed the souls of the dead.

CARD SYMBOLISM

The hieroglyph describes a human head, which emphasizes the usefulness of the axe supplied by the preceeding arcanum. The head is now free to peer through the aperture cut in the roof of darkness by this axe, incited by the archetype, who has inspired the action: yet it was executed on the autonomous initiative of individual intelligence.

The angel in the upper portion of the card symbolizes the Lord, the Supreme Deity emanating peace and hope. The trumpet indicates the divine voice that calls humankind to its confrontation with God. At the sound of the trumpet the spirit is freed from the prison walls of the body.

The angel's flag is divided into four portions by means of a cross. This symbolizes not only the four cardinal points but the reconciliation, that is, the reintegration of opposites. The great conjunction of the philosophers' stone has ceased to turn.

The symbol of solar light worn by the angel on its head represents the creative force in the communion between the individual mind and the collective intelligence of all humankind.

The *Mutationes in Tempore* implied in another of the arcanum's titles indicates the temporal quality of transformation. All processes require time, to germinate and evolve. If the intentions are well ordered, says the Great Hermes, Nature will offer its inevitable collaboration, by creating conditions of time and space that propitiate the journey. The influence of the archetype is such that our implicit godliness must necessarily be impelled toward fruition, in a new integration with Unmanifested Perfection.

LAMATL XX

MYTHOLOGY OF CE-ACATL
(THE REED OR CANE)

The jaguar throne was consecrated in this thirteen-day period, in the emblem of the arrow, or *acatl*, fashioned from the slim reeds of cane and water grasses. This arrow, or a quiver of arrows, served to indicate the justice administered by the royal office, at the hands of a king in royal garb, who sat on the jaguar couch, at his feet a fully extended jaguar pelt, head intact, teeth bared, claws curved, obsidian beads for its eyes.

The golden arrows and the bow beside the throne further emphasized the exercise of power and the administration of justice. This lamatl, associated with crime and punishment, is in fact defined in the judgment, for its patron is Ixquimil Itztlacoliuhqui, "Twisted Obsidian with Blindfolded Eyes."

This apparition of Tezcatlipoca the Black, the "smoking mirror" endowed with the gift of prophecy and divination, who judged the good and punished the transgressor, was identified with a vision of men and women after the Fall. Before his downfall he had been called Cipactonal. He had lived with Oxomoco, his wife. Yet she broke the codes of morality and rectitude and became Itzpapalotl, "The Obsidian Butterfly," an advocation of Tlazoltéotl, the lustful goddess-regent of this sign.

The ceremonies which took place during this period were devoted to Quetzalcoatl, Prophet of Enlightenment, who appeared at the four cardinal points. His various manifestations were indicated in the colors associated with Tezcatlipoca, Prince of Darkness, known as lurking evil, imminent danger, the misery of the spirit, mourning and gloom. Yet Tezcatlipoca was red or white, green, blue and yellow as well as black, for he could be burdensome, gallant, dauntless or crass, depending on the message implied or the worshipper's interpretation.

As Quetzalcoatl, however, he was richly adorned, grandly attired, feted, and honored with flowers, bundles of reeds, and incense. This sign was associated with honor and deification, the potential godliness in all humans, a release from the burden of temptation or temper, and redemption in the penance of the Creator Gods, whose sacrifice was intended to guide humankind along the way of righteousness.

The various incarnations of Quetzalcoatl-Tezcatlipoca, like Brahma and Siva, encompassed the full extent of the soul's struggle to define its labors and the nature of its goal, while the gods explored the far regions of the sky. If Tezcatlipoca aided Quetzalcoatl in the creation of the world, and in fact lost his left foot wrestling with the Primal Dragon, if he assisted in the raising of the sky after the deluge, he was also a god of afternoon and betrayal. He appeared when the Sun was about to be devoured by the nether-regions and disappeared before the eruption of the dawn. He thus represented both shores, the east and the west, where the Sun rose and fell.

He was lame, resentful, and malicious. He devised a ruse to disgrace Quetzalcoatl. Yet he offered his counsel to a forlorn little group of people, which permitted them to survive the flood. He allowed them the use of fire. He ruled the world, this "shadow by the shoulder." He was venerated and feared. He seduced, perverted, and dismayed. He knew the secrets in the hearts of men and women. The mystic clouding of his mirror permitted a vision beyond any other. As Itztlacoliuhqui, he was the god of biting cold, of ice, and of winter. He was a warrior god, of volcanic eruptions, "like pillars of fire," of disaster and destruction. He was the hurricane. He was blighted vegetation. Yet he was also witty and wise. He was the spotted fur of the rare black jaguar, like the sky on a starry night.

For he was Quetzalcoatl, the spirit of repentance, whose soul left his body "without a trace," when he became the Morning Star. He was the One God of the Toltecs, the Supreme Deity who lived beyond the Milky Way. He obliged the cipactli, the lizard or dragon, to come down from the heavens and form the trees, the valleys, and the rivers from the substance of its body. He was clouds and the breeze, cosmic polarity, the first priest, wisdom, and goodness, the red glow of dawn, the Earth itself. He had been born, according to the codices, of Mixcoatl—another advocation of Tezcatlipoca—and the virgin Chimalman, "Reclining Shield," of an "immaculate conception." He went to war with his father and when his sire had been killed, avenged his death before the "Four Hundred *Mimixcoa*." He was Huitzilopochtli, the stars of the southern heavens. He was the sky of the north, the Sun itself. He was ritual and law.

And if he sinned and was symbolically associated with Tlazol-téotl, his sin was redeemed in Chalchiuhtlicue, "She of the Skirts of Precious Stones," the goddess of the skirts of jade or blue water, who personified rich pulque, a liquid bounty like the nourishing rains from Heaven, all that is succulent and that makes things flourish and grow ripe. For she was corn and water, the redeeming angel of purification, the midwives' prayer, an exoneration expressed in the recovery of the soul's pristine clarity—indulged at birth and recaptured throughout a lifetime, one day at a time.

LAMATL DESCRIPTION

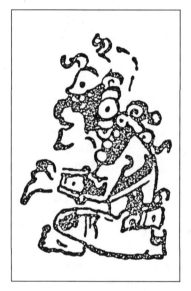

In the Books of the Divinatory Arts, the *Tonalamatl*, the goddess regent of the thirteen-day period called Ce-Acatl, One Reed, appears in the person of Chalchiuhtlicue, goddess of luminous precious stones, mistress of living water. She is often depicted with a mask, or with eye shadow in a variety of colors, usually red. She is crowned with a helmet of serpents and a headdress of short plumes. She is in a barge or kayak shown above a running stream of water, beside which appears the priest, Tlamacax-tli, with a bundle of reeds in his hand. The lamatl further illustrates various types of arrows or quivers of arrows. The goddess thus personifies justice. She is the priestess, that is the angel, of the Judgment.

The concept is confirmed in the Vatican and Borgia Codices, which illustrate arrows drawn along by a stream of water. They appear at the feet of the goddess, a woman seen to be weaving. Nearby a man is depicted. He bears a shield, a quiver of arrows and a coffer of jewels, an allusion to Chalchiuhtlicue.

In those codices specifically devoted to the culture of the Aztecs and Mexicas, the Bourbon and the Aubin, Chalchiuhtlicue accompanies a pair of adulterers, on whom she inflicts a severe punishment. Her chastisement is symbolized in the figure of the priest, who holds a quiver of arrows in his hand. He is the judge, whose divine powers are applied to punitive justice. He will deprive this couple of its

Figure 32. Chalchiuhtlicue, goddess of living water, springs and streams. From the Códice Borgia.

liberty, and will confiscate the worldly goods of those who transgress against the sacred dictates.

In certain codices, Chalchiuhtlicue accompanies the goddess Tlazoltéotl, who appears as a deity of forgiveness. Chalchiuhtlicue punished the transgressions described to her by the priests of Tlazoltéotl during public confession. Major sins, such as adultery, received the maximum punishment allowed by law, for the violation of the marriage bed was termed the clearest indication of social disorder, in a society which persistently stressed the stability of the family and the hierarchy of the clan.

LAMATL SYMBOLISM

The counterpoint of Quetzalcoatl and Tezcatlipoca, juxtaposed as the ascending and descending spirit, respectively, is synthesized in the reed shaft of the arrow. It may journey upward or downward, or strike precisely at its apparent goal. This target, however, may be revealed as an illusory prey.

Tlazoltéotl, the personification of lust and temptation, all that is corrupt and foul, becomes both sin and redemption. She is the transgressor and the transgressed. Just like the simultaneous Quetzalcoatl-Tezcatlipoca, she is guilt and the guilty, for the blameless, in the philosophy of the codices, is no less responsible in any action than the blamed.

The lamatl was presumed to indicate poverty of the spirit, the loss of material wealth, a decline in social position or even slavery, as rushing water in constant movement carries along everything in its path.

Life is therefore deemed transitory, ephemeral and fleeting. The Otomies, the oldest culture extant in Mesoamerica, still deny the burden of possession, while they refuse to build anything permanent. Thus, humankind is received in its nakedness, for in any case the gods strip the soul when it is judged at death.

This concept is confirmed in the legend of Tezcatlipoca, obsidian twisted and sightless, the implacable Itztlacoliuhqui, formed in the pillar of fire, who judges men and women and grants or denies their guilt, their freedom, the goods they own or claim, the privileges they presume, the position to which they aspire, their redemption, dismay, purification, or condemnation, in the lonely journey from one inconsolable existence to another.

PARALLEL SYMBOLISM

The Mesoamerican Books of the Dead, like comparable documents in other cultures, describe the aspiration to resurrection, the liberation from the pain or the suffering of this world by redemption in the next; and the spiritual desolation in materialism.

Abundant legends describe the nether-regions, and claim to satisfy humankind's unending curiosity regarding its fate after death. Yet even the tales which counsel wisdom, prudence, or righteousness fail to provide more than a glimmer of credibility for the "sinner," who will die confirmed in perversity. The path of moral rectitude, then, remains the province of the spiritually illuminated, who never doubt the nature of their goal.

These polarities in aim and method are symbolized in a whole network of divinities and their various representations. Yet most of them refer to men's and women's own betrayal by their unconscious mind. And while each religion absorbs the doctrines of its neighbors, and despite the dizzying pantheons of the Vedic or the Mesoamerican deities, all faiths essentially evolved from a solar cult, in which the earliest agricultural divinities were synthesized in the principle of One God, a unique and invisible being whose unutterable name obliged a multitude of euphemisms, hence the variety of forms and designations. This Supreme Deity, like mortal men and women on Earth, suffered many experiences, transformations, and incarnations, before He ultimately achieved pure enlightenment.

The Mexican jaguar, like Vishnu's boar, portrays a frightening vision of strength and power. Tezcatlipoca's volcano, like the pillar of

Figure 33. Tezcatlipoca-Ixquimilli, the blindfolded god known as lord of punitive justice.

fire implicit in the lingam, emphasizes respect, even fear. Yet eventually the deities, having consolidated their power, reveal themselves in goodness, generosity, and tenderness.

If filial devotion and conjugal regard were considered as laudable as a deliverance in duty, then abstinence and renunciation of material comforts and goods were prescribed in the teachings of the Masters, as an essential condition for religious and philosophic integration. The priests themselves were assigned the strictest modesty, even humility, under the guidance of Tlazoltéotl, herself "sin" and "the sinner"—like Brahma—who heard their confessions and pardoned their transgressions.

Water, as the symbol of purification, carried wealth, riches and vanity along with sin, poverty, or pain to a point at which all beings, the privileged as well as the humble, remained equally naked, and equally defenseless, before the Judgment. The arrow in the lamatl, like the trumpet in the twentieth arcanum, calls the dispossessed and the alienated, or the exalted, the fearful, the proud, and the misguided, to hear the verdict of a dispassionate yet bountiful emissary of the Supreme Deity.

The king on his jaguar throne, like Buddha prescribing the recommended postures, may dispense his authority from any or all of the cardinal points, in any sphere or dimension, envisioned in any color. Yet the final authority is one's own and Judgment is a private affair. A singular Hell, a solitary Heaven, are dispensed by the mind itself, in the full—however unwitting—awareness of the polarity of good and evil.

ARCANUM XXI

MYTHOLOGY OF THE FOOL

The twenty-first arcanum, a complex and mysterious card presumably included long after the other twenty in the major arcana, was only introduced after the sixteenth century.[1] It was often designated as "O," or "Zero," and was intended to be viewed independently of the remainder of the collection.

The card is referred to as *Furca*, the Fork, indicating the peculiar shape of the Hebrew letter *Shin*, and the unique position of the arcanum within the philosophical framework of the tarot. It is commonly denominated The Fool. The figure is normally associated with Dionysus during his spells of "madness" or "illumination," his rebellion against the established order and his errant life in the Middle East, which were seen as a metaphysical quest, according to the legend, for the weapon of light with which to confound the dark forces of evil.

The enigma of the "card without number" is encompassed in the notion of the ubiquitous, like the Joker in the modern deck, a warming and convenient presence that fits anywhere and serves many purposes. Therefore the arcanum was intended to imply the ambivalent factors of fire and light. As with Black Tezcatlipoca — the personification of terrestrial fire, the "twisted obsidian" of the lava flow, with those terrifying pillars of flame — the Greeks identified "the very young," an epithet of *Agni*, the Vedic god of fire, with Hephaestus, and translated his name from the Sanskrit *Yavishtha*.

This ill-made god, lame and twisted, conceived in the "illicit union" of brother and sister Zeus and Hera, "before their marriage," was, like Black Tezcatlipoca or the Egyptian Seth, the vision of the warped. His stumbling gait, his rage and fury, often equated him with madness, or at least the foolish and eccentric. He was ugly. Therefore, said the Greeks, he was evil.

Contrary to the official statement from Olympus, Hephaestus' infirmity was not the result of an accident. He was lame from birth. Homer recounts that Hera, ashamed of her son, tried to hide him

---

[1]Authors' Note: Guided by the Mouni Sadhu Tarot, I have chosen for purposes of correlation, to assign number XXI to The Fool, traditionally given no number, and therefore to advance the numbering of The World to XXII.

from the Immortals. "He is lame and I have sinned." She threw him from the heights of Olympus into the sea, where he was taken in by Thetis, daughter of Nereus, and Eurynome, daughter of the old Ocean. For nine years, like the nine levels of the underworld, he remained concealed in a deep grotto, "forging a thousand ingenious objects for the two nymphs," while he plotted his cunning revenge.[2]

Under his graceless exterior a subtle and inventive spirit evolved in the unhappy child. One day Hera received a gift from her son, a golden throne artistically wrought and lovely to behold. She sat on it with delight, but when she tried to rise again she was suddenly gripped by invisible hands. The Immortals tried in vain "to extricate her from the throne" but only Hephaestus was capable of releasing her, and he refused to leave the depths of the Ocean. Ares tried to drag him up by force but was "put to flight by Hephaestus who threw burning brands at him."[3] Dionysus was more successful: he made Hephaestus drunk and in this state perched him on a mule, which returned him to Olympus. Even so, Hephaestus refused to release Hera unless the gods gave him the loveliest of brides, the exquisite Aphrodite, whom he married, and who kept him, as Tlazoltéotl kept Tezcatlipoca, or Cipactonal kept Oxomoco, in a practically permanent state of cuckoldry, usually with the virile and aggressive Ares (Mars).

After Hephaestus had extracted from Hera the secret of his birth, there was peace between mother and son, though until they finally came to terms, Zeus generally raged at the miserable figure and pitched him from the Olympian heights. Hephaestus eventually built the palaces of the gods on Olympus, thus ingratiating himself by means of his talent. He fashioned their weapons on his forge. For himself he constructed "a sparkling dwelling of glittering and incorruptible bronze,"[4] in order to impress them with the luxury and comfort with which he surrounded himself. Yet he was lonely.

He often left his anvil and his palace to wander on the Earth, "where he maintained various underground places of residence."[5] He apprenticed on Naxos and unsuccessfully disputed the possession of the island with Dionysus, yet they remained close friends. He was assisted at his work by the Sileni and the Satyrs, the dwarfs and misfits who made up Dionysus' retinue. He imprisoned Typhoeus, who, like Cipactli in Mexico, had been crushed under the weight of Etna by Zeus, when Quetzalcoatl trapped the primal dragon. Heph-

---

[2]*Larousse Encyclopedia of Mythology*, translated by Richard Aldington and Delano Ames (London: Hamlyn House, 1969), pp. 126–127.
[3]*New Larousse Encyclopedia of Mythology*, p. 127.
[4]*Larousse Encyclopedia of Mythology*, p. 127.
[5]Ibid.

aestus was aided in his labor by the Palici, the twins—like Xochipilli and Xochiquetzal—who shared his addiction to pleasure and beauty.

Hephaestus fashioned Zeus' golden throne, sceptre, and thunderbolts, and with equal inventiveness and dexterity the fearful aegis, the winged chariot of Helios, the arrows of Apollo and Artemis, Demeter's sickle, Herakles' cuirass, the arms of Perseus, the armor of Achilles, the necklace that Harmonia wore for her nuptials, Ariadne's diadem, Agamemnon's sceptre, the hypogeum or underground chamber of Oneopion, the golden goblet Zeus offered to Aphrodite and the vase given by Dionysus to Ariadne. He created bronze bulls whose nostrils spurted flame. He bound Prometheus to the Caucasus. He split Zeus' skull in order that Athene might emerge, then fell in love with her and was rejected. For him nothing but love was impossible. He could mold the body of a woman with water and clay, then give it life and a human voice, to "form from it a virgin of ravishing beauty,"[6] though she would never, in spirit, submit to him.

Yet despite his unhappiness, his loneliness in fealty, to all he preached submission and resignation, counseled the moderation of wrath, and recommended pacifying the temper of Zeus, his father, perhaps recalling his tumbles from Olympus. He avoided quarrels. "The finest feast is without pleasure when discord triumphs."[7]

The hieroglyph of the arcanum is an arrow, and while the weapon indicates the allusion to Hephaestus, the Fork, or Trident, refers to Poseidon, "the Earth-shaker."

On occasion this Lord of the Sea, to whom one-third of Cronus' domain fell, used his wile, his disruptive temper and complaining nature, in one or another attempt to dethrone Zeus, as Tezcatlipoca had deposed Quetzalcoatl. Yet, he fought the Titans and the Giants at Zeus' side, as Tezcatlipoca often made common cause with Quetzalcoatl, and in fact not only rivaled the Supreme Deity but was often confused with him.

His trident symbolized the thunderbolt. Horses and bulls were sacred to him. His waters supported the Earth. He split mountains, formed islands, and loved many women. He frequently suckled his offspring on mare's milk.[8]

Yet his thirst for possession maintained his conflict with the other gods, whose authority he repeatedly challenged. This god of fertility and vegetation was the master of gushing springs and running water, lakes, rivers, and streams. And though he was the equal of Zeus by birth and dignity, he was nonetheless subject to his brother's sover-

---

6*Larousse Encyclopedia of Mythology*, p. 128.
7Ibid.
8*Larousse Encyclopedia of Mythology*, p. 133.

eign power, as Seth was subject to Osiris, except that he was confined to the Sea, his domain. There he ordered made for himself "a magnificent palace, glittering with gold, which would endure forever." When he left the palace, he harnessed swift steeds with golden manes and shod with bronze to his wondrous chariot and there, clad in his golden armor and with his "cunningly wrought whip" he hurled "over the watery plain."[9]

When he was other than one of his beloved horses, a shape he often took, he frequently appeared in the form of a bird—like Quetzalcoatl's quetzal or Tezcatlipoca's turkey—and when he used this ruse to seduce Medusa in the very temple of Athene, that goddess turned Medusa's hair to serpents, a familiar Mesoamerican symbol.

Poseidon was wild, stormy, and rebellious, often foolish in his romantic affairs, occasionally careworn. He was tempestuous and unrelenting, tending to intransigence, even stubborn. He was quarrelsome, often raging and furious, which earned him an association with madness, jealousy, fearful monsters but more than anything else, with water's rapture and water's contradiction: the drought. No plotting or punishment was ever so terrible as the drying up of the rivers and streams or unrelieved dryness and vanishing springs.

Sobek, Sebek or, in Greek Suchos, was the crocodile divinity who, like Cipactli, the oversized lizard or alligator, was considered a supreme god, to be appeased in sacrifice and prayer. To their worshippers, both Sobek and Cipactli, like the primal dragon in every legendary history, represented the Demiurge who issued from the dark waters on the day of creation, in order to arrange the world, as the female crocodile emerges from the river to deposit her eggs on the bank.

Sobek was especially worshipped at a remarkable city in the Fayyum at Ombos, in Egypt, called Shedet or Crocodilopolis, Hellenized during the Greek occupation as Crocodroupoulous. He shared the evil reputation of Seth, the Tezcatlipoca of Egypt, and was further identified with Geb, qualified by Plutarch as a representation of Cronus. He was the Earth-god, the physical foundation of the world, the mountains and the undulation of the Earth's crust. His body was frequently covered with verdure. Other interpretations saw him as a bull, who fertilized the celestial cow. He was reputed to be the father of the Osirian gods.

Sobek as Seth, whom the Greeks called Typhon, was related to Osiris' dreadful brother, who finally became the incarnation of the spirit of evil, in eternal opposition to the spirit of good. He personified the ubiquitous adversary, drought and darkness, the negation of

---

[9]*Larousse Encyclopedia of Mythology*, p. 133.

abundance or life-bringing water and light, all that is destruction and perversity. He was the crocodile, worshipped in certain provinces and mercilessly hunted in others, and in whose body Seth hid himself after the murder of Osiris.

Seth was the scorpion and the black pig. He wounded Horus in the eye, as Tezcatlipoca had wounded Quetzalcoatl. Each month he attacked and devoured the Moon, where the soul of Osiris had taken refuge. He was the wicked manifestation of the plumed serpent, the Typhonian animal with a curved snout, square-cut ears and a stiff, forked tail. The legendary struggles between the brother gods Seth and Osiris—a parallel to the opposition of Tezcatlipoca and Quetzalcoatl—reflects historical as well as mythological juxtaposition, even in its racial overtones, for he was white, and therefore despised by the Egyptians, a symbol of the undesirable.

All that was creation and blessing, then, came from Osiris or Quetzalcoatl. All that was destruction, misery, and treachery came from Seth or Tezcatlipoca.

CARD DESCRIPTION

le fou W

On a rock leading to a precipice, a man walks hastily. He wears a foolish cap cocked to one side of his head. The cap is fashioned in three colors, white, red, and black, the three colors identified with the multiple manifestations of Tezcatlipoca.

The Fool's clothing fits him badly. This gives him the appearance of a clown. He is evidently a traveler, a wanderer, or a vagrant. A bag full of apparently useless objects is carried across the stick balanced on his shoulder. He holds a staff in his right hand.

He ignores the precipice. In fact, he seems to be gazing in the opposite direction. Yet waiting for him in a body of water, jaws wide open, lies a crocodile with enormous teeth, Sobek or Cipactli, whose lower jaw Tezcatlipoca was said to have torn away to keep the reptile from sinking back into the primal sea, therefore obliging him to form the Earth, the trees, the rivers, and the mountains, from the substance of his own body.

The Fool's left leg has been torn by a vicious dog, which follows him from behind, still snarling and threatening. Blood is flowing from the wound onto the stony ground, exactly as occurred when Tezcatlipoca was hurled from Heaven and made lame, or when his struggle with Cipactli cost him his left foot.

The man in the arcanum makes no effort to put his staff—the reed or acatl, symbolizing Quetzalcoatl himself—to its intended use. He neither leans on it nor repels the animal biting at him. The left hand of The Fool holds a stick which supports the heavy bag on his shoulder, but even so, the position of the stick on the *right* shoulder obviously adds to the man's burden and discomfort, unless he is left-handed, perhaps, as Huitzilopochtli was.

The Fool strides straight toward the abyss, where a monster awaits him. His clothes, which normally would cover the body, in his case are a collection of motley garments, with no match or sense to them. His journey seems tiresome and his face is worn with care, yet he makes no attempt to discard the presumably useless articles in the bag.

CARD SYMBOLISM

The intricate symbolism of the twenty-first arcanum, or Zero, *Furca*, The Fool, represents frustration, and humankind's incapacity to organize the most productive enterprise from the existing elements at its disposition. The card indicates wasted effort and wasted materials, emotions spent on fruitless causes, ripeness brought to a sterile product. In this sense, the *vast* is seen as empty rather than extensive. And talent, for all its wonder and skill, is lost if not carefully applied.

The inference refers not only to the crafting of a work but in its presentation, on whom it is bestowed and for what purpose. The inner contradiction, the frustration and unfulfilled yearnings in Hephaestus and Poseidon, the aimless wanderings of Dionysus, for all they contributed in grandeur, amusement, material splendor, or vanity to those around them, never manage to converge in the happiness or spiritual integration of the protagonist.

Therefore the man depicted in the arcanum remains stagnant, like motionless water, and goes stale. His future growth and fulfillment will lie forever beyond his grasp, for like Geb, Seth, or Black Tezcatlipoca, he is caught in a web of revenge, remorse, frustrated ambitions, aimless desires, vanity, and presumption, and is their victim rather than their master.

Even the kindly Hephaestus, an essentially conciliatory personality, fails to integrate his worldly body with the bodiless spirit, which has no concern either for beauty or ugliness, except in the quintessential and symbolic application of their product, for a well-directed action or a concentrated effort are more valid and laudable than physical grace and loveliness, manners or fashion, grandeur, wealth or luxury, which only serve to ensnare the lover of worldly goods and pleasure, as Hera was trapped in Hephaestus' golden throne.

Monstrous or destructive animals, especially reptiles or predators, the semiotic counterposition in the arcanum of the dog and the crocodile, represented the limits of human evolutionary ascendance. The "Devourer of the Souls" in ancient Egypt, venerated as Sobek, invoked the Great Genii, and was interpreted as the God of Male Fecundity, aquatic, terrestrial, and solar. He was aggression seen as virility. He was adored as he emerged, like Poseidon, from the waves of the sea, like the morning Sun, and revered as he devoured all the fish in the water, considered the Sun's enemies. Therefore, the eyes of the crocodile symbolized the dawn, its throat was butchery, its tail the shadows and death.

Plutarch described the crocodile as the symbol of divinity. The Bible portrays it as one of the monsters of chaos. In the tarot, the crocodile is the symbol of contradiction, and so accompanies The Fool in the twenty-first arcanum. Though the giant reptile lives in a fertile world, it lamentably devours and destroys its own benefits and becomes an inverted master of the mystery of life and death, the initiator, symbol of occult knowledge in the light it eclipses.

The figure of the dog in the arcanum is often depicted as a feline, that complex emblem of indifference, a Joker presumed to adapt to any situation or circumstance, that survives by guile and betrays its benefactor, yet equally, like the canine, is seen as a reflection of humankind's own counterposed traits. This lynx, tiger, or ocelot, another Mesoamerican symbol, is identified with the night and magic, the jaguar's triumph over the dragon, the secrets of the Cosmos, with Quetzalcoatl as Tezcatlipoca, the solstice of the universe, the capricious and unpredictable Infinite, the beyond.

The figure then becomes the active principle of ferocious energy and misdirected aggression, applied at whatever extreme of the good-evil binary, because in either case the effort expended will produce the opposite of the intended effect. Thus the figure on the card is the monster of darkness, the new moon, magic, and deception, as when Dionysus transformed himself successively into a bull, a lion, and a panther, in order to induce the daughters of Minyas of Orchomenus into his cult. He failed.

LAMATL XXI

MYTHOLOGY OF AMOZOAQUES OR AHUACHCUATLI (THE SOOTHSAYERS, SERPENT, AND CENTIPEDE)

After the first twenty cards, or lamatl, in the *Tonalamatl* of the Bourbon Codex, which originated in the Aztec highlands of the Central Mexican Plateau, two additional cards appeared, exactly as had occurred in the tarot. One refers to the Soothsayers, the Amozoaques or Ahuachcuatli, and the other to the Quetzalcoatl-Tezcatlipoca binary. A study of their composite wisdom adds depth and understanding to the philosophic and divinatory compendium in the total *Tonalpohualli*.

The two lamatl, taken jointly, explained the accounting of the fifty-two years which made up the Mexica half-century, that is, the period corresponding to a normal human lifespan. The subject's life was therefore viewed here on the basis of a projection of his or her experiences and accomplishments, and consequently, an all-encompassing relationship with the cosmos.

In order to interpret the reading a priest would toss nine kernels of corn—representing the nine Lords of the Night, or planets—over these two lamatl and, as the kernels fell, just as the coins of the *I Ching* fall, the subject's astrological destiny was determined. Since the symbols, like the language, the inference, and even the interpretation, were totally abstract, the priest or *Tonalpouhque*—"the counter of days"—was necessarily of exceptional culture and academic discipline, almost invariably male.

Certain concepts or premises were difficult to represent and were therefore illustrated by means of the head of the god who encompassed the synthesis, for example, of wind, rain, home, devotion, death. On the other hand, the Aztec scribes were remarkably gifted at expressing human activity: "speaking" or "commanding," accompanied by the symbol for "flower" indicated "singing."

The presence of Huitzilopochtli in the festival calendar confirms the Bourbon Codex, housed in the National Library in Paris, as a unique illustrated manuscript originating in the capital of the Aztec Empire. It is, furthermore, considered by many to be the most beautiful of all the codices. It contains thirty-eight accordian pleated pages of thirty-eight by thirty-nine centimeters each, roughly 15 inches square. Unfolded it measures nearly one hundred and fifteen feet. This, like others of the Aztec religious and calendrical documents, demonstrates an impressive intimacy with the deities and a singular regional and nationalist flavor.

The Borgia Codex, one of the treasures of the Vatican Library in Rome, contains thirty-nine pages, painted on both sides by the *tlacuilo*, or artists, who specialized in this task. The pages measure 27 by 26.5 centimeters (10 x 10.5 inches) each and are divided into five manuscripts. These were probably designed and produced in Tlaxcala or Cholula, important centers of science and learning. In any case, they reveal the extent and subtlety of Toltec wisdom, perception, and sensibility, which reflected on both the Aztec and Maya cultures and was in turn affected by the Mixtec and Zapotec civilizations in Oaxaca.

The wealth of material on these colorful, fanciful and fascinating pages is inexhaustible, usually beginning with the *Tonalpohualli*. The signs of the days are presented in fifty-two vertical columns of five signs each, whose augurial significance is indicated in relation to the symbols and figures of the gods, arranged above and below them.

The next section describes the twenty "signs of the days," with their regent gods and patrons. A record follows which indicates, according to five separate points of reference, the five sequential periods of Venus. These, like the four successive solar years, were determined by their initial or final dates, respectively.

A notably vivid description then analyzes the celestial and terrestrial polarities—light and darkness, rainy season and dry season, day and night—after which a paragraph deals with the influence of the rain gods on agriculture during four consecutive years. Then a representation, rich in graphic and aesthetic symbolism, describes the four terrestrial and celestial regions. Throughout both the Bourbon and Borgia Codices other, lesser drawings portray groups of gods or divine couples, the Sun, the Moon, the Morning Star and twice the celestial divinity Quetzalcoatl in his double advocation as Lord of Life and Lord of Death.

Between these various sections and the *Tonalamatl* a kind of catalog appears, in the form of a nineteen-page resumé, describing the epic religious and mythological history of the factors that governed Mesoamerican life. In the Borgia, for example, a voluminous exposi-

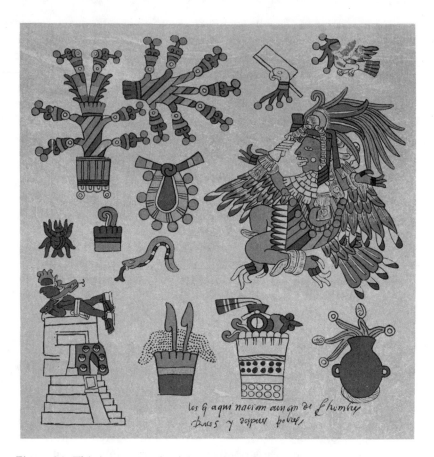

Figure 34. This is an example of the Bourbon Codex, a radically different style of art. The scene refers to the prediction that natives of this sign will grow up to be rich! (Reproduced from the Borbónico Códice, a facsimile edition published by Siglo XXI to accompany Francisco del Paso y Troncoso's documentation. Used by permission.)

tion appears in relation to the planet Venus in its role as the Morning and Evening Star, its journey through the underworld and its ascent to Heaven.

No Hesiod, Ovid, Plutarch, or Homer left a comparable interpretive documentation to be assimilated and analyzed over the years. Many of the codices have been damaged, or they perished during the various invasions and conquests, floods, earthquakes, and fires. Even the methodical manuscripts of the Franciscan friar Bernardino de Sahagún, or his counterpart in Yucatán, the Bishop Landa, are sadly sketchy, wondering but often limited, mystified by a culture so foreign to their own, and thoroughly confused and disrupted by the semiotic language of the abstract, more akin to the Far East or India than to a product of sixteenth-century Spain.

The ancient cultures of Mesoamerica, however, by the time of Cortez and the Conquest, had managed to qualify every detail, real or supposed, in their world, or the worlds exhausted before they ever appeared. Human existence, in the jurisdiction of the *Tonalamatl*, amounted to a philosophic and symbolic arithmetic not unlike the tarot, and took into account the totality of human experience. The central sections of the twenty-first and twenty-second lamatl, which emphasize the astrological interrelation of the cosmic and human cycles, were especially significant in relation to the divinatory arts. The peripheral areas of the cards were made up of a dual series of symbols: those which encompassed a precise number of years and the signs represented by the Nine Lords of the Night, alone or together with the regents of the years they "accompanied."

The contents of these two lamatl deal principally with what was termed Mundane or Civil Astrology, in its association with Temporal Astrology, but were used as much for determining an individual's future as for the resolution of matters of government or state.

For example, the year Tochtli, or One Rabbit, initiates the accounting of the twenty-first lamatl and serves as a resumé of all that went before. The sign is accompanied by Micantecuhtli, the God of Death, of Hell and the underworld, comparable to Hades in Greek mythology and corresponding to the planet Pluto, the astral body of subterranean energy, source of violence and death. The second year in this series is Two Reed, governed by Piltzintecuhtli, Lord Child, associated with the planet Mercury. The third year, Three Flint, is governed by Tlaloc, God of the Rain and the fertilizing waters of the Earth, who lives in the mountains or in the thunderheads which encircle their crown. His children—that is, the souls of those who entered his heaven or domain—are the *tlaloques*, who dispense thunder and lightning, characteristics associated with Zeus and with the planet Jupiter.

The fourth year is Four House, governed by Tlazoltéotl, Goddess of Carnal Love and Sensuality, associated with the planet Venus. The fifth year is Five Rabbit and is governed by Cintéotl, God of Corn and Sustenance, equivalent to Saturn. The sixth year, Six Reed, is governed by Xiuhtecuhtli, God and Fire and the celestial lightning of old Uranus, progenitor of all the gods.

The year Seven Flint is governed by Tepeyólotl, God of the Heart—or Spirit—of the Mountain, of the Echo and hidden water, carefully guarded in the mountain's core. Tepeyólotl, like Poseidon, or Neptune, God of the Sea, of oceans and springs, symbolizes all the animals and incarnates the principle of fecundity. This god is portrayed, or appears in the *nahualli* or disguise, of the jaguar or ocelot, as Poseidon's emblem or totemic manifestation was the horse, bull, or dolphin. Both represent the "Shaker of the Earth," or earthquake. The interaction of planets, that is, of cosmic time, was indicated by means of the Lords of the Night. The periods of worldly time—the years of the Earth and the human span—were established in the interrelation of men and women with their deities, their planet the Earth, and the Cosmos, as a form of quotidian space in the Mesoamerican world.

The twenty-first lamatl achieves a semiotic equation with the entire concept by means of a specific reference to "The Sorcerers" or "Soothsayers," Quetzalcoatl and Tezcatlipoca, the gods who created the world, expressed by means of Oxomoco and Cipactonal, a Mesoamerican Adam and Eve. This couple's identity, more than contradictory, even androgynous, indicates the wide range of abstract philosophy in duality.

Their synthesis occurs in the form of a primal binary, which explains that the couple was endowed by the Creator Gods with the faculties for creating the Earth, parting the waters, harnessing the wind, and generating fire. In addition, Oxomoco and Cipactonal were assigned the accounting of time and the devising of a Calendar. The gods then gave Oxomoco nine kernels of corn, the vehicle or apparatus of divination. They further lavished on Cipactonal other kernels for planting, along with the implements or tools necessary for the cultivation of the Earth, granted by Cipactli. According to the myth, this crocodile, alligator, sea serpent, or dragon asked in return only that it be named the symbol for the first day in the calendar and the designation assigned to those priests who practiced the divinatory arts. Thus Cipactli, the reptile, became one of the earliest advocations of Quetzalcoatl, the Plumed Serpent.

Oxomoco and Cipactonal were then conceived as human entities, descendants of the gods. As authors of the Books of Divination they were also the masters of culture and knowledge, the Guardians of Wisdom. They were therefore considered the *Amozoaques*, or Wise Men, who disembarked on the Gulf of Mexico coast of Tamaulipas looking for Paradise on Earth and a unique dwelling. This they discovered on the highest peaks of a mountain, *Citlaltepetl*, "The Mountain with its Head in the Stars," which brushes, they said, very close to the moon.[10]

---

[10]Citlaltepetl, or Peak of Orizaba, in Mexico's state of Veracruz overlooking the coastal plains and jungles, measures 18,701 feet (5700 meters), and after Mckinley and North Peak in Alaska, is the highest mountain on the North American continent.

LAMATAL DESCRIPTION

The *Amozoaques*, or *Ahuachcuatli*, as masters of the divinatory arts, were indicated by various symbols: a small gourd or calabash hung over the shoulder on a strap; by two picks fashioned from the antlers of a young deer or from deer bone, indicating a state of penitence. A pouch was later added. This served to hold the highly prized incense, copal, which suggested "luxury" or "abundance."

Eventually the designers of the codex depicted the couple in the Central Section by means of a handful of herbs or a branch heavy with fruit, to suggest their power, success, fruitfulness, verdure, and inventive skill, as well as the negation implicit in the contrary: weakness, sterility, drought, or frustration.

The two human figures in the center of the lamatl, depending on the codex, can be facing each other on twin benches atop a mat or rug: a pair of thrones embellished with the customary indications. Squatting toward the right usually appears the ambivalent form of an androgynous Cipactonal, identified by the name illustrated under the picture of Cipactli, the fantastic animal that emerged from the primal sea to form life on Earth. The association lends the figure its connotation of venerable antiquity.

The figure often holds the *tlemáitlo*, or incense burner, in its right hand. Smoke and flames arise from the copal on the coals. The pouch which holds the copal hangs from the figure's left fist, which is clutched around a deer-horn pick. The figure has been transformed into the penitent, who will offer his fragrant vapors, and soon his self-sacrifice, to the gods.

The old Oxomoco faces the figure, which he views from his bench or throne. He occupies an area as well as the posture reserved for the women, on his knees, then seated back on his own heels. He carries the openwork crate called the *huacal* on his back, fashioned from slim branches or limbs, which symbolize the Spiritual Essence, the "box of

Figure 35. Oxomoco, the old magician or soothsayer, with Cipactonal, the sorceress clairvoyant. They occupy the center of the illustrated manuscript of the Borgia Codex, surrounded by pairs or couples of deities. From the Códice Borgia.

destiny." His elevated right arm indicates that his fate is not a prospect, but already an accomplished fact.

In his left hand he generally carries a small, flat earthenware dish normally used for pulque. Instead it contains nine kernels of corn, which can be seen falling over the mat. The soothsayer or wizard is reading his fortune, utilizing for the purpose as many kernels as there are pages or escorts of the night, or pairs of divinities, whose images adorn the periphery of the card. In each instance, their sequence indicates their function.

The striking of the kernels, and their manner of falling on the cards extended across the surface of the mat, augur the figure's destiny. Each grain of corn represents a planet. As they fall, they establish a planetary interrelation, considered from the standpoint of the temporality of the human span represented in the pictures. The two old deities, man and woman, are endowed with the faculties of the *auxhuatzin*, or soothsayer, indicated in the gourd each wears slung across his back or hung over his shoulder on a strap. The two miniscule deer-horn picks, seen in the uppermost portion of the card, indicate the fact that they are penitents, recounting the "original sin," as did Zeus and Hera on the occasion of the birth of their lame and deformed Hephaestus.

The divinity of the two figures is emphasized in their attributes as Lords of the Divinatory Arts—an honor reserved for the earliest progenitors of Mesoamerica, those who invented the calendar—illustrated in the midst of their complex retinue.

LAMATL SYMBOLISM

The Twenty-first lamatl symbolizes the creation of the world, and the gift of the gods for magic and divination, which permitted not only the formation of the Earth, but the trees and rivers, mountains and sky, human existence, everything to be revered in astonished gratitude, everything tangible or vagrant, viable or elusive, within the vital cycle of fifty-two years.

Cipactonal and Oxomoco represent the total concept of the creation as well as the computation of time, the art of analyzing dreams and the invention of judiciary astrology. In addition, they describe the beginning of agriculture, the divinity of corn—the essential staple—the development of art, architecture and illustrated language, and the formal structure of Good and Evil within a code, implicit in the notion of crime, or sin, and punishment or penance.

Yet if Cipactonal designed and confirmed the cultivation of corn he-she encompassed as well a concept verified in Roman law: "Every privilege implies an obligation." The "original transgression" required the exorcising of "sin," in a ritual established and fortified by divine dictate. Frustration and penance were therefore the product of the vicious or erroneous application of these dictates, and the misuse or waste of life's essential components.

For unless they were ignored or rejected, these components were available equally to the rich or poor, the graceful or the awkward, the blessed or the damned. And if everything was accountable, therefore everything was redeemable. Yet redemption involved specific processes and precepts, an abstract network onto which was woven the quintessential substance of a lifetime.

PARALLEL SYMBOLISM

The subtleties in the symbolic inferences involving Hephaestus, Osiris, Poseidon, Sobek, Geb, and Seth, like the parallel associations with Quetzalcoatl and Tezcatlipoca, or Oxomoco and Cipactonal, imply the contradictions, even the juxtaposition, of fire and light, good and evil; and considered creation as much an entity in itself as it is a counterposition to destruction.

The primal beasts, Typhon and Cipactli, like the dragon and the crocodile, were equally significant as representations of knowledge or its negation, wisdom from a distant and inexplicable source, yet whose impact determined all of life's potential on the Earth, within the computation of the span assigned to each individual. Brahma said:

> This (world) was darkness, unknowable, without form, beyond reason, as if utterly asleep. Then the august and self-existing Being, he who never unfolded, having unfolded this (universe) under the form of the great elements and others, having shown his energy, appeared to scatter the shades of darkness. The (Being) whom only the spirit can perceive, subtle, without distinct parts, eternal, including in himself all creatures, incomprehensible, appeared spontaneously. Wishing to draw different creatures from his body he first by thought produced the waters and deposited his seed in them. This (seed) became a golden egg as brilliant as the sun, in which he himself was born . . . the first father of all worlds.[11]

From himself this primal being drew the Spirit, "including in itself being and not-being," and from the Spirit he "drew the feeling of self which is conscious of personality and is master." And also "the great principle of the Soul, and all objects, especially the four Vedas, the disk, the alms dish and the sacrificial spoon," and then the five organs of the senses which perceive material things."[12]

The worlds of Heaven, air, and Earth are seen as a work of art, derived from an organic process of development. Humankind, ac-

---

[11]Felix Guirand, ed., *New Larousse Encyclopedia of Mythology*, translated by Richard Aldington and Delano Ames (London: Hamlyn House, 1969), p. 344.
[12]Ibid.

cording to this philosophy, is less concerned with power over nature than in freeing itself from the basis of existence, the law of transmigration, and the doctrine of salvation. For this purpose, then, humans are allowed, in fact privileged, to make use of the resources at their disposition. They may use them well or foolishly, but the responsibility is their own.

Remorse, regret, revenge, the lucid awareness of right and wrong, like the application of judgment or the definition of a course of action, may be doubly interpreted at all times, and like all dual principles—such as aggression and virility, conciliation, even redemption—encompass the total gamut of the philosophic panorama.

The attachment to the material world and its goods is therefore as complex and frightening, or charged with cosmic significance, as revitalizing or paralyzing, as the individual's application of certain well-defined principles, associated with the nature of his or her goal, in this or any other world. Truth and mendacity are thus as flexible as the absurd or the irrational. Understanding or knowledge can be as frustrating as ignorance. Even awareness, badly applied, represents an obstacle.

The repeated symbolism of the enduring and the indestructible indicates an attempt to make permanent the temporary: a house, palace, body, objects, position, love, sorrow, joy, even fulfillment, and integration. Yet these are fragile principles, to be won and earned each moment during a lifetime, like emotional stability or honor, and to be considered as intangible and ephemeral as life itself.

The staff of the man in the arcanum, like scepters, wands or whips, may be considered a device, a symbolic clutching in the hand of the reed, or *acatl*, Quetzalcoatl himself. Yet without its polarity even this key to Supreme Wisdom is worthless. For as life and death or creation and destruction are indivisible, so wisdom and foolishness, rage and serenity, an object and its application, in effect, mastery of the spirit and a spirit to master, are polarities in the abstraction of the dual concept. Without the one, the other ceases to exist. Therefore nothing, not even creation, stands alone.

Everything, even the august and self-existing Being, are itself and its opposite. Objects, in themselves, are useless, unless conceived or applied in relation to something else—in fact or by implication: of elegance, superiority, beauty, success, dignity—the appearance as opposed to the essence.

The twenty-first arcanum, like the corresponding lamatl, interwoven and intricate, thus describes the fundamental difference between the verbs "to have" and "to be." And therein lies the secret of Supreme Wisdom.

ARCANUM XXII

MYTHOLOGY OF THE WORLD

Absolutum, the sum of the upper triangle of the Great Arcanum of Magic, or the Magic Crown — *Corona Magica* — is usually termed "The World."

The Italian Visconti Tarot saw the card as the omnipotence of nature. The French version, around 1500, ignored the presence of the fundamental elements — air, earth, fire and water — to interpret in the arcanum a dual opposition between the generative forces of matter and spirituality, thus picturing the card as a romantic figure, a lyrical representation of the symbol of the Sun.

The modern tarot tends to either consider the card the essence of the elements manifest in a garland of success; or to see the world enveloped by a serpent, biting its own tail, representing the infinite captured, *everything* enclosed in the evolutionary ebb and flow of the universe. In both versions, an androgynous figure with magical powers is depicted on the card, symbolizing the metaphysical premise for the creation of life and the world.

This arcanum is consequently seen as Unity, The World containing everything, a self-supporting system, self-perpetuating and autonomous, the *Omnipotentia Naturalis* in which humankind is the adaptation of the Great Operation — that is, the Hermetic victory, of the self, or awareness, who desires exactly that which will, and therefore must, be.

Within such a hypothesis, humankind ceases "to be in pain" and becomes "pain" itself. We are no longer obliged "to be happy"; we become "happiness." There is no wanting "to be successful." We are success. We need not light up the sky with our names, for our names are the sky, and we are the sky.

Anshar, the male principle and Kishar, the female, who represented the celestial and terrestrial worlds, were born of Lakhmu and Lakhamu, the pair of monstrous serpents that encircled the world in the Tiamat, the sea which filled the Apsu, or enveloping abyss. So The World began and so it continues. Marduk created humanity "for the rejoicing of the gods" and fashioned the first man with the blood of Kingu. He constructed a dwelling-place for the gods in the sky and placed there the stars, which were their image. Osiris or Quetzalcoatl, like Marduk, fixed the length of the year and regulated the course of the heavenly bodies. They combined power and justice. Before Marduk's throne were laid the insignias of royalty: the scepter, the diadem, the crown, and the staff of command.

Yet the essential privilege of the gods was immortaltity, for humankind unattainable. Even Gilgamesh, who brought up the prickly plant of eternal youth—the maguey fashioned by Quetzalcoatl—from the bottom of the sea, found the branch, after all his trouble, had been stolen by a snake.

"In the beginning," it was said, "there was Time, then Desire and Darkness. From the union of these principles were born *Aer* (air), pure intelligence; and *Aura* (breath), the first living creature proceeding therefrom by movement." Cosmic time, according to the Phoenicians, the Mesopotamians before them, and the Aryans who devised the concept, contained all things.

This process is repeated in every act on Earth, in tears and fruit, wine and grain, the rainbow, flame, pomp, gardens, words, a heartbeat, a glance, the open hand, every miracle, every day, perpetuated and regenerated in seashells, sunsets, pillars, perfume. If the world is perfect then everything in it, on the Earth, in the sky, in the human mind, is sublime.

It remains, then, never to strive for perfection, quest for truth nor seek understanding. All of it, in ready and ample abundance, is already here. It always has been. We need only be silent. It whispers, like the breeze off the desert through the columns of Karnak. The breeze, or voices, telling how it always has been, and how it will be forever.

CARD DESCRIPTION

In the center of most cards a nude woman dances triumphantly, supported lightly on one graceful foot, which is balanced on the body of a serpent, which generally encircles the space she occupies in a perfect and serene oval, biting its own tail.

She sometimes appears crowned with a garland of large green leaves decorated with two red ribbons; they form a cross. The serpent in most decks is marked with thirty-three perfectly matched pairs of square-shaped scales.

The woman's body is partially covered with a light veil over her left shoulder. This drapes across her undefined sex, indicating her androgynous or youthful quality. She carries two small rods, reeds or twigs in her left hand. She holds them parallel to each other. Occasionally, in place of the rods, she holds a container of elixir.

Four mystical animals usually occupy the four corners of the picture. Their different forms indicate the kingdom of nature, emphasizing the quaternary of the Sphinx—to dare, to know, to be silent, to will—or the four elements or cardinal points: the eagle or dove is the east, morning, the spring equinox; the lion is the south, the summer solstice; a bull or horse indicates the west, afternoon, and the fall equinox; the angel represents the north night, and the winter solstice.

The card generally appears with the strongest possible colors, bright yellow indicating the Sun; brilliant blue, the heavens, and vivid red, the spirit of evolution.

CARD SYMBOLISM

The forces of nature which govern human life are encompassed in the card, expressed in the cycles of harmonic evolution, repeated in constant death and rebirth.

The fulfillment of purpose, and a favorable cosmic presence, are indicated in the fixed signs of the zodiac represented by the figures in the four corners of the card: the bull for Taurus, the lion for Leo, the eagle or dove for an evolved and positive Scorpio, the angel for Aquarius.

The presence of the female figure dancing euphorically in her self-contained world indicates the metaphysical synthesis of Absolute Truth, which needs no further protection and which lies beyond all deceit or consternation. This woman, bearer of life, holds the binary in her hand, within the closed circle of the serpent—that is, the astral realm, biting its own tail, enclosing the evolutionary current of the universe.

This figure is therefore omnipotent because it is released from desire, and desires only what will be and must be, what is inevitable and ordained within natural and eternal law.

LAMATL XXII

MYTHOLOGY OF QUETZALCOATL-TEZCATLIPOCA (THE PLUMED SERPENT/THE SMOKING MIRROR)

The twenty-second lamatl depicts the figure of Ehécatl Quetzalcoatl, the oracular Quetzalcoatl, of the Wind; and Tezcatlipoca, represented here as the astral truth of Providence.

Quetzalcoatl is the god of the Earth, of science, and of the arts, the breath of life in the wind and the word. His symbols are associated with purity in Maya as well as Aztec and Toltec mythology. In Yucatán he appears as K'ukamatz, "The Heart—the 'spirit' or vital essence—of the Sea." In Belize, Chiapas, and Guatemala he is Kukulkán, (Kukulcán) "the serpent who swims in the water." This serpent is the master of terrestrial knowledge, the five-pointed morning star of wisdom, magic, the mysteries of the universe, the representation of the four elements, and the four cosmic spaces, of which he occupies the center, for he was the First Priest, the sum of priestly wisdom.

On the card he appears inextricably bound to his divine twin, Tezcatlipoca, god of Heaven and Hell, of good and evil, of giving and withdrawing, the cosmic messenger of the Supreme Gods who knows—because he is night and mystery, the shadow, the "twisted leg" of the south, the First Priest of the True Serpent of the Nocturnal Sky—the arts of magic and death.

Together these gods were "night and the wind," the Morning Star and its death, Yohualli Ehécatl. Quetzalcoatl in his disguise, or *nahual*, of the plumed serpent, or as the "serpent of the clouds" (water) or the "obsidian serpent" (fire), exercised his powers over thunder and lightning, over water and vegetation, rain, the zodiac, and shared with Tezcatlipoca the dominion of the starry sky. Together they manifest cosmic polarity—darkness and light, water and fire, male and female—and then distributed the polarities among the four cardinal points. They became the night and the daytime sky, the One God with infinite advocations, especially, and eventually, the essential Ehécatl, "The Wind," as the *age of the Earth* at the end of the disastrous cosmic upheavals, when life and humankind, culture and abundance, were ordained in harmonic proliferation. He thus personified the triumphant dance of the tourbillon in which nothing is detained, for all is contained.

The myth was synthesized by the Maya in the figure of Hunab Ku, the "mouth and eyes of the Sun," whose son, a civilizing hero like Tezcatlipoca-Quetzalcoatl, invented drawing and letters. He was represented in the form of a red hand, to which the infirm offered their prayers.[1]

The wind gods, "pillars of heaven," were eventually integrated with Kukulkán, god of life and vice, who came from the west with nineteen companions. Two among these were gods of fish and two others gods of agriculture. There was also a god of thunder. They remained ten years in Yucatán. Kukulkán, according to the myths, made wise laws, then set sail and disappeared in the direction of the rising sun. He had been, they said, a god of creation, benefactor of the world, the son of two flowers, perpetually at war with an evil deity, the enemy of humankind. He would return, they asserted, when men and women had discovered harmony, within the "perfect circle" which envelops "all dreams, for then they would be dreams no longer."

---

[1]There is, in fact, in the southern portion of the Mexican state of Campeche, within the precinct of an *ejido*, or collective farm along the Chetumal-Escarcega Highway, ruins of a Maya site called "Manos Rojas," or "Red Hands." The name is drawn from the myth though the red handprints on the stucco walls of one of the temples is probably just paint and the product of a local hoax.

Thus the principle of light, or Quetzalcoatl, like Vishnu, crosses the whole universe in three steps. The wealth of such a world, said the Mesoamericans, was its fecundity, like Mayahúel, of the four hundred breasts, or Hariti, the Vedic goddess, suckling five hundred demons. Here there would be no need for fear, thirst, famine, charity, worship, compassion, or wisdom as isolated entities, and more, as we saw on the previous card, were encompassed in the inherent condition of the total, the Absolute.

LAMATL DESCRIPTION

The two central figures of the twenty-second lamatl face each other. Their arms are extended and opened wide, to encompass the intervening space. The figure on the left appears with his face partially covered with the mask of Ehécatl Quetzalcoatl. He wears the peaked jaguar skin cap of the Huastec gods and a spiral breastplate formed of a conch, indicating the tourbillon.

His posture reaffirms the principle of movement, source of the first living creature. He is about to drop on one knee, but as yet has not completed the gesture. Quetzalcoatl bears in his hands the instruments of penitence described with regard to Cipactonal in the previous lamatl: the pouch of copal, the incense-burner, and other appliances which assign him in this context to the role of the inferior deity.

At this moment the figure he faces represents the superior power, Tezcatlipoca, his hands unburdened, his arms free. He bears no

Figure 36. Left: Quetzalcoatl as the god of the wind and the rain from the east. Right: Tezcatlipoca, god of the night and the rain of the north.

instruments of penitence or adoration, nothing to protect or support him. His headdress is surrounded by stars.

LAMATL SYMBOLISM

The two figures on the card describe the myth that tells of Quetzal-coatl's flight after his moral defeat at the hands of a shrewd and unscrupulous Tezcatlipoca. The enlightened Creator God, author and exponent of supreme wisdom, who taught his people religion and the harnessing of the elements, was led by a ruse into degradation and dismay, and as a result, to a lamentable degree of excess. The story claims he abused the sacred pulque and the prescribed rituals with regard to the body. In short, he sinned.

Tezcatlipoca the Black exhibited Quetzalcoatl's downfall before the people of his capital, in Tula, and they demanded his expulsion. Quetzalcoatl then left them, it was told, to wander over the face of the Earth. Yet everywhere, despite his disgrace, he was adored as the Supreme God. He was pursued and questioned, petitioned at every step to reveal the secrets of the universe. He finally reached the edge of the sea, from whence everyone had come, he explained, and there, according to the legend, he was "self-immolated" and became the Evening Star.

In the telling of the tale Quetzalcoatl, at the height of his promi-nence in Tula, looked one day upon himself in the mirror, that clouded mirror that was the wily Tezcatlipoca—an obsidian mirror—and he was revealed as wrinkled and decrepit. For a time, he went mad. In his desperation, he had allowed himself to be seduced by the illusion in drink and fornication, despairing because his vitality had waned. If he were truly a god, he said, he would have entered the realm of the immortals. Thus he "propitiated his transmigration" in order "to establish his immortality in the stars, and the wisdom he had sowed among the men on the earth."[2]

PARALLEL SYMBOLISM

The serpent, that emerged from the sea, became life on this Earth, wisdom, and the gods, who dwelled in the stars. Tezcatlipoca, the "devil," apparently defeated Quetzalcoatl—as the vain and the vacil-

---

[2]Fr. Bernardino de Sahagún in *Historia General de las Cosas de la Nueva España*, Book 1, Chapter V (Mexico: Editorial Porrua, 1979), p. 32.

lating in all of us may potentially defeat the resolved—by reminding him of his worldly self. Ultimately, however, the godlike quality in Quetzalcoatl, in all men, searched until it found the unthreatened and enduring realm of the soul, in the stars of the sky.

If The Fool in the twenty-first arcanum represents the transformation of The Magician in the first arcanum, then The Fool himself is finally resolved in Unity—in the abandoning of his powers, ambition, the somnambulistic state of the unreal—in his identification with the Absolute.

The Magician, like Quetzalcoatl, would have us believe his dominance and control over the affairs of life on the Earth. The Fool, with his mismatched garments and ridiculous cap, seems to indicate the opposite, the rumpled version on the far side of the mirror: Tezcatlipoca.

The adept, however, the person of true privilege, in effect penetrates the perfect wisdom of the gods and nature, to become one with the Sun, according to Hermetic precepts, the only unconquerable force. He is therefore the true Magician. More than a soothsayer, a wizard, or a philosopher, "the magician" brings solace, dominates anger and passion, enjoys the secret of riches as their possessor but never their slave. He can foresee even that which depends on fate. He overcomes all obstacles. For him there are no mysteries. His intuition remains eternally intact. He is magnetism, healing, wise counsel, revelation and discovery. He is perfecting and perfection.

His body, then, is as if dissolved in the mirage beyond the Absolute. Totality becomes his very life. There is nothing inside or outside, no past or future, no relativity in truth. The truth now exists independently of his knowledge or ignorance of it. He *is* Truth. There is no longer a separation between humankind and the gods. The whole wealth of experience of everything that has lived, or lives, or will live is part of this being, for "the magician" is as integrated into the wholeness of The World as The World itself. Nothing lies beyond. He *is* the beyond. And while he is everything, he is nothing.

EPILOGUE

In the middle of the Western Desert in Egypt lie the ruins of an ancient city. Once it was grand, shaded by trees, with broad avenues and fountains. Now it is sand, russet and gold, crumbling into the desert from whence it came. Its color is all that remains of a splendor long past.

All through history people have built great cities and legends, temples and towers, but eventually all of them, the richest, the highest, have been glutted by the jungle or returned to the desert, or were blasted to pieces by strange battles in foreign centuries, to be sacked by others who knew little of those previous gods or leaders, until nothing was left, sometimes not even the name.

Gods and kings, cups and gold, have gone the way of their sanctuaries and palaces. Yet if anything remains it may be defined in the quest, for something beyond cold stone or bright gilt, the idea, a dream, the Way, not of the flesh or of glory, but of the spirit, which needs no temple.

Towers have tumbled, but The Word remains, and with it the teachings of curiously similar precepts, strikingly common in their essence or in the abstract implication of all cultures. Many of these words have been distorted. The images have been blurred, in order to serve the immediate interests of another passing leader, battle, conquest, or imposition, so the basis of what went before has been obscured. Still a part of the grandeur, like the light of the Sun these people worshipped in one form or another, has managed to survive, to guide us yet.

We have led the traveler of the mind through the passageways of the tarot and the *Tonalamatl*, studies of philosophy through divination and the occult arts, but more, much more, lies in the myths of the Mayas. The correlation of the stories of the Greeks, the Mesopotamians, or from the Far East with those others, products of the people called "The Greeks of Mesoamerica," is material for another study, for these extraordinary people on the jungle acropolis of now crumbled cities, long ago discovered what modern societies are still trying to define.

They forgot to look, these civilized, industrialized, urban people of today. The "precise and exact science of mythology," said Goethe, supplied all the answers, again and again. It only remains to apply this wisdom, the experience of the past and the vision of the future, deciphered in the depths of deep green wells and dense forests.

Whether this knowledge originated in Mesoamerica or was brought from Japan or Polynesia, Mongolia, India, or China remains to be confirmed, and maybe it never will be. Whether this perception of life was native or imported, assimilated and exported again, has never been verified but at this late date can only be considered of very little consequence. It was there. And it is there still, on the walls of fallen buildings, or in the pages of badly translated books, in the erroneous interpretations, documents withered or partially destroyed, defamed, deformed, and dismaying, but it is there.

Like the richest of treasures, the tombs and coffers of kings or the Books of the Dead, it is ours to behold, secrets no longer hidden, the pulse of yesterday, life everlasting, the world's labor, the Moon's orbit and our own, patterns, promises, the outstretched hands of the Universe.

It is ours for the taking.

GLOSSARY OF TERMS

ácatl (áh-caht-tuhl): "Cane" or "reed," emblem of Quetzalcoatl (Coo-wetz-ahl-cóe-ah-tuhl), and when capitalized, a sign in the Almanac of Days.

acicintli (ah-see-sceént-lee): A type of plant that lives in or near the water.

Atlantéotl (Aht-lahn-téh-oh-tuhl): Giant deities, like a phalanx of Atlases, who hold the world upon their shoulders.

axolotl (ash-oh-lóh-tuhl): Salamander.

Camaxtli (Cah-másht-lee): One of the many names for Tezcatlipoca (Tess-caht-lee-póh-cah), used among the tribes of Tlaxcala and Huex-otzingo, near the present-day city of Puebla.

Ce-Acatl Topiltzin (Say-áh-caht-tuhl Toe-peélt-seen): "Lord of Tula" (Quetzalcoatl).

Chalchiuhtlicue (chawl-chewt-leék-kuay): "Skirts of Jade," the goddess of water.

Chalchiuhtotolin (Chawl-chew-tote-toe-leán): "The Jade Turkey," another manifestation of Tezcatlipoca.

Chántico (Chánt-tea-coe): "The Hearth."

Chicnahui Ehécatl (Chick-now-we Eh-héck-cat-tuhl): "Nine Wind," calendrical description of Quetzalcoatl.

Cintéotl (Seen-téh-oh-tuhl): The corn deity.

Cipactli (See-páct-lee): Primal dragon, in effect, Mother Earth.

Cipactonal (See-pact-toe-náhl): "Day of Cipactli," honoring the first or primary man or woman on Earth—from whose depths emerge the hatched eggs of the alligator or dragon, considered the Mother of All Things.

Citallantonali (seat-all-toe-nahli): Another name for Tonacatecuhtli, appearing as a nocturnal warrior god.

Citlalinicui (Seat-lah-lean-knée-kwee): "Skirts of Stars."

Coatepec (Kwaht-teh-péck): Literally, "Place of the Serpents," the origin or womb which gave birth to *Huitzilopochtli* (Wheat-zeal-oh-póached-lee), Aztec "Hummingbird of the South," in effect, the Sun God, by means of Immaculate Conception.

Coatlicue (Kwaht-líck-kway): "Skirts of Serpents," the mother of Huitzilopochtli.

Colhua (Cóal-wah): One of the tribes in the Aztec group.

Cuezaltzin (Coo-west-salt-séen): "Flame."

Ehécatl (Eh-héck-cah-tuhl): "The Wind," one of the manifestations of Quetzalcoatl.

Huehuecoyotl (Way-way-coh-yó-tuhl): "The Old Coyote," considered to have been the "first man" or the "the wise man," also "The Wise Old Man."

lámatl (láh-mah-tuhl): "Laminate" or "card" in the deck of the *Tonalamátl* (Toe-nah-láh-mah-tuhl), seen in total as the "almanac" or "Book of Days."

Huitzilopochtli (Wheat-zeal-oh-poáched-lee): "The Left-Handed Hummingbird" or "The Hummingbird of the South," one of the four Creator Gods, founder of the *Mexica* (Mesh-éek-cah) people.

Huixotzinca (We-hoat-séen-cah): One of the tribes encompassed in the Aztec nation or Alliance.

Huihuitéotl (Way-way-táy-oh-tuhl): "The Old God," considered to be the presence, or the essence, of "Fire."

Huitznahua (Wheatz-náh-wah): Huitzilopochtli's "four hundred siblings," the army that opposed the Aztec deity—in effect, a Victory figure—and who protested Coatlicue's "immaculate conception," which they described as a hoax.

Itztlacoliuhqui (Eats-lah-coal-liéu-key): "Twisted Obsidian," the "God of the Cold," another and more sinister manifestation of Black Tezcatlipoca.

Itzli (Eáts-lee): Obsidian, "The Stone Forged in Hell," therefore both a concept and object of great value and emblematic versatility.

Itzpapalotl (Eats-papa-lóe-tuhl): "The Obsidian Butterfly," the essence of female desirability seen as hard, cold, "a Treasure from Hell."

Ixcozauhqui (Its-coe-sów-key): "Yellow Face," in effect, a deity figure seen as the essence of "fire."

Ixcuina (Its-queén-nah): "Lascivious Woman," the "first" or "primary" woman, another manifestation of *Tlazoltéotl* (Tuh-láh-soul-téh-oh-tuhl).

Mamalhuaztli (Mama-wáltz-lee): Blowtorch.

Maguey (Mah-gáy): The *agave* (ah-gáh-vey) cactus, source of fiber and "honey-water" or *pulque* (poól-kay), a fermented and therefore intoxicating beverage, considered a sacred gift of the gods, equivalent to Greek "nectar."

Maquixcoatl (Mah-keys-coe-áh-tuhl): "Two-headed serpent," another name for Huitzilopochtli.

Mayahuel (Mah-yah-hoo-éll): "Goddess of the Maguey."

Mexica (Mesh-éek-cah): Dominant tribe among the Aztec group.

Mictlacacihuatl (Micked-lack-cah-sée-wah-tuhl): "Infernal Woman," Queen of the Underworld.

Mictlán (Micked-láhn): "Hell" or "Underworld," a legendary "Place of the Dead."

Mictlantecuhtli (Micked-lahn-teh-cóot-lee): "Lord of the Underworld."

Mixcoatl (Mees-coe-áh-tuhl): One of the names associated with Tezcatlipoca, especially among the tribes of Tlaxcala and Huexotzingo.

Moyocoyani (Moe-yo-coe-yáwn-knee): The "Almighty," one of the many forms of Tezcatlipoca.

Nahua or *Nohua* (Náh-wah or Nóh-wah): Ethnic nation of the Central Mexican highland plateau.

Nanahuatzin (Nana-wáht-seen): The priest named the "pustule," who became "The Sun" in a legendary ceremony.

Nonoaloas Tlacochcalcas (No-no-wall-lów-as Tuhlah-coach-cáll-cass): A tribe that came from the region known as *Chalco* (Chawl-coh), not far from present-day Mexico City.

Ocelotl (Oh-say-lóh-tuhl): The Jaguar God, a primal deity among the Olmecs, considered as a Supreme Commander, a transformation or earthly manifestation of the Almighty, as in the disguises of Zeus as he appeared among mortals.

Olmec (Ohl-meck): The culture generally considered to be the oldest in Mesoamerica, whose origins are to this day obliterated by time and distance, though one theory assigns their beginnings to El Salvador in Central America, from which they migrated to the Mexican Gulf Coast; and another places them among the collection of peoples known as the "Mayas," whose culture was in effect influenced by their Jaguar deity and priesthood.

Omecihuatl (Oh-may-see-wáh-tuhl): "Alma Mater," the "Mother Goddess," female half of the "Supreme Couple."

Ometecuhtli (Oh-may-teh-cúht-lee): "Lord God," male half of the "Supreme Couple."

Omeyocan (Oh-may-yóh-cahn): Resting place or "Paradise" of the "Supreme Couple," Ometecuhtli and Omecihuatl, a kind of Aztec "Olympus" for a Mesoamerican Zeus and Hera.

Omitecuhtli (Oh-me-teh-cóot-lee): "Lord Bone," another name for Aztec deity Huitzilopochtli.

Oxomoco (Oh-show-móe-coe): First man or woman, assigned the authorship of the "Original Sin"; another version of Tezcatlipoca.

Pachtli (Pátched-lee): A kind of moss or straw.

Patécatl (Pah-téh-cah-tuhl): "He of the Herbs," in effect, the God of pulque, a fermented ceremonial beverage.

Piltzintecuhtli (Peel-scent-teh-coot-lee): "Lord Child," the young Quetzalcoatl.

Pulque (Póol-kay): A beverage fermented from the honey-water of the maguey and generally applied in ceremonies and commemorations.

Quetzalcoatl (Coo-wetz-ahl-coe-áh-tuhl): "The Plumed Serpent," manifestation of God seen as Goodness, "The Illuminated," implying "Grace" and "Forgiveness." Generally interpreted as the "opposite" or "complement" of Tezcatlipoca, in which case both are seen collectively as "God" and "The Devil," or two sides of the "good-evil" dichotomy. "The Plumed Serpent" was also the "Lord of Tula," the Toltec capital, author of crafts, the metallurgic arts, philosophic and esoteric wisdom, and the knowledge of healing through herbs and plants.

Quiyauhtecuhtli (Key-yow-teh-cóot-lee):"Lord of the Rain."

Tecciztecatl (Tex-sees-téh-cah-tuhl): "He From the Resting-Place of the Seashell," priest converted ceremonially into the Moon.

Tecpaneca (Teck-pah-néck-cah): A tribe from the Central Mexican Plateau.

Técpatl (Téck-pat-tuhl): Flintstone.

Tlacaxipchauliztli (Tah-lah-cash-eep-chaw-uhl-its-lee): The month during which the largest number of sacrifices were celebrated, although also interpreted as a kind of "Lent," the "sacrifice" in this case assumed to imply only "penitence" or "renunciation of temptation."

Tlahuicac Mamalhuazocan (Tah-lah-wéek-ack Mamahl-wah-zóe-cahn): The "Heaven" or "Paradise" of the "fire forgers," that is, vulcanizers or smiths.

Tlahuizcalpantecuhtli (Tah-lah-wees-call-pant-leh-cóot-lee): "Lord of the Dawn."

Tlaloc (Tah-láw-loak): "The Rain God."

Tlalocan (Tah-lah-lów-cahn): "Resting-Place of the Rain" or "Paradise," a "Garden of Eden" of green growing things and running water, tantamount to Nirvana or an Islamic paradise of flowering vines and splashing fountains.

Tlatauhqui Tezcatlipoca (Tah-lahtah-úh-key Tess-caht-lee-póh-cah): "Smoke from the Red Mirror." "Tezcatlipoca the Red" is associated with *Xipe-Totec* (Shíp-pee Tóe-teck), a Zapotec deity from Oaxaca, symbolizing a vengeful victory, but also a semiotic triumph of the will over physical pain and adversity.

Tlaltecuhtli (Taw-lawl-teh-cóot-lee): "Lord" or "Lady" Earth.

Tlalxicco (Tah-lawl-shé-coh): Nahuatl linguistic adjustment of the Olmec concept of the "Center of the Earth" or "Earth's Navel," as Apollo conceived Delphi or in the Chinese sense of the "Middle Kingdom."

Tlaxcalteca (Tah-lass-cahl-téh-cah): Tribe within the Aztec group, associated with the present-day state or region of Tlaxcala.

Tlazoltéotl (Tah-lass-soul-téh-oh-tuhl): "The Mexican Aphrodite," goddess of carnal love and everything denominated "dirty" or "sinful," associated with "filth" and the "excrecia of the plastic world," in other words, "pornography."

Tochtli (Tóacht-lee): Rabbit (implying as well a state of inebriation).

Toci (Tóe-chee): Midwife, also "Goddess of Old Women," always appearing wrinkled and decrepit.

Tonacacihutal (Toe-nah-cah-see-wáh-tuhl): "Divine Mother," the female half of the Supreme Couple, later reinterpreted as the Virgin of Guadalupe, perfect and blameless, but still endowed with Pre-Hispanic emblems and attributes.

Tonacatecuhtli (Toe-nah-cah-teh-cóot-lee): God Almighty, the male half of the Supreme Couple, the sublime authority or father figure, later transposed to Christianity.

Tonalámatl (Toe-nah-láh-mah-tuhl): "Book of Days," anthology of the sum of the twenty-two "cards" or "laminates."

Tonalpohualli (Toe-nah-poh-wáhl-lee): The "Count" or "Accounting" of the lunar calendar.

Tonan Tlaltecuhtli (Tóe-nahn Tah-lahl-teh-cóot-lee): "Our Lady of the Mother Earth."

Tonatiuh (Toe-nah-tee-óu): "Solar Fire."

Tzizimime (Tzee-see-mee-meh): The Stars.

Tzolkin Augurs (Tzóhl-keen Ah-ghours): Maya books of destiny or prophesies of humankind.

Xipe-Totec (She-pee Tóe-teck): "Our Lord encased in Human Skin," generally—though in the metaphoric sense—assumed to dress in the skin of his vanquished victim, symbolically associated with the triumph of one person, battle, or cause over another. A manifestation of Tezcatlipoca, the Red.

Xiuhcoatl (Shoe-coh-áh-tuhl): "Serpents of Fire."

Xiuhtecuhtli (Shoe-teh-cóot-lee): "Lord Turquoise," the God of Fire.

Xochipilli (So-chee-péal-lee): "Prince of Flowers," a young and vigorous god, associated with the height of virility.

Xochiquetzal (So-chee-ket-sáhl): The fresh and youthful goddess of virginity and loveliness, Springtime, the female half of the venerated "Young Couple," the ideal of newly-wedded bliss and trust.

Xolotl (Show-lów-tuhl): An escort or page, who generally accompanies Mixcoatl, often illustrated as a jackal or canine figure.

Yayauhqui Tezcatlipoca (Yah-yów-key Tess-caht-lee-poh-cah): "Smoke from the Black (Obsidian) Mirror," the deity of Evil, the Devil, the reflection of the negative in oneself.

Yeotl (Yeah-óh-tuhl): Warrior god, one of the manifestations of Tezcatlipoca. Also known as Yaotl (Yah-oh-tull): the enemy.

Zapotec (Sáw-poh-teck): One of the oldest and most intellectual cultures in Mesoamerica, concentrated in the area of Oaxaca in the south.

BIBLIOGRAPHY AND RECOMMENDED READING

Alba, Víctor. *Politics and the Labor Movement in Latin America*. Carol Miller, trans. Stanford: Stanford University Press, 1968.

Alemán Velasco, Miguel. *La Isla de los Perros*. Mexico: Editorial Diana, 1983.

André-Bonnet, Léonard: *La Divination Chez les Aztlantes*. France: Adyard-Paris, 1950.

Augur, Helen. *Zapotec*. New York: Doubleday, 1954.

Calderón de la Barca, Mme. (Fanny). *Life in Mexico*. New York: Dutton, 1940.

Campbell, Joseph. *Creative Mythology*. Volume 4 of *The Masks of God*. London, Arkana, Penguin, 1991.

_____. *Myths to Live By*. New York: Bantam, 1972.

_____. *Occidental Mythology*. Volume 3 of *The Masks of God*. London: Arkana, Penguin, 1991.

_____. *Oriental Mythology*. Volume 2 of *The Masks of God*. London: Arkana, Penguin, 1991.

_____. *Primitive Mythology*. Volume 1 of *The Masks of God*. London: Arkana, Penguin, 1991.

Caso, Alfonso. *El Pueblo del Sol*. Mexico: Fondo de Cultura Económica, 1978.

_____. *Reyes y Reinas de la Mixteca*, Vols. 1 & 2. Mexico: Fondo de Cultura Económica, 1977.

Castiglioni, Arturo. *Encantamiento y Magia*. Milan: A. Mandatori, 1943; Mexico: Fondo de Cultura Económica, 1947.

Cartas de Indias, 5 vols. (*Carta de las Antillas, Seno Mejicano y Costas de Tierra Firme y de la América Setentrional*). Mexico: Secretaría de Hacienda y Crédito Público, 1981.

Ceram, C. W. *Gods, Graves & Scholars: The Story of Archeology*. Trans. from German, E.G. Garside. New York: Alfred A. Knopf, 1952; revised edition published 1967.

Chilam Balam (El Libro de los Libros de . . .). Barrera Vázquez, Alfredo and Rendón, Silvia, trans. Mexico: Fondo de Cultura Económica, 1948.

Chavero, Alfredo. *Resumen Integral de México a Través de los Siglos*, Volume 1. Mexico: Cía. General de Ediciones, 1974.

Clark, Kenneth. *Civilization*. New York: Harper & Row, 1969.

College of Mexico. *Historia General de México* (2 volumes), 1981.

Cotterell, Arthur. *A Dictionary of World Mythology.* New York: Perigee, G. P. Putnam & Sons, 1982.

Crim, Keith. *The Perennial Dictionary of World Religions.* San Francisco: HarperCollins, 1989.

del Paso y Troncoso, Francisco. *Códice Borbónico,* facsimile edition including description, history and analysis. Mexico: Siglo XXI Editores, 1993.

de la Fuente, Beatriz. "Introducción al Simposio 'Recientes Investigaciones sobre la Civilización Olmeca,'" *Arqueología* magazine, National Institute of Anthropology and History, Mexico, No. 3, Jan.-June 1990.

de Chardin, Teilhard. *The Phenomenon of Man.* Intro. Sir Julian Huxley. New York: Harper & Row, 1961.

Díaz del Castillo, Bernal. *The Discovery and Conquest of Mexico.* New York: Grove Press, 1958.

Enciso, Jorge. *Designs From Pre-Columbian Mexico.* New York: Dover Publications, 1971.

Ferguson, Marilyn. *The Aquarian Conspiracy, Personal and Social Transformation in the 1980's.* Los Angeles: J.P. Tarcher, 1980.

Flaum, Eric. *Discovery, Exploration through the Centuries.* New York: Gallery Books, 1990.

Forrest, W.G. *The Emergence of Greek Democracy.* London: Weidenfeld & Nicolson, 1979.

Frazer, Sir James G. *The Golden Bough.* New York: Macmillan, 15th printing, 1979. Orig. 1922.

Fuentes, Carlos. *The Buried Mirror: Reflections on Spain and the New World.* New York: Houghton Mifflin, 1992.

Gonçalves de Lima, Osvaldo. *El Maguey y el Pulque en los Codices Mexicanos.* Mexico: Fondo de Cultura Económica, 1978.

Graves, Robert. *The Greek Myths,* 2 volumes. New York and London: Penguin Books, 1955. Revised and reprinted 1990.

_____. *Los Mitos Griegos.* Mexico: Alianza Editorial, 1992.

Guillén, Ann Cyphers. "Figurillas femeninas del Preclásico en Chalcatzingo." *Arqueología* magazine, National Institute of Anthropology and History, Mexico, No. 3, Jan.-June, 1990.

Guirand, Felix, ed. *Larousse Mythologie Générale.* France: Librairie Larousse, 1959. Richard Aldington and Delano Ames, trans., with a panel of editorial advisers: *New Larousse Encyclopedia of Mythology.* Intro. Robert Graves. London: Hamlyn Publishing Group, 1968.

Haberland, Wolfgang. *Culturas de la América Indígena/Mesoamérica y América Central.* Frankfurt am Main: Akademische Verlagsgesellschaft Athenaion, 1969. Mexico: Fondo de Cultura Económica, 1974.

Hagen, Víctor W. von. *The Aztec, Man and Tribe.* New York: Mentor, New American Library, 1958.

_____. *Maya Explorer: John Lloyd Stephens and the Lost Cities of Central America and Yucatán.* San Francisco: Chronicle Books, 1990.

_____. *World of the Maya.* New York: Mentor, New American Library, 1960.

Hamilton, Edith. *Mythology: Timeless Tales of Gods and Heroes.* New York: New American Library, 1969.

Hawking, Stephen. *A Brief History of Time, From the Big Bang to the Black Holes.* Intro. by Carl Sagan. New York: Bantam Books, 1990.

Hofstadter, Douglas R. *Gödel, Escher, Bach: An Eternal Golden Braid.* New York: Vintage Books, 1980.

Homer. *The Iliad.* E. V. Rieu, trans. New York: Penguin, 1979.

_____. *The Odyssey.* E. V. Rieu, trans. London: Penguin, 1979.

Jensen, Ad. E. *Mitos y Culto Entre Pueblos Primitivos.* Weisbaden: Franz Steiner Verlag, 1960; Mexico: Fondo de Cultura Económica, 1966.

Johnson, John J. *The Military and Society in Latin America.* Stanford, CA: Stanford University Press, 1964.

Karen, Ruth. *Feathered Serpent, The Rise and Fall of the Aztecs.* New York: Four Winds Press, 1979.

Kingsborough, Lord (Sir Edward King, Viscount of Kingsborough). *Antigüedades de México,* 4 vols. Mexico: Secretaría de Hacienda y Crédito Público, 1964.

Kerler, Richard & Christa María. *El Horóscopo Azteca.* Germany: Falken-Verlag (Aztekenhoroskop), 1981; Mexico: EDAF Mexicana, 1984.

Koldeway, Robert. *The House of the Foundation of Heaven and Earth.* Germany, 1898. Cited in Ceram, C.W.: *Gods, Graves & Scholars.*

Krickeberg, Walter. *Etnología de América.* Mexico: Fondo de Cultura Económica, 1982.

_____. *Las Antiguas Culturas Mexicanas.* Berlin: Safari Verlag, 1956; Mexico: Fondo de Cultura Económica, 1982.

_____. *Mitos y Leyendas de los Aztecas, Mayas y Muiscas.* Dusseldorf: Diederichs Verlag, 1968; Mexico: Fondo de Cultura Económica, 1980.

Landa, Friar Diego de. *Yucatán Before and After the Conquest.* Translated and with notes by William Gates. New York: Dover, 1978. Based on material compiled by Landa c. 1540.

Leander, Birgitta. *Herencia Cultural del Mundo Nahuatl.* Mexico: SepSetentas, 1972.

Leeming, David Adams. *Mythology, The Voyage of the Hero.* New York: Harper & Row, 1981.

León-Portilla, Miguel. *Toltecayotl, Aspectos de la Cultura Nahuatl.* Mexico: Fondo de Cultura Económica, 1980.

Lévi-Strauss, Claude. *Mitologías, de la Miel a las Cenizas.* Paris: Librairie Plon, 1966; Mexico: Fondo de Cultura Económica, 1978.

_____. *Mitologías, Lo Crudo y lo Cocido.* Paris: Librairie Plon, 1966; Mexico: Fondo de Cultura Económica, 1968.

Lindsey, Hal (with Carlson, C.C.). *The Late Great Planet Earth.* Grand Rapids, MI: Zondervan, 1972.

Luxton, Richard and Pablo Balam. *The Mystery of the Mayan Hieroglyphs: The Vision of an Ancient Tradition.* San Francisco: HarperCollins, 1981.

Malraux, André. *The Voices of Silence.* Gilbert Stuart, trans. New York: Doubleday, 1953.

Markman, Robert H. & Markman, Peter T. *The Flayed God, The Mythology of Mesoamerica.* San Francisco: HarperCollins, 1992.

Matos Moctezuma, Eduardo. *El Rostro de la Muerte.* Mexico: GV Editores, 1987.

_____. *El Templo Mayor de México, Crónicas del Siglo XVI.* Mexico: Asociación Nacional de Libreros, 1981.

McHenry, J. Patrick. *A Short History of Mexico.* New York: Doubleday, 1962.

Medina, Jesús, ed. *México: Leyendas, Costumbres, Trajes y Danzas.* Mexico: Medina Hermanos, 1970.

Méndez, Conny. *Metafísica al Alcance de Todos,* 4 vols. Mexico: Asociación Civil Pro Enseñanzas Parasicológicas, 1985.

Miller, Carol. *El Profeta Alado.* Mexico: Editorial Diana, 1990.

_____. *Mundo Maya: Viajes.* Mexico: Publicaciones El Día, 1993.

_____. *Más Viajes por el Mundo Maya: la Península de Yucatán, Belice y El Salvador.* Mexico: Lotería Nacional, 1994.

Miller, Mary and Karl Taube. *The Gods and Symbols of Ancient Mexico and the Maya.* London: Thames & Hudson, 1993.

Montejo, Víctor. *The Bird Who Cleans the World and Other Mayan Fables.* Willimantic, CT: Curbstone Press, 1992.

Morley, Sylvanus G. *The Ancient Maya.* Stanford, CA: Stanford University Press, 1946.

Palerm, Angel and Wolf, Eric. *Agricultura y Civilización en Mesoamérica.* Mexico: SepSetentas, 1972.

Parsons, Talcott, ed. *Knowledge and Society.* Washington, DC: Voice of America Forum Lectures, May 1968.

Peck, M. Scott. *The Road Less Traveled.* New York: Touchstone, 1978.

Peñalosa, Joaquín A. *El Mexicano y los 7 Pecados Capitales*. Mexico: Ediciones Paulinas, 1972.

Piña Chan, Román. *Historia, Arqueología y Arte Prehispánico*. Mexico: Fondo de Cultura Económica, 1980.

_____. *Quetzalcoatl, Serpiente Emplumada*. Mexico: Fondo de Cultura Económica, 1981.

Plutarch. *The Lives of the Noble Grecians and Romans in Great Books*, Vol. 14 (Dryden Translation). Chicago: Enclyclopaedia Britanica, 1952.

Popol Vuh: Las Antiguas Historias del Quiché (Maya). Recinos, Adrián, trans. Mexico: Fondo de Cultura Económica, 1952.

Renfrew, Colin. *Before Civilization*. New York: Alfred A. Knopf, 1973.

Reed, Alma M. *The Ancient Past of Mexico*. New York: Crown, 1966.

Rieu, E.V. (Livy). *Rome and the Mediterranean*. London: Penguin, 1978.

Rodríguez Vallejo, José. *Ixcatl, El Algodón Mexicano*. Mexico: Fondo de Cultura Económica, 1963.

Sadhu, Mouni. *The Tarot: A Contemporary Course of the Quintessence of Hermetic Occultism*. North Hollywood, CA: Wilshire, 1962.

Sahagún, Fr. Bernardino de. *Historia General de las cosas de Nueva España*. Mexico: Editorial Porrua, 1979. This book is a 16th century compilation of the language and customs by a Franciscan friar, with annotations and indexing by Angel María Garibay K. Available in English as *Florentine Codex, General History of the Things of New Spain*, translated by Arthur J. Anderson and Charles E. Dibble. Salt Lake City, UT: University of Utah Press, 1982.

Seler, Eduard. *Comentarios al Codice Borgia*, 3 volumes. Mexico: Fondo de Cultura Económica, 1980. Orginally published in German, Codex Borgia, Eine Altmexikanische Bilderschrift der Bibliothek der Congregatio de Propaganda Fidel, 1904.

Shri Purohit Swámi. *The Geetá, The Gospel of the Lord Shri Krishna*. London: Faber and Faber, 1973 (first published 1935).

Shri Patanjali, and William Butler Yeats. *Ten Principal Upanishads*. New York: Faber and Faber, 1970.

Smart, Ninian. *The Long Search*. Boston: Little Brown, 1977.

Smith, Bradley. *Mexico: Arte e Historia*. Mexico: Editora Cultural y Educativa, 1969.

Sodi Morales, Demetrio. *The Maya World*. Mexico: Editorial Minutiae, 1976.

Soustelle, Jacques. *La Vida Cotidiana de los Aztecas en Vísperas de la Conquista*. Paris: Hachette, 1955; Mexico: Fondo de Cultura Económica, 1982.

Spranz, Bodo. *Los Dioses en los Códices Mexicanos del Grupo Borgia.* Mexico: Fondo de Cultura Económica, 1973. (Originally published in German).

Stephens, John L. *Incidents of Travel in Central America, Chiapas & Yucatán.* New Brunswick, NJ: Rutgers University Press, 1949.

Tejera Gaona, Héctor. "Antropología y etnología en Mexico." Article published in Mexico, *Antropológicas* Magazine, National Autonomous University in Mexico City, Oct. 1993.

Thoorens, León. *De Sumer a la Grecia Clásica.* Barcelona: Manuel Tamayo, 1977.

Toor, Frances. *A Treasury of Mexican Folkways.* New York: Crown, 1960.

Toscano, Salvador. *Cuauhtemoc.* Mexico: Fondo de Cultura Económica, 1982. Originally published in 1953.

Tripp, Edward, ed. *The Meridan Handbook of Classical Mythology.* New York: New American Library, 1974.

Vaillant, G.C. *Aztecs of Mexico.* New York: Penguin, 1962.

Valentini, Norberto and Clara Di Meglio. *El Sexo en el Confesionario.* Mexico: Editorial Grijalbo, 1974.

Van Over, Raymond. *Sun Songs: Creation Myths from Around the World.* New York: Mentor, New World Library, 1980.

Velikovsky, Immanual. *Mundos en Colisión.* Mexico: Editorial Diana, 6th ed., 1964; New York: Dell, 1950.

Warner, Rex. *The Stories of the Greeks.* New York: Farrar, Straus, & Giroux, 1967.

Weaver, Muriel Porter. *The Aztecs, Maya and their Predecessors.* New York: Academic Press, 1981.

Wilhelm, Richard, trans. (Baynes, Cary F., English). *The I Ching or Book of Changes.* Bollingen Series XIX, Princeton, NJ: Princeton University Press, 1950.

Wolf, Eric. *Pueblos y Culturas de Mesoamérica.* Chicago: University of Chicago Press, 1959; Mexico: Ediciones Era, 1967.

INDEX

Carol Miller was born in Los Angeles, California. She first traveled to Mexico as a correspondent and travel writer for *LIFE* magazine and fell permanently in love with the color and history of this culture. For over forty years, Mexico has been her home, and her fascination with its character and diversity has inspired many travel articles, critiques, and commentaries that have appeared in magazines and newspapers in Mexico and around the world. A woman of many talents, Miller has also received international recognition for her achievements as a sculptor. Her unique bronze figures have been exhibited in Mexico's Museum of Modern Art and Palace of Fine Arts, and are featured in the Permanent Collection of Art of the Organization of American States in Washington, D.C. She has traveled the world on what she calls a "quest for cultural convergence," venturing to cultural centers and archeological sites in Latin America, Europe, Africa and the Middle East. In addition to *The Winged Prophet from Hermes to Quetzacoatl*, she is the author of *Travels in the Maya World*, a two part odyssey published in Spanish in 1993 and 1994.

Guadalupe Rivera experienced a unique childhood as the daughter of the renowned and controversial painter Diego Rivera. She was exposed from an early age to discussions of art, politics, history, and culture among some of the most colorful and influential individuals to inhabit Mexico in the early part of this century, developing an especially close relationship with the painter and cult figure Frida Kahlo. As an adult, Rivera has made significant contributions to the politics and culture of her homeland. Rivera earned a doctorate in law and published several scholarly works involving law and history. Intensely involved in Mexican politics, Rivera served as a Congresswoman and currently heads the Institute for Historical Studies on the Mexican Revolution. Her interest in pre-Colombian culture led to her collaborative research on the topic with her late husband, Dr. Ignacio Iturbe-Zabaleta. Their study provided the foundation for what Rivera and Carol Miller would later develop into *The Winged Prophet from Hermes to Quetzacoatl*. Rivera is also the author of the recently published *Dining with Diego and Frida*. Photo courtesy of Grupo Editorial Armonia.